SOUTHERN BIOGRAPHY SERIES
Bertram Wyatt-Brown
Editor

GENTEEL REBEL

The Life of Mary Greenhow Lee

SHEILA R. PHIPPS

LOUISIANA STATE UNIVERSITY PRESS

BATON ROUGE

Copyright © 2004 by Louisiana State University Press

Manufactured in the United States of America
First printing
Cloth
13 12 11 10 09 08 07 06 05 04
5 4 3 2 1
Paper
13 12 11 10 09 08 07 06 05 04
5 4 3 2 1
Designer: Melanie O'Quinn Samaha
Typeface: Janson, Arcana GMM Std Manuscript
Typesetter: Coghill Composition Co., Inc.
Printer and binder: Thomson-Shore, Inc.

Library of Congress Cataloging-in-Publication Data:

Phipps, Sheila R., 1948–
    Genteel rebel : the life of Mary Greenhow Lee / Sheila R. Phipps.
        p.   cm.
Includes bibliographical references and index.
    ISBN 0-8071-2885-6 (cloth : alk. paper)—ISBN 0-8071-2927-5 (pbk. :
alk. paper)
    1. Lee, Mary Greenhow, b. 1819.   2. Winchester (Va.)—Biography.   3.
Women—Virginia—Winchester—Biography.   4. Winchester
(Va.)—History—19th century.   5. Virginia—History—Civil War,
1861–1865.   I. Title.
    F234.W8P47   2004
    975.5'99103'092—dc21

                                                    2003009440

To Shirlie Islay Smith Baber
and to Brandi Rae Phipps, Brian Dale Phipps,
and Hunter James Lloyd Phipps

Contents

Illustrations

Acknowledgments

This book has developed through several phases, and I am greatly indebted to all who have pointed me toward sources, offered advice, read portions of the manuscript, and listened to my often agonized musings over interpretation. I want to first express my appreciation to James P. Whittenburg of the College of William and Mary for his administrative and scholarly guidance, his willingness to patiently listen to all of the problems and questions that arose during the dissertation stage of this project, and his sage counsel toward finding solutions. Leisa D. Meyer, Philip J. Funigiello, and Ludwell H. Johnson III of the College of William and Mary, and Elizabeth R. Varon of Wellesley College also gave essential advice as well as direction for broadening this project to its present form. For their interest and assistance, I am especially grateful. Colleagues and friends have been both helpful and patient, reading portions of the revised manuscript, listening to my concerns, and offering scholarly solutions. They are Nancy Baumgartner, Janine Lanza, Dorothea Martin, Myra Pennell, Neva Specht, Marie Strawser, Mary Valante, and Antoinette Van Zelm.

Without assistance from the archivists at the several repositories and libraries I pestered, this biography would be much less complete. I want to express special appreciation, however, to the efficient and congenial staff at the Virginia Historical Society in Richmond and to the accommodating staff of the Albert and Shirley Small Special Collections Library at the University of Virginia. Two archivists in particular deserve my grateful acknowledgment. Margaret Cook of the Swem Library at the College of William and Mary pointed me first to the Civil War diary of Laura Lee and heartily encouraged my further research into the life of Laura's sister-in-law, Mary. And Rebecca Ebert of the Handley Library in Winchester offered patient assistance each time I visited, "introduced" me to Mary Greenhow Lee's neighbors, gave directions to landmarks, offered information on lodging, pointed me in the direction of more fruitful research paths, and even taught me the correct pronunciation of Frederick County's most intimate place names, including "Opequon" (which sounds very different than one might think).

In seeing this biography to completion, I am indebted to Appalachian State University for a generous University Research Council Competitive Grant, which funded my final research stage. I am also indebted to Bertram Wyatt-Brown, senior editor of the Southern Biography Series of Louisiana State University Press, for offering to publish Mary Greenhow Lee's life story, providing the wider public with this intimate view of the nineteenth-century South.

Finally, my family merits special thanks for their belief in me and for their patience while I completed work on this book. My son, Brian, offered calm and thoughtful assurances. My daughter, Brandi, took an active interest in my progress and offered her artistic talent to the finished product. Finally, I offer heartfelt gratitude to my mother, Shirlie Islay Smith Baber, for her invaluable assistance in researching, gathering tax data, computing numbers, proofreading, and even cooking for me when necessary. Her most valuable gift to me, however, has been her example of courage, upon which I have drawn countless times.

Abbreviations

CWF   The John D. Rockefeller Jr. Library, Colonial Williamsburg Foundation, Williamsburg, Va.

CWM   Special Collections, Swem Library, College of William and Mary, Williamsburg, Va.

ESB   Eleanor S. Brockenbrough Library, Museum of the Confederacy, Richmond, Va.

HHG   Harriet Hollingsworth Griffith Diary. Harriet Hollingsworth Griffith Collection (1179 WFCH), Handley Library, Winchester, Va.

HL   The Archives Room, Handley Library, Winchester, Va.

JC   Julia Chase, "War Time Diary of Miss Julia Chase, Winchester, Virginia," typescript. Julia Chase Collection (544 THL), Handley Library, Winchester, Va.

JHU   Special Collections, Milton S. Eisenhower Library, Johns Hopkins University, Baltimore, Md.

JPC   John Peyton Clark Journal, typescript. Louisa Crawford Collection (424 WFCHS), Handley Library, Winchester, Va.

LC   Manuscripts Division, Library of Congress, Washington, D.C.

LL   Laura Lee Diary, "The History of Our Captivity," March 1862–April 1865. Special Collections, Swem Library, College of William and Mary, Williamsburg, Va.

LOV   Archives, Library of Virginia, Richmond.

MCS   "Minutes of the Cerulean Society." Special Collections, Swem Library, College of William and Mary, Williamsburg, Va.

MGL   Mary Greenhow Lee (Mrs. Hugh Holmes Lee) Diary, typescript. Mrs. Hugh Lee Collection (1182 WFCHS), Handley Library, Winchester, Va.

MHS   Manuscripts Department, Maryland Historical Society, Baltimore.

MJCG/LC   Mary Greenhow Diary, original, microfilm. Mary Greenhow Lee Papers, Manuscripts Division, Library of Congress, Washington, D.C.

MJCG/MHS   Mary Greenhow Diary, 1837, typescript. Greenhow-Lee Papers (MS 534), Manuscripts Department, Maryland Historical Society, Baltimore.

MLG   Mary Lorraine Greenhow (Mrs. Robert Greenhow Sr.) Commonplace Book, 1829–50. Greenhow-Lee Papers (MS 534), Manuscripts Department, Maryland Historical Society, Baltimore.

MSA   Maryland State Archives, Annapolis.

OR   U.S. War Department. *The War of the Rebellion: A Compilation of the Official Records of the Union and Confederate Armies*, 70 vols. in 128 pts. (Washington, D.C.: Government Printing Office, 1880–1901). All citations are to series 1 unless otherwise indicated.

RG   Robert Greenhow Jr. Diary, "An Account of His Journey from Washington, D.C., to Mexico City in 1837." Special Collections, Swem Library, College of William and Mary, Williamsburg, Va.

SHC   Manuscripts Department, Southern Historical Collection, Wilson Library, University of North Carolina at Chapel Hill.

UVA   The Albert and Shirley Small Special Collections Library, University of Virginia Library, Charlottesville.

VHS   Manuscripts and Archives, Virginia Historical Society, Richmond.

GENTEEL REBEL

Introduction

*O*n the afternoon of January 12, 1865, widow Mary Greenhow Lee went shopping for oranges to give to convalescing Confederate soldiers at the hospital the next day. Winchester, Virginia, had been under Union occupation for some time, and the only merchants allowed to do business were sutlers, merchants who followed the Union army and who had the right to refuse service to disloyal citizens, which applied to Lee. When she entered one particular establishment, the "Yankee shop keeper," as she called him, became "so busy patronizing" her that she "assumed a grand air & asked for the porter to carry" her purchases home for her, knowing full well that the merchant, running a temporary business during wartime, had no porter available. Regardless, she continued playing the role of a "most helpless fine lady" until the man scrambled to find someone to carry her "bundle home" and apologized profusely for not having a porter on hand to provide the services a lady such as herself would obviously require. The significant elements of this scene are that Lee used her status as a "fine lady" to gain her oranges and also a bit of amusement at the expense of the shopkeeper, that she could tell herself later that "Yankees" had provided the fruit she would offer to her "Rebel" soldiers, and that she had to pretend to be "helpless," which she did only when it suited her. For the most part, she hid the northerners' effect on her and wanted nothing from them but to go away. She used a complex blend of gender and status roles to fulfill her obligations to both her family and the Confederacy while at the same time turning those roles into weapons to use against her enemies. The life story of this "genteel Rebel" uncovers the complicated interaction between both the "genteel" and the "Rebel" facets of this nineteenth-century southern woman.[1]

To explain Mary Greenhow Lee's "genteel" status, I have borrowed two words from her personal lexicon: *visitable* and *connexion*. The thread of Lee's *visitable connexion* that runs through this biography complicates the normal attributes given to the term *elite* because economic standing and political power had less to do with this network's self-perception of social status than did various other factors. *Visitable*, a term she adopted at an early age, was the contemporary rubric symbolizing qualities that safeguarded gentility, precluding indiscriminate socializing. These qualities included strong family heritage, a good education, piety, and an easy familiarity with the social graces.[2]

The term *connexion* had been used in Lee's family for some time. In an 1812 advertisement announcing the expansion of his medical practice, Mary's uncle, James Greenhow, publicized that he would "receive into his shop as students two young gentlemen of respectable connexions, and good educations." *Connexion*, in its nineteenth-century usage, meant kinship. Cousins married cousins, as happened frequently at a time when distances between kin necessitated visits over an extended period. They also married neighbors (their own or those of their relatives), married children of their fathers' business associates, or the daughters of their mentors. The effect was a wide network of family members among the elite that was a self-perpetuating social class. For the sake of brevity, I use *connexion* in Lee's biography to denote her social equals, those who were *visitable*, that is, those who fit into her social comfort zone.[3]

1. MGL, 762 (Jan. 12, 1865). The manuscript copy of MGL is also located at HL. Portions of this chapter reprinted from Sheila Phipps, "'Their Desire to Visit the Southerners': Mary Greenhow Lee's Visiting Connexion," in *Negotiating Boundaries of Southern Womanhood: Dealing with the Powers That Be*, ed. Janet Coryell, Thomas Appleton Jr., Anastatia Sims, and Sandra Gioia Treadway (Columbia: University of Missouri Press, 2000), by permission of the University of Missouri Press.

2. Ibid., 866 (Sept. 7, 1865); *Etiquette at Washington: Together with the Customs Adopted by Polite Society in the Other Cities of the United States*, 3d ed. (Baltimore: Murphy, 1857), 45–50; MJCG/MHS, 12 (Sept. 23, 1837).

3. *The Enquirer*, Nov. 6, 1812; Jane Turner Censer, *North Carolina Planters and Their Children* (Baton Rouge: Louisiana State University Press, 1984), 65, 84–86; John Thomas Schlotterbeck, *Plantation and Farm: Social and Economic Change in Orange and Greene Counties, Virginia, 1716 to 1850* (Ann Arbor, Mich.: University Microfilms International, 1980), 243; Bill Cecil-

But Lee used the word "class" to express difference, the difference between others and herself. "That class" for Lee could mean various groups of people: those with less education and less prominent heritage, northerners, or Union officers and soldiers during the war. She even assigned people to "that class" if they betrayed less optimistic hopes for the South during the war than she held. In other words, Lee rarely used "class" as a term for her own group but more for those who were outside of the category to which she assigned herself.

Lee's use of "class" agrees with studies of southern social structure. Although by the time of the Civil War the South had developed an aristocracy of sorts, privileged southerners merely operated under the assumption that they existed primarily as independent, self-sufficient units only occasionally benefiting from being included in the society of comparably advantaged people. In other words, the southern aristocracy was not a self-conscious class. Southern whites who would not be termed "elite" were also unaware of their membership in any category. Small slaveholders and nonslaveholders, likewise, did not think of themselves as members of a clear-cut social group.[4]

This seeming unawareness of stratification begs the question of how these people had any sense of social place. Class consciousness develops, however, only in opposition to another class. Indeed, a class is usually "other-defined," initially located and labeled by those not included; "class" for nineteenth-century southerners meant people in whose company they did not feel at ease and with whom they did not relate. For Mary Greenhow Lee, *connexion* referred to those with whom she did feel comfortable, those who met her requirements for social inclusion.[5]

Fronsman, *The Common Whites: Class and Culture in Antebellum North Carolina*, (Ann Arbor, Mich.: University Microfilms International, 1985), 3; Joan E. Cashin, *A Family Venture: Men and Women on the Southern Frontier* (Baltimore: Johns Hopkins University Press, 1991), 16–20. See also David Hackett Fischer, *Albion's Seed: Four British Folkways in America* (New York: Oxford University Press, 1989), 219–25.

4. Wilbur J. Cash, *The Mind of the South* (New York: Alfred A. Knopf, 1941), 7, 11, 34, 35, 39; Bertram Wyatt-Brown, "W. J. Cash and Southern Culture," in *From the Old South to the New: Essays on the Transitional South*, ed. Walter J. Fraser Jr. and Winfred B. Moore Jr. (Westport, Conn.: Greenwood, 1981), 195–214; Cecil-Fronsman, *Common Whites*, 3. See also Randolph B. Campbell, "Planters and Plain Folks: The Social Structure of the Antebellum South," in *Interpreting Southern History: Historiographical Essays in Honor of Sanford W. Higginbotham*, ed. John B. Boles and Evelyn Thomas Nolen (Baton Rouge: Louisiana State University Press, 1987), 48–77.

5. For a discussion of class identification, see Edward P. Thompson, "Eighteenth-Century English Society: Class Struggle without Class?" *Social History* 3 (1978): 149; and Edward P. Thompson, *The Making of the English Working Class* (New York: Random House, 1963), 9–13. For a postmodernist dialogue on the topic, see Stuart Hall, "Gramsci's Relevance for the Study

Diminishing fortunes did not seem to make a difference within Lee's *connexion;* disparity in economic power was an acknowledged fact of life. A history of family wealth—or obvious economic potential—could earn one a place in the group. Although her father ranked in the ninety-eighth percentile of taxable wealth for Richmond when Lee was born in 1819, her own economic holdings ranged near the bottom of the *connexion* relative to her own generation.[6]

Looking at 1860 in isolation, all of Lee's friends owned slaves, but in Winchester several claimed only one or two, while others in the town owned as many as five. Lee paid personal property taxes on two slaves for her household. For those of her friends who lived in rural areas, slave ownership ranged from four to thirty-nine. Personal property values spread from the lowest (her cousin George Charlton in Petersburg) at 0.03 percent of the total taxable wealth of his community to her neighbor Philip Williams at 5 percent. Lee herself hovered near the lower end at 0.08 percent. For land taxes, Joseph Sherrard held the lowest position in her *connexion* at 0.01 percent, with the highest, Nathaniel Meade, editor of the *Winchester Republican* and a farmer in Clark County, assessed at 2.8 percent of that district's total taxes on land. Lee paid 0.3 percent of Winchester's land taxes for her house on Market Street. Clearly, uniformity of wealth was not a characteristic of this group of Virginians. Even through widowhood and war, Lee's social position as a member of this group—the *visitable connexion*—remained a constant throughout her life; it is a continuing thread in her biography.[7]

An analysis of Lee's *connexion* is also the study of a community. Of over 650 names taken from her diaries and journals, the known population of her

---

of Race and Ethnicity," in *Stuart Hall: Critical Dialogues in Cultural Studies*, ed. David Morley and Kuan-Hsing Chen, 411–40 (London: Routledge, 1996).

6. Marianne Patricia Buroff Sheldon, *Richmond, Virginia: The Town and Henrico County to 1820* (Ann Arbor, Mich.: Xerox University Microfilms, 1975), 124; Land Tax Records and Personal Property Tax Records, Richmond and Henrico County, 1819, 1830, LOV; Personal Property and Land Tax Records for Richmond, Staunton, Winchester, and the counties of Albemarle, Augusta, Clark, Dinwiddie, Fairfax, Frederick, Harrison, Henrico, and Loudoun,1860, LOV.

7. Land Tax Records and Personal Property Tax Records, Richmond and Henrico County, 1819, 1830, LOV; Personal Property and Land Tax Records for Richmond, Staunton, Winchester, and the counties of Albemarle, Augusta, Clark, Dinwiddie, Fairfax, Frederick, Harrison, Henrico, and Loudoun, 1860, LOV. In order to draw economic comparisons between the members of this group, and because they were from various jurisdictions, I divided each person's tax liability for slaves, personal property, and land taxes by the aggregate assessment for his or her particular jurisdiction. Admittedly, this is still a rough comparison, but it does give some indication of how widely the valuations of economic wealth differed within the group.

world, approximately one-third have been identified in some detail. Several members played vital roles in Lee's life; many moved only on its periphery. In addition, Lee's South was not the plantation but rather the urban South. The *connexion* tied these areas together. Some of this population farmed, but the property owned by many in the group was measured in lots rather than acres, and their primary income came from professions, not crop yields. They were lawyers, doctors, merchants, and coal dealers. Some sold tobacco in various forms. Others were respected clergymen. Still others taught in universities and wrote textbooks.[8]

Lee's own life supports this picture of the urban *connexion*. She was born and grew up in Richmond, Virginia, yet also spent time with friends and family in Williamsburg and Washington, D.C., during her youth. After marrying Hugh Holmes Lee in 1843, she moved to his home in Winchester, in the Lower Shenandoah Valley, where her husband practiced law until his death in 1856. Their house remained Mary Greenhow Lee's home until Maj. Gen. Philip H. Sheridan banished her from Winchester in 1865. After wandering in exile throughout that summer, she finally relocated in Baltimore, where she lived out the rest of her life.

Lee admits her "Rebel" identity in her lengthy Civil War journal—a predominant source for her biography—but this study reveals that she evidenced a rebellious nature throughout her life. In fact, her family background, her family's political activities, her *connexions*, and the southern culture in which she developed serve to explain not only Lee's spirited nature but also the ethic of rebellion that she, as well as most of her *connexion*, adopted when Virginia seceded from the Union.

Other than a small number of letters found in a few archives, the three most important sources available for this biography are a journal Lee kept from September 1837 to April 1838 while she was eighteen years old, a small diary kept in the fall of 1842, and her Civil War journal. The latter begins on March 11, 1862, on the eve of the first Union occupation of Winchester, and ends on page 891 in November 1865 on the day she signed a lease on her first house in Baltimore. If Lee had borne children, then there might be a repository somewhere that houses several feet of her papers. She did not, and there is not. Without children to save a person's mementos, the difficulty of finding sources is sometimes enormous. Much of what I have learned of Mary Greenhow Lee has come through epiphanies (or, maybe, divine guidance) and sometimes just plain sleuthing out the sources. For example, in her Civil

8. MGL, 873 (Sept. 27, 1865).

War journal, the entry for October 24, 1863, mentions that she had spent the evening reading through a diary she had written some twenty years earlier while she had been enjoying "the gay scenes" of Williamsburg. After having checked repositories from New Jersey to North Carolina and not having found her "1843 diary" (as I termed it), I realized that the "mock chevalier society" she mentioned in her Civil War journal bore a close resemblance to the "Minutes of the Cerulean Society" at Swem Library's Special Collections I had looked at earlier. When I read the "Minutes" more closely, I found two very brief diaries of the trips Lee took to Williamsburg and Winchester in 1842 in the back of the small bound volume. Then I found, almost verbatim, passages she mentioned in her Civil War journal. Many such investigative leaps have been necessary throughout the research process.[9]

Research into what other people had to say about Lee proved productive to a very limited extent. Sources written by some of her best friends have not surfaced, and there are almost none that give the critical view of Lee that might have balanced the picture shown here. One example in particular illustrates the problem. Lee's best friend as a young woman was Edmonia "Eddie" Christian, who, as a mature married woman, became known as "Mona" Warren. Research has not uncovered correspondence by either "Eddie Christian" or "Mona Warren." Like Lee, Edmonia Christian Warren had no children, the typical source of archival collections. Absent a rich collection of sources revealing what others had to say about Mary, I approached her diaries and journals as though they were tools she used to explain herself to others and, therefore, to us.[10]

When a rich and detailed journal like Mary Greenhow Lee's is available, it is appropriate to sift her words finely for a clue to the dynamic effect of war on women. One insightful woman's journal can be a psychological road map to her emotional and physical struggles throughout the conflict. Historians such as George C. Rable and Drew Gilpin Faust have tapped this journal for insight into women's wartime experiences; Winchester historians have made

9. Ibid., 500 (Oct. 24, 1863); MCS.

10. See MJCG/MHS, 9 (Sept. 1837); James Balfour Tubbs, *Rennie Family Connections*, vol. 1 (privately printed, 1993), 161; Michael W. Berry and Ann Arsell Wheat Hunter, "Collier and Christian of Charles City and New Kent Counties," *Virginia Genealogist* 34, no. 2 (Apr.–June 1990); *Christian Family of Virginia* (Richmond, Va.: Whittet and Shepperson, 1901); Andrew H. Christian Jr., *A Brief History of the Christian, Dunscomb, and Duval Families* (Richmond, Va.: Dietz, 1909); and MGL, 545 (Jan. 23, 1864), 559 (Feb. 19, 1864), 564 (May 1864), 863 (Aug. 29, 1865), 866 (Sept. 7, 1865).

extensive use of it to study the events that kept the town in turmoil throughout the Civil War.[11]

Many southern women took up pen and what paper they could find to record their experiences during the Civil War. Mary Chesnut's war journal is well known, but the journal that went into print was not the one she wrote during the war. For almost twenty years, Chesnut stewed over how she should present her account of the war to the public. Adhering to the standards of model behavior for nineteenth-century women, Chesnut felt she should not have a public voice, so she worked at leaving references to her own feelings out of the journal while still recreating her wartime experiences. Her solution was to assign some of her own judgments to a friend, thereby exposing her opinions to public view without risking condemnation for having them, and to leave others completely out of her published work.[12]

Mary Greenhow Lee had no problem claiming her identity, even though she suspected that her journal might eventually be read by others. Her entry for October 27, 1862, begins: "What do you think—all you who may hereafter read my journal, what do you think has happened to-day—I must lead you to it by degrees," introducing her account of a visit from Maj. Gen. "Stonewall" Jackson. Already gaining a reputation as a staunch and assertive Confederate, she assumed Jackson's visit to be a high compliment to her for her efforts. The beginning of her entry for that day reveals that she had begun to imagine an audience for her musings. Clearly not shy about revealing her opinions on public policy, Lee learned to create a dramatic effect to reflect the position in which she perceived her "Self" to be.[13]

11. George C. Rable, *Civil Wars: Women and the Crisis of Southern Nationalism* (Urbana: University of Illinois Press, 1989); Drew Gilpin Faust, *Mothers of Invention: Women of the Slaveholding South in the American Civil War* (Chapel Hill: University of North Carolina Press, 1996); Roger U. Delauter Jr., *Winchester in the Civil War* (Lynchburg, Va.: H. E. Howard, 1992); A. Bentley Kenney, "The Devil Diarists of Winchester," *Winchester–Frederick County Historical Society Journal* 5 (1990); Garland R. Quarles, *Occupied Winchester: 1861–1865* (Winchester, Va.: Farmers and Merchants Bank, 1976). Since Faust uses Mary Greenhow Lee's Civil War journal extensively for her work in *Mothers of Invention,* and since she uses many of the same direct quotations that I use here, some readers might wonder why I do not cite Faust more often in this biography. Many of the interpretations I make here I had made in my study "'As If I Were a Confederate Soldier': Mary Greenhow Lee and the Civil War She Waged in Winchester, Virginia" (master's thesis, College of William and Mary, 1996), completed at the time *Mothers of Invention* appeared. Therefore, I did not draw on Faust's work, but on my own.

12. Melissa Mentzer, "Rewriting Herself: Mary Chesnut's Narrative Strategies," *Connecticut Review* 14, no. 1 (1992): 49–56, 50–52.

13. MGL, 249 (Oct. 27, 1862).

When Lee began her journal, she was really beginning a letter to no one in particular to "pass away . . . dreadful hours of suspense" once she knew that Confederate troops were evacuating Winchester and Union troops were just outside of town. She then decided to write it for her dear friend in exile, Jeannie Mason. Eventually, though, she clearly appropriated the journal as a place to "talk over" the events of her day with her "Self." Lee did not make an entry in her journal for Friday, January 23, 1863. She reported the next night, "as I had nothing particular to say to myself in my journal, I skipped a day."[14]

In a sense, journals are a forum for writers to display their actions and feelings for reappraisal. On another level, a journal can be a stage for interaction where writers can reconstruct the scenes of important events between themselves and an "Other," the responses of which help define a writer's definition of his or her "Self." If the reactions of a friend are positive, the writer will note a level of affirmation about his or her "Self." Likewise, if the recorded reactions of an enemy are negative, the writer's words will reflect some satisfaction as well. Whatever the case, a journal can be searched for clues about the writer's expectations, both of the "Self" and of the "Other," in each situation. To her journal, for example, Lee continually reiterated that the Yankees had no control over her because she "never ask[ed] favors of them." Instead of asking, she stated, "I *make* them do . . . for me." Lee believed this about her "Self," and her belief was reinforced as she played the scenes over in her journal, thus giving her the quality of control she aspired to and confidence for her next confrontation. In addition, the way that Lee obtained personal power in these situations could help scholars redefine power for use in women's history, to replace the generalized notion of women as being oppressed and powerless with a picture of how women of the past found control over their own lives and politicized their needs to acquire at least a perception of strength. As Linda Gordon has suggested, "to be less powerful is not to be powerless," and Lee's story illustrates the unique ways she found to take command in her own life. A woman who stated, "I do what I think right & am willing to take the consequence," does not fit the image of the helpless, powerless "Southern Lady."[15]

14. Ibid., 301 (Jan. 24, 1863).

15. Richard D. Logan, "Reflections on Changes in Self-Apprehension and Construction of the 'Other' in Western History," *Psychohistory Review* 19, no. 3 (spring 1991): 295, 298; MGL, 7 (Mar. 13, 1862), 733 (Dec. 7, 1864), 730 (Dec. 3, 1864), 763 (Jan. 23, 1865), 697 (Sept. 30, 1864, emphasis added); Linda Gordon, "What's New in Women's History," in *A Reader in Feminist*

Mary Greenhow Lee was a fascinating and lively woman, but what can a biography of one woman, no matter how interesting, contribute to our understanding of the past? A biography is a microscopic look at the past. As Joan W. Scott has argued, the impressions of historic events upon women can change "the standards of historical significance" by showing how personal experiences can act on public matters as much as the reverse. Furthermore, while thematic history searches for change through time, a biography often locates constants through change, as I have done for Lee's life in the form of her sense of social place—her *connexion*—and her strong character.[16]

Furthermore, a biography of a woman who lived through the Civil War can dissect the elements of debate concerning where southern women stood at the end of the conflict, whether empowered, further subjugated, or remaining in place on the pedestal they had occupied in the Old South. A more intensive study of one woman's experiences, though unable to sort out the confusion, at least can help explain it. Lee did not lose faith in the cause, nor did she resent the sacrifices she made for it. She put her energy into Lost Cause associations after the war for the same reason she agreed to secession: to protect and preserve the Old South's traditions, including her gendered position. Although, from a twenty-first-century vantage point, we might argue with Lee that the work she performed during the war proved her right to a political voice, that would have been a radical notion for a woman steeped in nineteenth-century southern culture. She wanted her men to regain their political power, and she wanted to retain her right to be exempt from that responsibility. To request more of her would be asking too much.[17]

Additionally, while composite studies claim that women soon became tired of the war and wished it over, won or lost, Lee's story sheds light on the realities of their days. It is true that she at times became disheartened and depressed and wanted the war to end; but her experience provides insight into why she might have left the impression that she was giving up. "I always write at night, when completely fagged out," she explained, and "I fear I give a weary view of matters." There was only one outcome of the war that she

Knowledge, ed. Sneja Gunew (London and New York: Routledge, 1991), 75–77; MGL, 552 (Feb. 6, 1864).

16. Joan W. Scott, *Gender and the Politics of History* (New York: Columbia University Press, 1988), 20.

17. See Rable, *Civil Wars*, 227, 288; Anne Firor Scott, *The Southern Lady: From Pedestal to Politics, 1830–1930* (Chicago: University of Chicago Press, 1970), 81–102; Faust, *Mothers of Invention*, 251.

could accept, but the time of day when she wrote her thoughts shadowed her reflections with weariness. She wanted her readers to understand, however, that she felt more optimistic than her words might imply. Possibly, other women's Civil War diaries were similarly tainted. Southern nationalism has been measured mostly from defeat backward, looking only for the reasons for failure. Historians are now beginning to ask, though, how the South held on for so long in such a lopsided struggle, and Lee's personal struggle provides at least some answers. The dark and brooding comments that scholars have tallied up into a general surrender of will might be explained in part by the lateness of the day as much as by the length of the war.[18]

Born in 1819 and living until 1907, Mary Greenhow Lee was indeed a nineteenth-century woman. Her story is a window into the world of that era. We cannot know everything about her life since the sources do not reveal them. For instance, although women of the time felt destined to fill roles as wives and mothers in order to be complete, Lee had no children. She lived through sad anniversaries that do not match the deaths of her known family, which might point to dates when she lost children or miscarried pregnancies; we will never know. She "mothered" nieces and nephews, however, and does not seem to have lacked a sense of identity for being childless. Her identity as "wife" was important to her. After her husband's death, she never remarried, choosing to be known as the widow of Hugh Holmes Lee. We will never know whether she remained a widow for reasons of sentiment, economics, or something else. Similar to other areas of her life, she probably had very complex reasons for remaining identified as a widow.

But there are several elements to her life that can be known. Readers will find that she preferred the company of young people; they tapped into her youthful spirit and sense of fun. Lee was a woman of courage who had a horror of mice and bats but refused to fear invading armies. She exhibited a willful character, high intelligence, and quick wit and appreciated well-written books, bright people, and good music. In her youth she was slightly irreverent. As a mature woman, her faith was sometimes her only comfort. She had a fondness for champagne and oysters and a passion for ice cream. Although she could be very critical of others, she also had a lovely ability to laugh at herself. Since Lee was a slaveowner who revealed in her musings the very complicated relationship between whites and blacks in the antebellum South,

18. MGL, 419 (June 19, 1863); Gary W. Gallagher, *The Confederate War* (Cambridge: Harvard University Press, 1997), 31–34.

readers might be offended by her obvious racism, but one should remember that she was the product of a culture that had always included this oppressive "peculiar institution." Mary Greenhow Lee lived in a world unfamiliar to us now, but the story of how she placed her "Self" in that world also reveals seamless similarities between the present and the past.[19]

19. MGL, 305 (Feb. 3, 1863), 457 (Aug. 12, 1863), 874 (Oct. 1, 1865), 890 (Nov. 12, 1865), 891 (Nov. 14, 1865), 586 (Apr. 30, 1864), 637 (July 12, 1864), 838 (June 21, 1865); MJCG/ MHS, 71 (Mar. 12, 1838), 72 (Mar. 15, 1838), 73 (Mar. 21, 1838), 75 (Mar. 25, 1838), 76 (Mar. 25, 1838). For the historical construction of "race," and thus "racism," see Barbara Jeanne Fields, "Slavery, Race, and Ideology in the United States of America," *New Left Review* 181 (May–June 1990): 95–118.

I

"My Birthday—I Have Spent It Profitably"

*O*n September 9, 1819, in Richmond, Virginia, at that time of evening when autumn competes with summer for dominance, candlelight could be seen through a few of the many windows of the large house on Capitol Street; smoke rose from the central chimney. Passersby would not have guessed the heightened level of anticipation circulating throughout the home. Most of the twelve household slaves were no doubt carrying out their customary evening duties; but some hastened to perform special tasks, on orders of the people attending to Mary Lorraine Greenhow, concentrating on the labor of giving birth. Candlelight blended shadows in the room as she met each contraction, and it flickered deep golden lights on the mahogany bedstead supporting her.[1]

Downstairs, Robert Greenhow probably waited for word on his wife's progress. He might have passed the time working at his desk, trying to concentrate on many of the business details demanded of a merchant and landlord, while he sipped coffee hot enough to scald most people, just the way he

1. Richmond Personal Property Tax Lists, 1815, 1819, LOV.

liked it. Or it is possible that he filled the time standing at one of the windows facing the state capitol, contemplating the world his newest child fought to enter.[2]

Gazing past the trees and shadows of the capitol lawn, Greenhow might have pondered the economic problems Richmond faced. Indeed, the whole nation had been experiencing bank and business failures to an alarming degree. Greenhow's own extensive properties had plunged in value by 20 percent from the previous year, but others were facing difficulties more severe; some had lost half the values on their property. Prices on "necessaries" were rising too. The cost of flour at fifteen to sixteen dollars a barrel was four to five times more than it had been just a few years earlier. Richmond itself was thinning out as citizens moved off to find better opportunities elsewhere. The financial panic was one of the first depressions of its kind for the United States, a new nation feeling its way into modern capitalism, realizing how erratic the economic cycles could be.[3]

The city lived under the threat of a deadly disease as well. From the domed building across the way, Greenhow's friend Peter V. Daniel, Virginia's lieutenant governor, had issued an order of quarantine for all ships entering state ports from Baltimore, Charleston, and Cuba to protect Virginians from the "malignant and contagious fever" raging in those areas.[4]

Although Greenhow might have been concerned as he waited for word on his wife, he no doubt reasoned that he had the intelligence and resources to provide the best protection possible for his youngest child. Surveying his surroundings, his experienced eye would have taken in the mahogany dining table in the next room, remembered that he had enough matching chairs on hand to seat sixty guests, and relished memories of the "beautiful dinner parties" held there. The piano offered hours of entertainment, the silver tea service added luster to their afternoon ritual, carpets cushioned the step in various rooms through the house, and a carriage with two horses was avail-

2. MJCG/MHS, 78 (Apr. 11, 1838); list of family births and deaths, MJCG/LC; Mary Wingfield Scott, *Houses of Old Richmond* (Richmond, Virginia: Valentine Museum, 1941), 57–61. The manuscript copy of MJCG/LC includes a list of family births and deaths and a list of parties that the typescript located at MHS omits.

3. Sheldon, *Richmond, Virginia*, 294, 295, 298; Richmond Personal Property Tax Lists, 1818, 1819, LOV. On the reasons for the Panic of 1819, see Steven Watts, *The Republic Reborn: War and the Making of Liberal America, 1790–1820* (Baltimore: Johns Hopkins University Press, 1987), 319.

4. *Richmond Enquirer*, Sept. 11, 1819. Orders were issued on Aug. 19, 1819.

able to take the family wherever they needed or wanted to go. His home, at least, would offer a comfortable immediate world to the newest Greenhow, no matter what evils raged outside.[5]

At twenty minutes to nine, any worries that might have been plaguing Robert Greenhow were probably interrupted by the piercing infant cry cutting through the stillness. He checked his gold watch to note the time, then waited to be summoned to his wife's side.[6]

When this particular child entered into the relatively abrasive world of sheeting, light, drafts, and human hands, her cry probably did not require much encouragement. Given the control she attempted to maintain over her environment throughout the rest of her eighty-seven years, it would have been uncharacteristic of Mary Jane Charlton Greenhow to remain silent at her very first opportunity to protest.

To understand Mary Greenhow Lee, the first step is to study the world of her origin. Who Robert Greenhow was, how he conducted his life, and the degree to which he felt comfortable in his environment says a great deal about the strong woman he raised, providing the example of the patrician values of civic obligations she would later exhibit. Additionally, although raised in one of the wealthiest surroundings in Richmond, Mary Greenhow Lee would one day feel just as satisfied with her "comfortable little room" in her modest Winchester home. Ultimately, it was not the extent of material possessions that mattered to her, but the degree to which she had the power to control her surroundings.[7]

The world of wealth and public responsibility Robert Greenhow provided for his family was, in part, a legacy of his own beginnings: the first from his father, John Greenhow; the second arising out of the time and place of his boyhood. Mary's grandfather migrated to America from Staunton, near Kendall, in Westmoreland County, England, during the middle of the eighteenth century, settling at Williamsburg, Virginia's colonial capital. Greenhow opened a store near Bruton Parish Church on Main Street about 1754. The establishment proved a success, offering "wine by the pipe, cask, gallon, or quart"; beaver traps; yard goods; salt sacks; frying pans; and corks, among various other merchandise for home and farm. Greenhow advertised his

5. Richmond Personal Property Tax Lists, 1815, 1819, LOV; MGL, 865 (Sept. 3, 1865).

6. Richmond Personal Property Tax Lists, 1815, 1819, LOV; list of family births and deaths, MJCG/LC.

7. MGL, 490 (Oct. 9, 1863).

store's location "near the Church" in 1755; but a sign of his success is that other Williamsburg proprietors began using Greenhow's store as a landmark in their advertisements by 1767. John Greenhow married Judith Davenport, daughter of Joseph and Margaret Davenport of Williamsburg, in November 1759, signifying that the immigrant from England had proven himself sufficiently worthy in both financial and social terms to gain acceptance by the Davenports. Judith's father served as clerk of the Hustings Court for James City County and as the Williamsburg town clerk.[8]

John and Judith Greenhow had two children, Robert, born in May 1761, and daughter, Ann, before Judith, "a sincere Christian . . . lov'd [and] valu'd," died on January 4, 1765. John married again, this time to Elizabeth Tyler of Charles City County, aunt of the John Tyler who would become president of the United States. Out of this marriage Robert Greenhow gained five half-brothers and three half-sisters. When Elizabeth died of smallpox in 1781, John Greenhow married Rebecca Harman, daughter of Benskin Harman, with whom he had one more daughter.[9]

Before John Greenhow died in 1787, he had fathered eleven children in three marriages, accumulated property in and around Williamsburg, and extended his holdings to a store and four lots on Shockoe Hill in Richmond. The Greenhows lived in the "large and commodious Dwelling House on the main street" of Williamsburg, but their patriarch also owned at least six houses on the back street and four hundred acres on the east end of town adjacent to the "Public Gaol" and framed on the north and west by streets that were both named for him. According to the advertisement announcing the sale of his estate, John Greenhow owned "a number of valuable slaves"; livestock; "elegant household Furniture," including "a beautiful keyed chamber Organ and a Spinnet"; and "london built town" silver coffee and teapots monogrammed with the initials "JG."[10]

8. Gravestone, John Greenhow, Bruton Parish Church, Williamsburg, Va. According to the inscription, Greenhow was born Nov. 12, 1724. Kendal is located in northern England, an area sparsely populated at the beginning of the eighteenth century and noted for its woolen industry. See *Historical Atlas of the World*, newly rev. ed. (Maplewood, N.J.: Hammond, 1995), 36; Mary A. Stephenson, "The John Greenhow House Historical Report, Block 13-2, Building 23E, Lot 159," Report 1265, CWF, 1947; Mary A. Stephenson, "The General Store (18th Century)," Report 90, Research Department, CWF, 1954; and "Davenport Family," *William and Mary Quarterly*, 1st ser., 7 (1898–99): 17.

9. "Davenport Family," *William and Mary Quarterly*, 1st ser., 7 (1898–99): 17; gravestones, Judith Greenhow and John and Elizabeth Greenhow, Bruton Parish Church, Williamsburg, Va.

10. Lyon G. Tyler, Williamsburg Plat, in "Williamsburg, the Old Colonial Capitol," CWF, photostatic copy; Stephenson, "John Greenhow House"; "Last Will of Robert Greenhow," Richmond Hustings Court Book 8:263, LOV.

Mary's father grew up, then, the oldest child in a sizeable family of comfortable circumstances in a town that had been designed to reflect its importance to both the Virginia colonists and England's Crown. He also grew up during the era when colonists struggled to separate themselves from that Crown. By the time Robert Greenhow was born, Williamsburg had a population of one thousand residents and about two hundred dwellings. When the Virginia assembly was in session, the town swelled significantly in numbers, as burgesses arrived to conduct the colony's business. Men who had stood for election in their home counties, who had taken over leadership roles in the colony, came to Williamsburg when the governor called. As young Robert Greenhow grew up learning within his home how to create and maintain a successful business, he also no doubt watched with interest as, just outside of his house, political leaders gathered to discuss the issues of the day.[11]

In 1771 lightning struck John Greenhow's house, splitting the chimney and shattering some of the windows. That same year John Murray, the earl of Dunmore, arrived in Williamsburg to assume his duties as governor of the colony. One can imagine the disturbance in the Greenhow household caused by the former event. But Dunmore's stay in Williamsburg precipitated further excitement on the streets of the town, and his departure in the middle of one night in May 1775 signaled the beginning of the end for Virginia's colonial status.[12]

At just the point in a child's life when he or she realizes that there are such things as political issues and persuasive skills, Robert Greenhow witnessed one of the most tumultuous political events in Virginia's history, as his daughter would one day witness another. The town and times of his boyhood clearly pulsed with the atmosphere of change, with both the anxiety and the hope that only rapid change can generate. From church to tavern, revolutionary rhetoric bounced off of walls and must have affected the young boy. The Raleigh Tavern, among other establishments in town, housed some of the legislators or hosted them as they gathered for discussion and debate. Since Robert Greenhow's uncle Anthony Hay owned and managed the Raleigh Tavern, it is logical to assume that young Robert spent some of his free time

11. Norman K. Risjord, *Jefferson's America, 1760–1815* (Madison, Wis.: Madison House, 1991), 22–23; Jack P. Greene, *Pursuits of Happiness: The Social Development of Early Modern British Colonies and the Formation of American Culture* (Chapel Hill: University of North Carolina Press, 1988), 85, 93.

12. *Virginia Gazette*, Aug. 19, 1771; Virginius Dabney, *Virginia: The New Dominion* (Charlottesville: University Press of Virginia, 1989), 119, 128, 130; Rhys Isaac, *The Transformation of Virginia, 1740–1790* (New York: W. W. Norton, 1982), 257.

there and probably witnessed the frenzy of debate. It could even be possible that he watched as the burgesses, after resolving to set June 7, 1774, as a day of fasting and prayer in sympathy for Boston's blockaded port, were prorogued by Lord Dunmore from the Hall of the Capitol. On a scale of momentous events, watching the disbanded burgesses walking resolutely down the street from the capitol to Raleigh Tavern to conduct their extralegal business must have been close to the top for an eighteenth-century lad.[13]

Clearly, Robert Greenhow did become aware of the events surrounding him and caught the fervor of patriotism. If, as historian Rhys Isaac argues, being a member of a community "unanimously roused in support of its dearest rights" communicated to those citizens the "Anglo-American ideal of civic virtue," then the revolutionary generation helped style Robert Greenhow's future as a civic leader. And if, as Isaac also suggests, military exercises "provided opportunities for the self-presentation of the warrior that was expected to exist in every free man," then Greenhow was further impressed with the responsibilities of leadership.[14]

In June 1775, at fourteen years of age, Robert Greenhow joined a group of young men who formed a military corps in Williamsburg. They chose Henry Nicholson as their captain and adopted the backcountry uniform of hunting shirts and cockades, fastening the "Liberty or Death" motto to their breasts. On June 3, soon after Virginia's colonial governor, Lord Dunmore, fled from Williamsburg to a British man-of-war in the York River, this group of young men broke into the "magazine and armed themselves with . . . blue painted stock guns," believing that "they could . . . perform all the evolutions of the manual exercise far better than the soldiers who were daily arriving from the adjacent counties." Unfortunately for three of the boys, two of the spring guns were fixed with trip cords set to fire the weapons if anyone approached the stockpile behind them. Citizens of the town did not approve of the boys' overly ardent behavior but approved less the malicious trap that wounded three of them. Robert Greenhow had his first and last experience with open warfare that night. Although others in the group went on to fight within the ranks of the state service during the Revolution, Robert Greenhow, or more probably his father, purchased "the services of a substitute" and remained at home. Although Robert served in a "junior company whose duty was confined to the immediate protection of Williamsburg and the neighboring

13. Isaac, *Transformation of Virginia*, 216, 217, 243, 254; "Davenport Family," *William and Mary Quarterly*, 1st ser., 7 (1898–99): 17; Dabney, *Virginia*, 119–21.
14. Isaac, *Transformation of Virginia*, 255–56.

banks of the James River," his ability to avoid actual combat points to the limits of patriotism among some members of the elite. It might also be evidence of John's, if not Robert's, reluctance to see the colonies separate from England.[15]

After attending the College of William and Mary, Robert worked with his father in the store and took on civic obligations in Williamsburg, serving several years as mayor and two terms as the representative of James City County in the state legislature. Greenhow's public service reflects the ideology of republicanism that emerged out of the struggles of rebellion, war, and state and nation building. For the Revolutionary generation, republicanism meant that politics, economics, and society were interdependent. Civic virtue lay at the heart of this ideology, demanding that personal success equaled a moral obligation to serve society. For the Greenhows, that translated into success as merchants and active participation in community.[16]

In June 1786 Robert married Mary Ann Wills, daughter of Elias Wills from Fluvanna County. On August 29 of the next year, John Greenhow died "after a very short illness," leaving Robert sole executor of his estate. Robert advertised the public sale of his father's property that September but then purchased the property himself, or at least a portion of it, at auction. He then began advertising as "Robert Greenhow, Merchant in Williamsburg" in the *Virginia Gazette and Richmond Chronicle* but moved his family, which by this time included their ten-year-old son, Robert Greenhow Jr., to Richmond in 1810. In effect, he followed the capital, for it had been moved to Richmond from Williamsburg in 1780. Other friends and family members had migrated

15. Dabney, *Virginia*, 130; Robert Greenhow's obituary, *Richmond Enquirer*, July 3, 1840; "Affidavit of Robert Greenhow," *Genealogies of Virginia Families from the William and Mary College Quarterly Historical Magazine*, vols. 3–4 (Baltimore: Genealogical Publishing, 1982), 4:15–16.

16. John B. Danforth and Herbert A. Claiborne, *Historical Sketch of the Mutual Assurance Society of Richmond, Va., from Its Organization in 1794 to 1879* (Richmond, Va.: William Ellis Jones, 1879; reproduced by duopage process, Wooster, Ohio: Micropublishers, Micro-Photo Division, 1971), 126 [original at LOV]; *Richmond Enquirer*, July 2, 1840; advertisement (announcing that those who had been selling lottery tickets for the college should turn the money over to Robert Greenhow), *Virginia Argus*, June 6, 1804, reprinted in *William and Mary Quarterly*, 2d ser., 4 (1924): 121–22; Drew R. McCoy, *The Elusive Republic: Political Economy in Jeffersonian America* (New York: W. W. Norton, 1980), 6–8. Danforth and Claiborne state that all of John Greenhow's sons attended the College of William and Mary but do not give the dates; their names do not appear in college records. Given his polished writing skills and his fluency in French, it is probable that Robert was educated in a college setting, and it makes sense that he would have attended the institution closest to home. There is no record, however, of when he did. The fact that Claiborne was a friend of the family lends weight to his personal assertion that Greenhow did attend William and Mary.

to Richmond earlier, and Greenhow's business dealings, involvement in establishing the Academy of Science and Fine Arts in Richmond in 1786, and social visits to friends and family there had already provided the Greenhows an easy familiarity with the city. In a form of cultural exchange, the Greenhows replicated the social activities they enjoyed in Richmond at their home in Williamsburg. In 1808 a Julia F. Pagaud attended a "tearing Ball at Mr. Greenhow's," characterized by another guest as a "six hundred squeeze; *a la mode de* Richmond."[17]

The family settled into a home on West Franklin Street and prepared to take an active part in the development of Virginia's new and growing capital. This *connexion* created a strong link between Williamsburg and Richmond. Family already situated in Richmond probably helped in the transition. Brothers John, George, Samuel, and James Greenhow had moved from Williamsburg before the turn of the century. Most of them, like Robert, followed in their father's footsteps. All but James opened stores in Richmond, then added to their income through the accumulation of real property. By supporting their families through more than one source and by taking an active part in their community, they were living up to the ideal of civic humanism within which they had grown to adulthood. Those who believed in the patrician ideal of virtue felt obliged to extend themselves in economic pursuits, not just for the good of their families but also to afford them the time and resources for public service. Economic advantage coupled with civic responsibility meant that republicanism was working. The Greenhow men of this generation all seemed to fit this ideal. Economically flexible and patriotic, they supported their families through more than one means and served their community when asked.[18]

17. "Robert Greenhow, Merchant in Williamsburg," *William and Mary Quarterly*, 2d ser., 5 (1925): 125–26; Michael E. Pollock, *Marriage Bonds of Henrico County, Virginia, 1782–1853* (Baltimore: Genealogical Publishing, 1984), 71; gravestone, John Greenhow, Bruton Parish Church, Williamsburg, Va.; Stephenson, "John Greenhow House," 6; Fillmore Norfleet, *Saint-Mémin in Virginia: Portraits and Biographies* (Richmond, Va.: Dietz, 1942), 169, 168, 11, 37–42, 72; Henrico County Land Tax Lists, 1809, 1810, LOV; Julia F. Pagaud to Joseph Prentis, Suffolk, Mar. 21, 1808, CWF. In 1788 Robert Greenhow's name appears in the tax transfers as the owner of "4 lots via John Greenhow." John Greenhow's estate paid taxes on 296 acres in 1788 but on only 141 acres in the years 1789–93. Tax records also show that the estate paid no taxes on land in 1794, but Robert Greenhow paid taxes on the 141 acres that year. In 1801 Greenhow insured his property, which matches the location of his father's house and also the "Lumber House," for a total of $9,200, his estimate for replacing the buildings.

18. Mary Wingfield Scott, *Houses*, 59; Stanley Elkins and Eric McKitrick, *The Age of Federalism* (New York: Oxford University Press, 1993), 8–9, 23–24, 693; Walter Lippman, *A Preface to*

Brother John died in 1795, at only twenty-six years of age, but had entered the mercantile trade in Richmond and in Fredericksburg before his death. Samuel and George also continued in their father's trade, opening stores and buying up property. James, however, set up a medical practice, eventually moving into a small brick-and-frame house on Fifth and Clay Streets, with his office on the corner. James Greenhow did not become the financial success that his father and older brother did, but he built a solid reputation as a physician, often called on to attend to some of the most respected people in the community. For example, George Wythe, the revered law professor from the College of William and Mary, migrated to Richmond in 1789 and settled into a yellow house on the corner of Fifth and Grace Streets. When his grandnephew George Wythe Swinney added yellow arsenic to Wythe's coffee one morning in 1806 in hopes of using his inheritance to pay off gambling debts, James Greenhow helped perform the autopsy on the body.[19]

In 1815, just before he died, Dr. Greenhow was mentioned as one of the "most eminent physicians" in Richmond, though a "bold phlebotomist" due to his habit of bleeding patients in the winter months, considered a risky practice by some doctors. James traveled to Philadelphia late that year for special medical attention. Writing to his wife, Lucy, in December, he reported that two weeks earlier the doctors there had performed an operation on him for his "fistulous affections," and he felt much better within a few days. By the time of this letter, however, he felt so weak from "chills & fevers & a most troublesome cough" that he had to dictate the letter rather than write it himself. Although he had good hopes for his progress at the time, he had probably died before the letter reached home with his "best wishes" for his wife and "Dear children," of which he left eight, one as yet unborn. Lucy Greenhow and her children remained in Richmond, important influences in Mary Jane Greenhow's childhood.[20]

Samuel Greenhow died in 1815 as well. Like his older brother, Samuel

Politics (Ann Arbor: University of Michigan Press, Ann Arbor Paperbacks, 1962), 18; McCoy, *Elusive Republic*, 17–19, 21, 22, 45.

19. Sheldon, *Richmond, Virginia*, 270; "Greenhow Family Papers," *William and Mary Quarterly*, 1st ser., 7 (1898–99): 17; Mary Wingfield Scott, *Old Richmond Neighborhoods* (Richmond, Va.: Whittet and Shepperson, 1950), 279; Julian P. Boyd, "The Murder of George Wythe," *William and Mary Quarterly*, 3d ser., 12, no. 4 (Oct. 1955): 518, 519, 527; W. Edwin Hemphill, "Examinations of George Wythe Swinney for Forgery and Murder: A Documentary Essay," *William and Mary Quarterly*, 3d ser., 12, no. 4 (Oct. 1955): 557.

20. Quoted in Wyndham B. Blanton, *Medicine in Virginia in the Nineteenth Century* (Richmond, Va.: Garrett and Massie, 1933), 246; James Greenhow to Lucy Greenhow, Dec. 11, 1815, Claiborne Family Papers, VHS; "Hayes Family," *Genealogies of Virginia Families*, 3:959–60.

had added Richmond property to his assets through the years, one of which he rented to Aaron Burr for a time, but never amassed holdings equal to Robert's. A successful merchant in both Richmond and Fredericksburg, Samuel served on the city council, as vestryman for St. John's Church, and as treasurer of the Bible Society of Virginia, while becoming principal agent for the Mutual Assurance Society in 1808. As agent, Samuel corresponded with Thomas Jefferson regarding some misgivings the ex-president had about the future of the company. Hoping to insure his mills, Jefferson had sent in a report on their size and construction but then heard that the society was close to bankruptcy. Although Greenhow assured him of the company's solvency, Jefferson decided to wait longer before signing on. Greenhow had more success in persuading Jefferson to donate money to the Bible Society of Virginia, although not without effort. The former president was reticent for several reasons, not the least of which was his fear that the society advanced the goals of a single denomination. Greenhow assured him that the membership was broad based, "the result of that perfect toleration secured to us, in all matters relative to religion." Finally agreeing with Greenhow that "there never was a more . . . sublime system of morality delivered to man than is to be found in the four evangelists," Jefferson sent him fifty dollars.[21]

George Greenhow advertised "Family flour, of superior quality, for sale" in June 1812. The flour might have been stock he sold through his store or that he produced on his farm in Henrico County. George also built homes for rental and for sale; the high-quality workmanship of these structures gave them a reputation for durable construction. But his property holdings dwindled until there were none listed in the city land-tax lists in 1835, four years before his death. George's main civic importance to the town lay in his role as commissioner of the revenue, making him an important member of municipal government and a household name throughout the city, at least once a year.[22]

21. *Richmond Portraits in an Exhibition of Makers of Richmond, 1737–1860* (Richmond, Va.: Valentine Museum, 1949), 83; Sheldon, *Richmond, Virginia*, 270; Danforth and Claiborne, *Historical Sketch*, 126; W. Asbury Christian, D.D., *Richmond, Her Past and Present* (Spartanburg, S.C.: Reprint Company, 1973), 46–47; Thomas Jefferson to Samuel Greenhow, Nov. 7, 1809, Thomas Jefferson Papers, Presidential Series, LC (microfilm, VHS); Greenhow to Jefferson, Nov. 11, 1813, ibid.; Jefferson to Greenhow, Jan. 31, 1814, ibid.; Greenhow to Jefferson, Feb. 4, 1814, ibid. The Mutual Assurance Society was begun by W. F. Ast, originally from Prussia, and chartered by the state legislature in 1794.

22. *Enquirer*, June 12, Oct. 9, 1812; Henrico County Land Tax Registers, 1815–26, LOV; Richmond Land Tax Registers, 1810–35, LOV; Mary Wingfield Scott, *Neighborhoods*, 150; Danforth and Claiborne, *Historical Sketch*, 126.

Given that all of the Greenhow brothers were occupied in the same profession in such close proximity to each other, one might suspect that they
would have indulged in a healthy competition, but, in fact, a letter from
George Greenhow to Gen. John Preston in 1802, while Robert was still
doing business in Williamsburg, reflects just the opposite. Preston had asked
George to supply goods to his brother Thomas, which he had done, but then,
considering Thomas Preston's location, suggested that he might find it
"more convenient to supply himself at Williamsburg," that is, at Robert's
store. Even after Robert moved to Richmond, there was still no apparent animosity between the fraternal merchants, suggesting that the affection of family members overrode considerations of finances for these men, even though
Robert threw himself into the business with a vengeance.[23]

When Robert Greenhow moved to Richmond, it could just barely be
called a city. Established by William Byrd II in 1733, Richmond's population
stood at a little under five thousand residents by 1810. Initially, merchants
like the Greenhows ran the city, but one of his first occupations there was the
accumulation of property. The city taxed him for $37,500 worth of property
on more than ten lots the year he moved to Richmond. Since he had been
taxed for only one lot worth $1,000 the year before, it is evident that Robert
Greenhow immediately reinvested capital from liquidation of his property in
Williamsburg. During his early years in Richmond, he ranked in the 99.8
percentile of taxable wealth. By 1819, the year Mary was born, he owned
twenty-one lots in Richmond, paying 1.35 percent of the aggregate assessed
on land that year. By 1825, he also owned $5,896 worth of property in sur-
rounding Henrico County.[24]

Robert Greenhow seems to have exercised sound business judgment in his
property management. Holdings he retained the longest consisted of two lots
near Rocketts Warehouse and Landing. Being a merchant, he understood the
importance of this property. Richmond had a geographic advantage because
it was located at the falls of the James River, supposedly the last site at which
ships could reach the interior from the coast. Establishment of a public warehouse at Shockoe Creek in 1737 had been intended by the colonial General
Assembly to facilitate movement of goods and crops, namely tobacco, between the Tidewater and the backcountry. Since the river becomes narrower

23. George Greenhow to Gen. John Preston, Jan. 19, 1802, Preston Family Papers (Mss1P9-
267fFA2), VHS.

24. Dabney, *Virginia*, 87, 180; Sheldon, *Richmond, Virginia*, 124, 382, 335–36; Norfleet,
Saint-Mémin, 168; Richmond and Henrico County Land Tax Registers, 1809–40, LOV.

and more shallow as it nears the falls, even smaller ships had to stop about one mile below Richmond at Rocketts Landing. Thus, for goods coming into the city from either direction, men such as Greenhow who owned property near Rocketts held a monopoly over trade. Between his other interests and the rents he collected on "pleasantly situated" and "neatly arranged" city buildings or an "agreeable, healthy, little Farm" just outside of town, Greenhow was able to provide well for his family and accumulate the resources necessary to address his civic responsibilities as well.[25]

One of Greenhow's first acts of community service was as overseer for the poor. Urban areas were the first to begin seeing poverty as a problem requiring institutionalization, and Richmond decided to build an almshouse in 1804, though not from purely altruistic concerns. In a society where social philosophy demanded that citizens had a duty to become productive, being contributing members in order to maintain the liberty for which they had struggled, almshouses became reforming institutions designed to instill a more responsible work ethic into the least productive members of society. Richmond aldermen identified people in need of such instruction and wrote orders for them to be placed in the almshouse, where they were required to work until they had produced enough to reimburse the city for their stay. It was in his capacity of alderman that Greenhow fulfilled these duties.[26]

Greenhow's servants found a baby in a basket on his front porch one morning, with a note attached, stating simply, "Alexander B. White." Soon, Greenhow learned that the baby was the son of Eliza White, daughter of a poor and dying widow; the daughter and her husband had left the city. Greenhow "sent the babe to the poor house, and directed a proper nurse to be provided for it." Informed by "the worthy matron there" that the child was doing well, he then used his influence and connections to locate the mother. In an earlier era or another place, he might have taken the child in to his own home, but by the early nineteenth century, there were other procedures in place for managing the situation. Clearly, Greenhow took on patriarchal responsibilities for Richmond as he did for his family. His financial and political power made him both expected and able to act benevolently

25. Richmond Legislative Petitions, Dec. 9, 1815, LOV; Sheldon, *Richmond, Virginia*, 222–26, 261–63; *Enquirer*, July 3, 28, 1812.

26. Sheldon, *Richmond, Virginia*, 416; Linda K. Kerber, "The Revolutionary Generation: Ideology, Politics, and Culture in the Early Republic," in *The New American History*, ed. Eric Foner, rev. and exp. ed., American Historical Association (Philadelphia: Temple University Press, 1997), 41. See also David J. Rothman, *The Discovery of the Asylum: Social Order and Disorder in the New Republic* (Boston: Little, Brown, 1971).

toward those who were less fortunate. Power and benevolence were inextricably entwined in the early Republic's definition of civic virtue. Although it is uncertain the extent to which Mary Jane Greenhow witnessed the public service her father performed, it would not be a stretch to imagine that he replicated at home the attitude of responsibility he displayed to the wider world.[27]

Research has not uncovered the political affiliation, if any, of Robert Greenhow. Being a successful merchant in Richmond during the early national period, when the city was a Federalist island in Republican Virginia, suggests that Greenhow might have been persuaded by Federalist goals. Merchants occupied most civic offices in Richmond until 1820, which was a normal trend in the initial years of urban formation, for the commercial sector of a city had the most to gain from development into a well-ordered urban society. Wealth was another common trait among the first leaders of Richmond since early officeholders did not receive salaries. Therefore, the fact that Greenhow advanced to public office in Federalist Richmond does not say as much about his political persuasion as it does about his economic motives and financial success.[28]

Greenhow served the city in several capacities, soon after arriving there, as councilman, alderman, recorder, and mayor. The city's voters did not elect him to any of these offices. When the state legislature incorporated Richmond as a city in 1782, the structure of government followed the form established in most English municipalities by the end of the seventeenth century. Freeholders elected a corporate body of twelve officers who then elected the councilmen, aldermen, recorder, and mayor. The combination of these officials constituted the Common Hall, or the governing body of Richmond. Prevailing fears of executive abuses following the Revolution circumscribed Greenhow's function as mayor to more judicial and ceremonial rather than executive powers. He was charged with maintaining the peace of the city and sitting on the Hustings Court.[29]

A study of his tour as mayor in 1812–13 reveals the best evidence for Robert Greenhow's political leanings. Events leading up to the War of 1812, and emergencies in Richmond during the war itself, provide clues that Greenhow was a Republican. The United States had become the target of both the French and the British in their war with each other, and American ships be-

27. Incident related in George Wythe Munford, *The Two Parsons; Cupid's Sports; the Dream; and the Jewels of Virginia* (Richmond: J. D. K. Sleight, 1884), 98–99.

28. Sheldon, *Richmond, Virginia*, 102, 112, 129, 130, 163.

29. Christian, *Richmond, Her Past*, 107, 117; Sheldon, *Richmond, Virginia*, 72–73, 79, 80, 124, 140.

came vulnerable to search and seizure from both sides in the European conflict. When the British warship HMS *Leopard* attacked the USS *Chesapeake* off the coast of Norfolk in 1807, it embarrassed and enraged Americans, but President Thomas Jefferson's response to the insult proved ineffective. The Embargo Act, lasting from December 1807 to March 1809, was meant to encourage domestic manufacturing while it attempted to damage England's market for manufactured goods. The embargo hurt England but crippled United States seaports more, leading to its repeal, which satisfied folks in Richmond, who had been more than a little annoyed with the "Dambargo."[30]

America was a nation still defining itself, and being bullied by France and England fostered frustration and embarrassment. Some of those with the least inclination to accept foreign insults to American shipping won during the 1810 congressional elections, and numbers of these new congressmen who arrived in Washington the next term were dubbed "war hawks." According to historian Steven Watts, these men were Liberal Republicans who had "unbending confidence in the strength of the young republic."[31]

Robert Greenhow's views of the situation were similar to the "war hawks." In May 1812 he served on a committee with William Wirt, Peyton Randolph, Thomas Ritchie, and Peter V. Daniel that issued a resolution stating that, not only were they willing to go to war with England again but also with France if necessary. When Congress declared war on Britain on June 3, 1812, Wirt wrote to James Monroe from Richmond, "there is not a man here who is not an inch taller since congress has done its duty."[32]

In fact, Richmond celebrated the declaration of war as if it had been an armistice. The Society of Friends of the Revolution met at Washington Tavern on June 20 to make plans for a special Fourth of July jubilee that would give the citizens a chance to celebrate both their first independence from England and the commencement of their second. Among the plans for the event was an illumination of the city at night, and it was on this point that Robert Greenhow's role as mayor came into conflict with the powers of the Common Hall. For one thing, the council questioned organizing an event cele-

30. Risjord, *Jefferson's America*, 265–69; McCoy, *Elusive Republic*, 210; Daniel P. Jordan, *Political Leadership in Jefferson's Virginia* (Charlottesville: University Press of Virginia, 1983), 27 (quote).

31. Risjord, *Jefferson's America*, 272, 273; Watts, *Republic Reborn*, xv, 257, 269.

32. Sheldon, *Richmond, Virginia*, 165; Christian, *Richmond, Her Past*, 84; John P. Frank, *Justice Daniel Dissenting: A Biography of Peter V. Daniel, 1784–1860* (Cambridge: Harvard University Press, 1964), 20, 22, 23; Risjord, *Jefferson's America*, 281, 282 (quote); McCoy, *Elusive Republic*, 235.

brating the onset of war, "the last resort of republicans," rather than waiting until they had won at least one battle. They also reminded Greenhow that late-night celebrations could sometimes get out of hand. Since the mayor's job was to protect the peace, it seemed incongruous for him to be planning events that could disturb it. Having said all of that, however, the council resolved to approve the event from their "feeling of highest personal respect for the Mayor."[33]

The celebration went on as planned, beginning with a gun salute at sunrise, then Governor Barbour's review of the troops, Peter V. Daniel's committee on toasts providing more than enough reasons to tip back the glass, readings of the Declaration of Independence and the war resolution, banquets throughout the city, and culminating with the city's illumination. Immediately afterward, eleven members of this *connexion* began a fund drive to provide supplies for Virginia soldiers. Samuel Greenhow took on the job as treasurer for the group and, by December 1812, had collected $2,910 with promises of $3,150 more. Of the money already collected, they had paid for shoes, socks, flannel under-jackets, books, postage, and a "Waggon to hire." Among the names on the subscribers list were the Greenhow brothers, Samuel, George, and Robert, all aiding efforts toward winning the war.[34]

As mayor during this time, Greenhow exercised his powers to maintain the peace to a greater degree. Upon reports that the British were inciting a slave insurrection, Greenhow called for more patrols and suggested that the powder magazine be removed to a safer location, actions reminiscent of his concerns as a young man during the Revolution. He also instituted a night watch to "prevent . . . the depredations committed . . . by the Nightly Robber." Further, conscious of the accelerated pace of economic change during war, Greenhow appealed to the virtuous side of society to overcome growing self-interest. He argued that the war had become a convenient excuse for engagement in "the Odious and Detestable Practices of the Monopolizer." Articles that "from long use of them, have become, Necessaries of Life" were either unavailable or "so-enhanced and increased" in price due to hoarding "that the poorer class of people are utterly unable to procure them." Greenhow the merchant and landlord asked for everyone to "discountenance, and by every possible means suppress . . . , speculation."[35]

33. Richmond Common Hall Records 3, LOV, 217–21 (July 3, 1812); Sheldon, *Richmond, Virginia,* 80; Christian, *Richmond, Her Past,* 84.

34. Frank, *Justice Daniel Dissenting,* 24–26; Samuel Greenhow, "Account of Subscribers to Fund Promoting Success of War with Great Britain," Dec. 18, 1812, Preston Family Papers.

35. Virginius Dabney, *Richmond: The Story of a City,* rev. and exp. ed. (Charlottesville: University Press of Virginia, 1990), 59–60; *Richmond Enquirer,* Jan. 13, 1814. See also McCoy, *Elusive Republic,* 210, 219–20.

The years from 1811 to Mary's birth in 1819 were the most tumultuous in Robert Greenhow's life. Deeply engaged with city business and war, he also experienced some of his highest and lowest personal events. He buried one wife, married another, buried an infant son a year later, moved into a new residence, and then was blessed with two more children.[36]

The day after Christmas, 1811, the Placide Stock Company offered a benefit performance at the new brick theater on Academy Square. Theatergoers, in a holiday mood and decked out in their finest attire, anticipated an exciting evening. Robert Greenhow attended with his wife and young Robert. When the curtain rose on the second act, Mary Wills Greenhow, "in the full tide of Health" and "looking better than" Robert "had seen her for some months," leaned back from her seat in the first row of their box, the third from the stage, and rested against Robert's knees. He circled her waist with his arms and prepared to enjoy the rest of the play, surrounded by friends and family.[37]

Instead of the expected artistry, however, the audience heard an announcement that "the house is on fire!" Although new and made of brick, the theater afforded only a few passages of escape. Doors and stairways were so narrow that amid the panic and terror, and choking from smoke, passage became virtually impossible. Charged with his wife's last words, "save my child," Robert Greenhow struggled to get his young son from the building. Leaving his wife in brother James's care, he carried the boy to the staircase, where he was pushed down to the floor by the crush of people trying to escape. Finally pulling himself up, he made his way past and over victims on the stairway until he reached the street. Although he went back into the building, he could not fight his way against the flow of people pushing out. Mary Wills Greenhow died in the fire along with seventy-one others.[38]

Robert Greenhow confessed his grief to friend John T. Mason in a letter dated February 7, 1812. Sentimental and dramatic, Greenhow portrayed his

36. List of family births and deaths, MJCG/LC. Robert Greenhow and his second wife, Mary, had a son born to them on June 17, 1814. Francis John Seymour Greenhow died before he reached his first birthday, on Mar. 26, 1815, Easter Sunday, and was buried "about 40 steps North of the church on Richmond Hill." See also Arthur Pierce Middleton, director of research, Colonial Williamsburg Foundation, to Cora B. Powell, July 8, 1952, CWF.

37. Dabney, *Virginia*, 267; Mary Newton Stannard, *Richmond: Its People and Its Story* (Philadelphia: J. B. Lippincott, 1923), 104–5; Robert Greenhow to John T. Mason, Feb. 7, 1812, in Norfleet, *Saint-Mémin*, 168–69.

38. Stannard, *Richmond*, 105; Christian, *Richmond, Her Past*, 80; Norfleet, *Saint-Mémin*, 168–69; John S. Salmon, comp., *A Guidebook to Virginia's Historical Markers* rev. and exp. ed. (Charlottesville: University Press of Virginia, 1994), 159. Dr. James Greenhow did not die in the fire, but there is no record of the circumstances of his rescue or of how he came to leave Robert's wife in the building.

sense of loss by measuring his grief against the happiness he had experienced with his wife. He wrote Mason that Mary had been his "wife for near 26-1/2 years! with whom I had enjoyed as much of connubial Bliss as ever fell to the Lot I dare venture to pronounce of any one pair! Suddenly & in a moment unlooked for & unexpected taken without one Sad last parting Adieu from my very arms!"[39]

Although his grief seemed deep, his mourning was short. Four months later Greenhow married Mary Lorraine Charlton of Yorktown and in 1814 moved his family into a prestigious home on Capitol and Tenth Streets in Richmond. Built in 1803 by Edmund Randolph, the two-story octagonal brick house, fifty-five feet long and twenty-seven feet wide, sported three-sided ends, giving the building an oval shape. This home was the first environment known to Mary Jane Charlton Greenhow.[40]

The closest circle of Mary Jane's *connexion* was her immediate family: her mother, father, and two-year-old brother, James Washington Greenhow. Her half-brother Robert, nineteen years old by the time Mary Jane was born, had already received a degree from the College of William and Mary and was at that point pursuing a medical degree at what became Columbia University in New York City.[41]

Mary Jane Greenhow's identity can also be traced from the gradually widening circle of her first world, beginning with her neighborhood. From the Greenhow home on Capitol Street, she could view the expanse of the capitol lawn, the trees and walkways, and the governor's mansion, which her father

39. Greenhow to Mason, Feb. 7, 1812, in Norfleet, *Saint-Mémin*, 168–69.

40. Mary Wingfield Scott, *Houses*, 59–61; Richmond Hustings Court Book 50:614–15, LOV; *Richmond Enquirer*, July 3, 1812. After Randolph died in 1813 while visiting his wife's family at Carter's Hall in Clarke County, his daughters liquidated the estate. There must have been several claims upon that property, however, because the full lot came into Greenhow's fee-simple ownership in three stages. His brother George, as commissioner of the revenue for Richmond, was charged with the responsibility of selling off Randolph's personal property in 1812. By May 1817, through purchase from Philip Norborne Nicholas, Peter V. Daniel, and Thomas Ritchie, Greenhow finally owned the total property, though the family had moved into the home in 1814.

41. List of family births and deaths, MJCG/LC; David Rankin Barbee, "Robert Greenhow," *William and Mary Quarterly*, 2d ser., 12, no. 1 (Jan. 1933): 182–83; U.S. Bureau of the Census, Fourth and Fifth Census, LOV, microfilm; MJCG/MHS, 11 (Sept. 22, 1837), 28 (Oct. 25, 1837), 30 (Nov. 5, 1837), 33 (Nov. 15, 1837), 40 (Dec. 3, 1837), 61 (Feb. 6, 1838), 68 (Mar. 5, 1838). There is evidence that one of Mary Jane's aunts, an "Aunt Jane" or "Aunt Greenhow," also lived in the home with them. Both the 1820 and 1830 U.S. Census for Richmond list a female in the same age group as Robert Greenhow, who would have been too old to be Robert's wife.

had helped commission. Just one block east of her home, local civic leaders bustled in and out of the new Richmond courthouse or stood outside discussing the issues of the day. On the other side stood the Virginia Museum, an imposing brick structure ninety-one feet long and fifty feet wide. Also nearby stood the Swan, a two-story frame inn taking up most of the block between Eighth and Ninth Streets, and the Washington Tavern, just down the hill on Ninth and Grace Streets, both of which hosted the movers and shakers of early nineteenth-century Virginia.[42]

The neighborhood in which she grew up included many of the economic and political elite of Richmond. Some of the children from these families became her lifelong friends. Peter V. Daniel, who served as lieutenant governor of Virginia for thirteen years, lived just a few blocks from the Greenhows. Daniel's children Elizabeth and Peter Jr. grew up as contemporaries of Mary Jane, and it is clear that the families spent a good deal of time together. John Tyler became governor of Virginia in 1825 and moved his family into the governor's mansion in Richmond. Although the Tylers and Greenhows were related by marriage and Mary Jane could have referred to Tyler's children as "cousin," she later introduced "Lilly" (Letitia) Tyler as her "friend," indicating that the two girls had formed a bond in their youth.[43]

Among other nearby neighbors, Col. John and Catherine Ambler and their family lived two blocks from the Greenhows in an octagon-shaped house built by Lewis Burwell on Twelfth and Clay Streets. Ambler and Greenhow were of the same age, had both served James City County in the Virginia General Assembly, and continued their associations after moving to Richmond, serving in city offices and other organizations together. Although Ambler lived in the city, he owned over two thousand acres in Henrico County along the James River on which he worked between twenty-nine and thirty-six slaves through the years. In addition to these holdings, Ambler maintained Ambler Hill in Winchester, property he obtained from his wife's first husband's estate. The Greenhows and Amblers socialized a great deal during Mary Jane's early years. Her connection to them continued even after

42. Stannard, *Richmond*, 67; Mary Wingfield Scott, *Neighborhoods*, 97, 104.

43. Frank, *Justice Daniel Dissenting*, vii, 38, 39, 48; MJCG/MHS, 5 (Sept. 13, 1837); Mary Wingfield Scott, *Neighborhoods*, 150; Paul Brandon Barringer, James Mercer Garnett, and Rosewell Page, eds., *University of Virginia: Its History, Influence, Equipment, and Characteristics, with Biographical Sketches and Portraits of Founders, Benefactors, Officers, and Alumni* (New York: Lewis, 1904), 324; Theodore C. DeLaney, "Julia Gardiner Tyler: A Nineteenth-Century Southern Woman" (Ph.D. diss., College of William and Mary, 1995), 214; MGL, 876 (Oct. 8, 1865), 883 (Oct. 21, 1865).

the end of her life by naming Ambler's grandson as the executor of her meager estate.[44]

John Marshall, related by marriage to John Ambler, lived nearby on Ninth Street. From all accounts he was a friendly neighbor, charming and engaging. Marshall made enemies among the Jeffersonians in town, but they had difficulty hating a man who, although a Federalist, dressed and treated his neighbors in a simple Republican fashion. One of the Jeffersonians who lived nearby was Thomas Ritchie, residing on Grace Street. Ritchie's newspaper, the *Enquirer*, was the chief political organ for the Richmond Junto.[45]

Although there are no sources stating that Mary Jane had many contacts with these powerful men, they were members of her father's world and frequently in his company. It is possible that her political awareness later in life came in part from listening to the ins and outs of politics discussed over tea or across the family dinner table. These powerful Virginians obviously made an impression on the young girl.

One of the most important neighborhood influences in young Mary Jane Greenhow's life was that of her church. She was baptized on October 27, 1819, at Monumental Church in Richmond. Administered by Bishop Richard Channing Moore, the baptism was witnessed by the baby's mother, father, and fifteen-year-old cousin Lucy Greenhow. Monumental Church, constructed on the site of the 1811 theater fire, was both an Episcopal church and a monument. Since many of the victims had been so consumed by the fire to be unidentifiable, their relatives determined that the spot should be consecrated and the remains buried there. The church became their memorial. When Monumental Church held its first service, Robert Greenhow had been one of its first two wardens; his wife Mary directed the Sunday school.[46]

Into this sandstone and stucco, octagon-shaped building Mary Jane Greenhow entered with her family regularly for worship. As the family

44. *Richmond Portraits*, 6–7; Mary Wingfield Scott, *Neighborhoods*, 94; Sheldon, *Richmond, Virginia*, 120; Henrico County Personal Property and Land Tax Records, 1811–35, LOV; John Jaquelin Ambler, *The Amblers of Virginia* (Richmond, Va., 1972); Garland R. Quarles, *The Story of One Hundred Old Homes in Winchester, Virginia* (Winchester, Va.: Farmers and Merchants Bank, 1967), 14–16; MGL, 242 (Oct. 14, 1863), 395 (June 3, 1863), 506 (Nov. 2, 1863); administration of estate, Mary Lee, 1908, MSA.

45. *Richmond Portraits*, 116, 170–71; Frank, *Justice Daniel Dissenting*, 39; Mary Wingfield Scott, *Neighborhoods*, 150.

46. List of family births and deaths, MJCG/LC; MGL, 877 (Oct. 8, 1865); Christian, *Richmond, Her Past*, 80, 81; Stannard, *Richmond*, 106; George D. Fisher, *History and Reminiscences of the Monumental Church, Richmond, Virginia, from 1814 to 1878* (Richmond: Whittet and Shepperson, 1880), 163.

walked down the center aisle, they saw ahead of them the raised pulpit centered between two green, marbleized Ionic columns, with stairways leading up on both sides. The colors inside the conservatively styled building matched the exterior: shades of pale gray. The Greenhows settled into the fourth pew on the right from the pulpit as comfortably as they could in the straight-backed seats to await the service.[47]

During services, young Mary Jane surely recognized several family friends, among them the Ambler family sitting across the center aisle and one row back. She probably became accustomed to seeing John Marshall unlatch his pew door during the service so that he could make room for his long legs or studied with interest young Edgar Allan Poe as he joined the John Allan family in their pew. Her keen appreciation of music might have begun here as she listened intently to the organ located in the rear balcony. If she did not dress warmly enough in winter, she might have fidgeted in her seat or cuddled next to another family member since the furnace in the basement was undersized and forced what little heat it generated through four small openings in the sanctuary. When she first learned to read, the young, ambitious child probably practiced on the words "Give Ear O Lord" above the chancel while half-listening to the message. Whatever else Mary Jane Greenhow did while attending this church, she noted the importance of it in her parents' lives and would one day assign the same weight to it in her own. As a young woman living with her parents, church attendance was automatic but an occasion more for socializing than spiritual strengthening. Her mother's chastising "Are you going to church today, my dear?" played in Mary's head whenever she was away from home. This would change. In fact, being a faithful Christian would one day be of foremost importance to her, and asking her Lord to "Give Ear" turned into a daily, sometimes hourly, ritual.[48]

The physical setting into which Mary Jane Greenhow was born, and the influence her father had in creating it, gave her beginnings an atmosphere of wealth, power, responsibility, and prestige. The more intimate relations she had with her family helped mold her character.

47. Stannard, *Richmond*, 107; Glave Newman Anderson and Associates, Inc., Architects, *An Adaptive Preservation Study for the Monumental Church* (1974), 9, 10, 11; Richmond Hustings Court Book 9:475–77, LOV. On May 13, 1814, Robert Greenhow paid $350 for the lease of pew 16 at Monumental Church. Fifteen percent of the money derived from leases went to pay the rector's salary.

48. Stannard, *Richmond*, 107; Receipt for use of pew 52, Col. John Ambler, June 1, 1835, Ambler Family Papers (Mss1Am167c), VHS; Glave Newman Anderson, *Preservation Study*, 11; MJCG/MHS, 20 (Oct. 8, 1837), 37 (Nov. 28, 1837), 66 (Feb. 28, 1838), 68 (Mar. 5, 1838).

2

"A Most Accurate Remembrance of My Wild Kicks"

The Early Development of a Rebel

*M*ary Greenhow Lee rarely let circumstances dampen her sense of control. Throughout her life, she willfully resisted circumstances that tired, bored, or intimidated her. That she would defy Union occupiers during the Civil War in Winchester is not surprising since, as a young woman, she had shown numerous signs of rebellion. Her ability to laugh both at herself and at cumbersome situations helped her diminish feelings of helplessness when needed. She asserted her independence and individuality when it suited her. Traits inherent in her adult character resembled her youthful "wild kicks," the phrase she applied to memories of childhood mischief. Her clear sense of identity fueled her nerve. She gained confidence from the safe environment of an affectionate and accepting family, the comfort she became accustomed to in the presence of powerful people, and the self-confidence instilled in her from a good education. Mary Jane Greenhow became an accomplished scholar in both academic pursuits and social decorum. Although she pulled at the restraints of societal rules, she appreciated the position she held in the structure.

The Greenhows represented the modern American family taking shape during the early national period. Its form emerged between the Revolution and the 1830s and exhibited at least four distinctions from earlier family structures: the marriage of the parents was based on affection; the wife's primary role was to nurture her children and manage her home; the parents concentrated their resources and time on parenting; and the family unit was smaller than those of the previous century.[1]

Robert Greenhow said of his first wife at her death, "My wife! & friend of my heart & warmest affections." To better understand Mary Jane Greenhow's childhood, it is critical to assess how he felt about her mother, his second wife. Thirty years younger than her husband, Mary Lorraine Greenhow had made several adjustments in her own life by the time her daughter was born. Only twenty-one when she married Robert Greenhow, a businessman and widower with a twelve-year-old son, she had assumed the domestic responsibilities of a wife in the highest social circles of a growing city. The daughter of Francis and Mary Charlton of Yorktown, Mary Lorraine left a village society and moved into her husband's politically and economically energetic world in Richmond.[2]

Robert Greenhow's relationship with his younger second wife is difficult to interpret because sources connecting the two are scarce. The thirty-year difference in their ages could have lessened the chances of Mary Lorraine Charlton also becoming the "friend of [his] heart." Clearly, he expected her to outlive him and worked to provide resources for her upon his death. Robert Greenhow took full charge of the family finances. According to custom, his wives did not concern themselves with the murky world of money.[3]

There is some evidence, however, that Mary Jane Greenhow's parents had an affectionate marriage. A concept of marriage derived from companionship and love of like-minded individuals, rather than couples conveniently linked

1. Carl Degler, *At Odds: Women and the Family in America from the Revolution to the Present* (New York: Oxford University Press, 1980), 8–9, 14; Jan Lewis, "Motherhood and the Construction of the Male Citizen in the United States, 1750–1850," in *Constructions of the Self*, ed. George Levine (New Brunswick, N.J.: Rutgers University Press, 1992), 145; Kerber, "Revolutionary Generation," 40.

2. Robert Greenhow to John T. Mason, Feb. 7, 1812, printed in Norfleet, *Saint-Mémin*, 168–69; Mary Wingfield Scott, *Houses*, 57–61; Greenhow Family Papers, Genealogical Collection, CWM.

3. John F. Kasson, *Rudeness and Civility: Manners in Nineteenth-Century Urban America* (New York: Hill and Wang, 1990), 68; Norfleet, *Saint-Mémin*, 168; Kerber, "Revolutionary Generation," 38; "Last Will of Robert Greenhow," Richmond Hustings Court Book 8:263, LOV. In none of the deeds of trust studied for this project was either of Greenhow's wives examined for their understanding of the vulnerability to their dower rights should the property in question be subject to foreclosure.

for the purposes of political or economic advantage, arose from the Revolutionary period. Revolutionaries rebelled against not only George III but also patriarchy. Americans governed themselves; thus, children began claiming the right to choose their mates, one of their first acts of asserting their individuality. Studies have shown that the companionate marriage indeed emerged in Richmond by the early nineteenth-century. Mary Greenhow Lee eventually developed into a woman who was naturally affectionate to close family members, was especially fond of both of her parents and her brothers, and ultimately cared for members of her husband's family as if they were her own. Affection is natural, but it is also easier to exhibit if a child grows up modeling herself after affectionate parents. If the poem Robert wrote in his wife's commonplace book in 1830 is any indication, Greenhow's relationship with her was respectful and romantic.[4]

> Oh, Woman! What bliss, what enchantment we owe,
> To the spell of thy heart to thy solace below,
> To thy truth so endearing—thy kindness and care
> In the morning of joy, in the night of despair!
>
> To thy soul's chosen love thou unchanged will remain,
> In health and in sickness, in pleasure and pain;
> And, when closed are his eyes in death's mortal eclipse,
> Even then, still is his the last kiss of thy lips!
>
> And, over his grave thou wilt mournfully keep
> Thy love vigil of sorrow, to pray and to weep;
> Yes! to pray—that his errors of heart be forgiven,
> And, that thou may'st yet meet him unsullied in Heaven![5]

Assuming that the pair placed great importance on the words he left for her in a book of memories, then their marriage was based on affection and romance. The poem also hints at his growing sense of mortality. By this time, Robert Greenhow was sixty years old and undoubtedly imagining his wife in the role of widow. Asking that his "errors of heart be forgiven" could be interpreted several ways, yet it is doubtful he would have displayed a dark confession in the pages of a book meant to circulate among friends and fam-

4. Degler, *At Odds*, 8–9, 14; Anya Jabour, *Marriage in the Early Republic: Elizabeth and William Wirt and the Companionate Ideal* (Baltimore: Johns Hopkins University Press, 1998).
5. MLG.

ily. "Errors" of Greenhow's heart could lie in a level of reservation, possibly believing that he had not given his second wife all of the love he had lavished on his first. Another possible interpretation could be that he felt less physically capable of fulfilling his role as husband.

Whether or not Mary Lorraine Greenhow felt cheated out of her husband's total devotion is difficult to judge. She has not emerged clearly from the evidence. In fact, although most sources correctly name her as Greenhow's second wife and Mary Greenhow Lee's mother, there are a few that give her an incorrect middle name and at least one that claims Robert married his brother George's wife, Elizabeth. Clearly, Mary Jane's mother has come down through history as merely a wife and mother but with no personal identity. The epitaph on her gravestone in Winchester, Virginia, states simply: "I have no will of my own. And when she had said this, she fell asleep." In remembrance of her mother, Mary Greenhow Lee's selection of these lines for her gravestone are surely in reference to Mary Lorraine's religiosity, if not her character.[6]

The passages recorded for her by friends and family in her commonplace book, if meant as a reflection of her personality and not merely as flattery, reveal Mary Lorraine Greenhow as a gracious woman: religious, intelligent, and vibrant. At the age of twelve, her son James Washington Greenhow presented the red album with gold embossing and contributed the first poem, signing it "Your Album." The message of the poem is that "lady fair" should treat the book "gently" because the memories collected on its pages would become a "chain of rosy bows." In fact, she did press leaves and flowers within the pages, revealing a sentimental side to her nature.[7]

Many of the poems contained in the commonplace book address the issue of a woman's place in nineteenth-century society, stressing the virtues of benevolence and hospitality. Another entry indicates that the gracious woman with "no will" of her own instead had a depth of feeling and possibly mystery. Washington Greenhow selected a poem by Lord Byron, left untitled, that lends insight to this deeper facet of his mother's nature: "As the bolt-bursts on high / From the black clouds that bound it / Flashes the soul of that eye / From the long lashes around it." Although sentimental, gracious, and fair, Mary Jane Greenhow's mother evidently also had fire, which would have given the daughter a model for both passion and tact.[8]

6. Norfleet, *Saint-Mémin*, 169; George D. Fisher, *Monumental Church*, 191; gravestone, Mary Lorraine Greenhow, Mount Hebron Cemetery, Winchester, Va.

7. MLG.

8. Ibid.

The second characteristic of the modern family, separate spheres, suggests that gender roles were diverging relative to space as well as occupation. Women began spending most of their time in the private world of home, concentrating on family, while men increasingly made their living and conducted their affairs outside of the home in public. This trend has been identified more in the Northeast than in the South, in urban rather than rural areas, and for the middle and upper classes more than the poor, artisan, or yeoman households. The model fits the Greenhows, however, a family of upper-middle-class financial standing, living in Virginia's most prominent example of urbanity. Robert Greenhow is found in sources dealing with the economic, legal, and political world, while neither of his wives appears in sources outside of the domestic realm, except as members of church organizations, which are interpreted by scholars as extensions of the home.[9]

Although consigned to domestic space, women of this class did have a political role to play. They were charged with the conservative task of maintaining civic virtue by inculcating it in their children. Most of the *connexion* grew up exposed to the behavior and skillful conversation that would mark them as genteel and followed the gender roles exhibited by their elders. Books for young children often detailed passive behavior for girls and active behavior for boys, intended to produce ladies and gentlemen who fit into their assigned roles easily and not slip from them for fear of losing prestige. True gentlemen were self-controlled, firm in their resolve, ambitious, honest, industrious, energetic, loyal, and chivalrous. A true lady was pious, a comfortable companion to her husband, agreeable, bright, affectionate, composed, attractive, self-controlled, and modest, probably the behavior expected of Mary Jane by her family.[10]

The third and fourth characteristics of the modern American family were in many respects connected. Parents had been for some time decreasing the

9. Degler, *At Odds*, 8; Nancy F. Cott, *The Bonds of Womanhood: "Woman's Sphere" in New England, 1780–1835* (New Haven: Yale University Press, 1977), 89–100; Mary P. Ryan, *Cradle of the Middle Class: The Family in Oneida County, New York, 1790–1865* (Cambridge: Cambridge University Press, 1981); Barbara Welter, "The Cult of True Womanhood: 1820–1860," *American Quarterly* 18 (1966): 133–55; George D. Fisher, *Monumental Church*, 163.

10. Kerber, "Revolutionary Generation," 36–37; Lewis, "Motherhood," 144, 145, 150, 151, 154–56; Cott, *Bonds of Womanhood*, 89–100; Linda K. Kerber, *Women of the Republic: Intellect and Ideology in Revolutionary America* (Chapel Hill: University of North Carolina Press, 1980), 284–88; Kasson, *Rudeness and Civility*, 57, 43; Sarah E. Newton, *Learning to Behave: A Guide to American Conduct Books before 1900*, Bibliographies and Indexes in American History, no. 28 (Westport, Conn.: Greenwood, 1994), 29, 50, 52, 53, 85; MGL, 230 (Sept. 13, 1862), 260 (Nov. 19, 1862), 693 (Sept. 26, 1864).

size of their family to provide for their children in a changing economy. Robert Greenhow did not follow his father's example of producing almost a dozen offspring. He sired only four children with two wives, raising three of them to adulthood.

It is also apparent that Robert and his wives participated in the fourth and connecting trend in the modern American family structure, the expenditure of more time, money, and energy parenting their children. In an era of industrialization, urbanization, and rapid economic changes, parents increasingly focused attention on preparing their children to meet the challenge of a new age. Additionally, with modernity came a belief in individuality. Parents began discerning their children's strengths and weaknesses and to channel their talents into careers or skills that would be the most profitable. Thus, on the one hand, the family became a comfortable, loving haven from the changing economic world outside. On the other hand, the family produced children more capable of adapting to that world. When charting societal changes through time, the family is the most compact social unit of study; it has historically adapted to change while concurrently conserving tradition.[11]

The most important means of preparing children for a changing world

11. Kerber, "Revolutionary Generation," 39; Degler, *At Odds*, 9; Sean Wilentz, "Society, Politics, and the Market Revolution, 1814–1848," in *The New American History*, ed. Eric Foner, rev. and exp. ed., American Historical Association (Philadelphia: Temple University Press, 1997), 63, 64; Censer, *North Carolina Planters*, 24, 19, 31; John Demos, *Past, Present, and Personal: The Family and the Life Course in American History* (New York: Oxford University Press, 1986), 33; Philippe Aries, *Centuries of Childhood: A Social History of Family Life*, trans. Robert Baldick (New York: Alfred A. Knopf, 1962), 132–33, 406–7; Tamara K. Hareven, "Family Time and Historical Time," in *The Family*, ed. Alice S. Rossi, Jerome Kagan, and Tamara K. Hareven (New York: W. W. Norton, 1978), 57, 58. Some sources state that Robert Greenhow and his first wife Mary had a daughter named Polly, who married French émigré and educator Louis H. Girardin. Polly Girardin and the couple's only son died in the Richmond Theater fire in December 1811. In her study of Girardin, Jane C. Slaughter argues that he was not married to Greenhow's daughter but to Polly Cole, daughter of Roscow Cole, Greenhow's business partner in Williamsburg. Although Greenhow and Girardin had several connections, it does not appear that they were related. Support for Slaughter's argument comes in the form of silence. Had Greenhow lost a daughter as well as his wife in the theater fire, at least some of the narratives of the disaster would have mentioned it. They do not. For more on Girardin, see Jane C. Slaughter, "Louis Hue Girardin: Educator, Historian, and Man-of-Letters" (Ph.D. diss., University of Virginia, 1935); Dabney, *Richmond*, 77; "L. H. Girardin," *William and Mary Quarterly*, 2d ser., 3 (1923): 50–51; "L. H. Girardin to Wm. Wirt," *William and Mary Quarterly*, 2d ser., 5 (1925): 105–6; Stephenson, "John Greenhow House," ill. 1; and Edith Philips, *Louis Hue Girardin and Nicholas Gouin Dufief and Their Relations with Thomas Jefferson, an Unknown Episode of the French Emigration in America*, extra vol. no. 3 (Baltimore: Johns Hopkins University Press, 1926).

was education. During the nineteenth century, parents in the *connexion* increasingly prepared their sons for professions rather than bequeathing land. They sent their sons to the College of William and Mary, the University of Virginia, Washington College, and Hampden-Sydney College—even to faraway Harvard. Education was the answer to Thomas Jefferson's question of "whether we are to leave this fair inheritance to barbarians or civilized men." Schooling in the South was still mostly a private endeavor, however. In fact, although Jefferson believed that the new nation could remain free only with an informed electorate, southern states did not publicly support education until after the Civil War. Therefore, education was an indicator of economic advantage and a deep concern for many parents.[12]

Like Jefferson, Robert Greenhow valued education. In 1786 he had been a subscriber to the new Academy of Science and Fine Arts in Richmond, had acted as agent and treasurer to the commissioner of the lottery for the College of William and Mary in 1806, and had served on the board of the experimental Lancastrian School in 1825. He sent his son Robert Jr. to William and Mary and then on to Columbia for a medical degree. He saw to the education of younger son James Washington by sending him to the new University of Virginia, where he studied moral philosophy and natural philosophy in preparation to practice law.[13]

The sources have been silent as to whom Robert Greenhow entrusted the education of his daughter. It seems clear that she was educated outside of the home because she mentions meeting or hearing from "old school mate[s]," indicating that she probably attended classes at a formal institution. Green-

12. Tyler Family Papers, Women of Virginia Project Records, CWM; Robert Greenhow Jr. Papers, CWM; Ryan, *Cradle of the Middle Class*, 62, 74, 184; Censer, *North Carolina Planters*, 48; Risjord, *Jefferson's America*, 187–88. Jefferson quoted in Jordan, *Political Leadership*, 206.

13. Norfleet, *Saint-Mémin*, 168; Quarles, *Occupied Winchester*, 14; Tyler Family Papers, Women of Virginia Project Records; Robert Greenhow Jr. Papers; Ludwell H. Johnson, "How Not to Run a College, 1812–1825," in *The College of William and Mary: A History, Vol. I. 1693–1888*, ed. Susan H. Godson, Ludwell H. Johnson, Richard B. Sherman, Thad W. Tate, Helen C. Walker (Williamsburg, Va.: King and Queen, 1993), 199–226; *The Fundamental Rules and Regulations of the Lancastrian Institution* (Richmond: Ritchie, Trueheart, and Du-Val, 1817); Barbara J. Griffin, "Thomas Ritchie and the Founding of the Richmond Lancastrian School," *Virginia Magazine of History and Biography* 86, no. 4 (Oct. 1978): 447–60; Robert Greenhow to Richard Gwathmey, Aug. 2, 1826, "Extract from the Journals of the Board of Trustees for the Lancastrian School Institution," Gwathmey Family Papers (Mss1G9957a), VHS; Capt. Joseph Van Holt Nash, comp., *Students of the University of Virginia: A Semi-Centennial Catalogue, with Brief Biographical Sketches* (Baltimore: Charles Harvey, 1878), 70; "A Catalogue of the Officers and Students of the University of Virginia, Tenth Session, 1833–1834" (Charlottesville, Va.: Chronicle Steam Book Printing House, 1880), 7.

how had several options when the time came to educate Mary Jane. Besides the schools available in Richmond, the Young Ladies' School at Charlottesville was also open for those "desirous of sending their daughters or wards." The Young Ladies' Seminary at Prince Edward Court House, Virginia, began in 1832, offering everything from rhetoric to natural theology and mineralogy. Gender biases in education were mostly based on an assumption that women were biologically unsuited for comprehending some subjects and less capable of reason than men. Curricula for women had expanded from the eighteenth-century practice of merging basics like rhetoric, grammar, and arithmetic with needlework, drawing, dancing, and music. Now, some female academies were adding mythology, universal history, and logic to their courses of study. By 1860, southern women's academies led northern schools in the addition of the classics to their curricula. Although rare, this indicates that some educators in the South believed women capable of understanding classical instruction. It could be that Greenhow sent Mary Jane out of state for study, but whatever the school, it would have followed a liberal curriculum. We know that she learned French and mythology and that she did not appreciate history books, finding them nothing but a "dry detail of facts."[14]

The Greenhows believed that education further refined their children, marking them with the stamp of gentility. A properly educated child grew up with enhanced earning potential, more confidence in public, more composure in crisis, and a greater sense of responsibility toward those in need. The practical application of this was controlled and civil behavior. Obligation was attached to membership in the *connexion*, a willingness to aid friends and provide for the welfare of dependents, from children to slaves. Mary Greenhow learned the lessons of self-denial, responsibility, and hospitality at her parents' hearth, all of these held together by a firm conviction that God was choreographing their movements.[15]

Mary Jane Greenhow's relationship with her parents was both affectionate and friendly. Although her 1837–38 diary is the only source on this subject, it portrays a daughter who felt confident in her parents' love and free to relate

14. MGL, 864 (Sept. 3, 1865), 872–73 (Sept. 24, 1865), 772 (Jan. 26, 1865), 678 (Sept. 6, 1864); MJCG/MHS, 2 (Sept. 6, 1837), 30 (Oct. 28, 1837), 51 (Jan. 3, 1838); *Richmond Enquirer*, May 27, 20, 1834; Kerber, *Women of the Republic*, 210–11, 215, 218, 220–21; Anne Firor Scott, *Southern Lady*, 69–75; Christie Anne Farnham, *The Education of the Southern Belle: Higher Education and Student Socialization in the Antebellum South* (New York: New York University Press, 1994), 2, 11, 151–54; Margaret Ripley Wolfe, *Daughters of Canaan: A Saga of Southern Women* (Lexington: University Press of Kentucky, 1995), 95–98.

15. Cash, *Mind of the South*, 68, 74–77.

to them as individuals. There are more entries referring to "Mother" than to "Father," but clearly she kept in touch with both through letters. References to her father were rather teasing, as though the family understood and respected some of his idiosyncrasies yet were allowed to poke fun at them. Mary Jane lightly connected some of her own activities to her father's behavior, from drinking scalding hot coffee to digressing in her entry until, as her father would say, she had to "resume the thread of [her] narrative." Robert Greenhow might have been somewhat indulgent with his daughter. When a friend worried that she would receive a scolding for staying out so late at night, Mary wrote in her journal, "*my father* would not scold me if I staid out till 10 o'clock." What and how Mary Jane wrote about her father leaves the impression that they had an easy, comfortable relationship.[16]

References to her mother were often more impassioned and sentimental. She obviously relied on her mother for comfort; worried about her "health and spirits," knowing that she could become "prey to ennui"; and was almost jealous of time spent away from her. She vowed during the Christmas season at her brother Robert's home in Washington that her next Christmas would "be with Mother." Two or three times that winter, Mary wrote of her mother, "I would give anything to see her," and once "wrote a terribly harsh letter" to her mother, "scolding her for not writing." After Mary Lorraine Greenhow asked her to write a remembrance of her in the commonplace book, Mary Jane's poem of response poured forth almost possessively. "What shall I write, my mother dear," she asked in meter, "Have I forgetfulness to fear? / Let others here in accents mild, your love and friendship claim / Tis in your heart, that I aspire to fill a loved one's place." Clearly, Mary Jane Greenhow was deeply attached to her mother.[17]

She was also devoted to, and affected by, both of her brothers. Their relationships are visible mainly in the pages of her 1837–38 diary, kept while visiting brother Robert and his family in Washington. By this time, Robert had made a name for himself in medicine and in government. After graduating from the College of William and Mary and Columbia University, he spent seven years in Europe, studying medicine in Edinburgh, London, and Paris while developing friendships with Lord Byron and other literary figures. In

16. MJCG/MHS, 34 (Nov. 19, 1837), 40 (Dec. 3, 1837), 78 (Apr. 10, 1838), 23 (Oct. 16, 1837, emphasis hers).

17. Ibid., 11 (Sept. 23, 1837), 27 (Oct. 24, 1837), 32 (Nov. 10, 1837), 33–34 (Nov. 15, 1837), 40 (Dec. 3, 1837), 44 (Dec. 13, 1837), 47 (Dec. 24, 1837), 52 (Jan. 3, 1838), 56 (Jan. 9, 1838), 58 (Jan. 23, 1838), 61 (Feb. 3, 1838), 63 (Feb. 6, 1838), 68 (Mar. 5, 1838), 76 (Mar. 25, 1838); poem by Mary Greenhow Lee, MLG, Sept. 25, 1846.

1825 he returned to the United States and began practicing medicine in New York City.[18]

During the period Robert Greenhow Jr. spent in New York, he became involved in Thomas Jefferson's project to establish a medical school at the new University of Virginia. Greenhow gathered information from Europe on the materials needed for the school and found models of organs, skeletons, "a series of figures . . . representing the foetus during various periods of utero gestation, [and] . . . a decomposable brain." In the end, Greenhow extended to Jefferson his hopes for the new school, "that it may prosper and that you may see the tree which you have planted bring forth fruit."[19]

In 1830 Greenhow's interest in the liberal revolution in France prompted him to found a newspaper entitled *The Tricolor* to inform the public about the changes in French rule. Stating that "the weak and misguided monarch" had been "hurled from" the throne and "driven into exile," Greenhow applauded the revolution in France, claiming that the "great nation" once again stood "forth the advocate of resistance and oppression." Fond of neither "the old Monarchical times" nor the "savage ferocity which marked the reign of terror," Greenhow praised France for joining "the march of liberal institutions." Mary Jane's brother condoned rebellion when necessary.[20]

Through his friendship with Robert Livingston, Andrew Jackson's secretary of state, Greenhow's career shifted gears. Livingston obtained an appointment for Greenhow to the State Department. Fluent in French, Spanish, Italian, and German, Greenhow served as interpreter for the diplomats and as librarian. The cultured manners he had acquired in his father's household went a long way toward making him a favorite in Washington society as well.[21]

Mary Jane Greenhow arrived in Washington in the fall of 1837, after brother Robert returned from a diplomatic mission for President Martin Van Buren, who had selected him to deliver a formal note to Mexico's foreign affairs minister detailing grievances against the new government by U.S. citizens living in Mexico. Instability following Mexico's independence from

18. Barbee, "Robert Greenhow," 182–83.

19. Jefferson to Greenhow, Mar. 8, 1825, Thomas Jefferson Papers, Presidential Series, LC (microfilm, VHS); Greenhow to Jefferson, Mar. 22, 1825, ibid.

20. Robert Greenhow, *The Tricolor: Devoted to the Politics, Literature, &c of Continental Europe, Nos. I to IV Inclusive, Containing a Full Account of the Late Revolution in France, and a Summary of Its Causes—the Constitutional Charter, with Its Amendments, and Other Matters* (New York: Ludwig and Tolefree, 1830), 16 (Sept. 13, 1830), 26 (Sept. 20, 1830); Barbee, "Robert Greenhow," 182.

21. Barbee, "Robert Greenhow," 182.

Spain had made Americans' property there vulnerable to bands of robbers. That, coupled with Mexican resentment over their loss of Texas, had exacerbated tensions between the United States and its southern neighbor. The letter listed over fifty-seven claims, and Greenhow was instructed to enlighten the minister as to Van Buren's firm requirement that the Mexican government show an earnest desire to settle them. Additionally, Secretary of War Joel Poinsett charged Greenhow with the responsibility of delivering a personal letter to Mexican president Anastasio Bustamante.[22]

Like his sister, Robert was an interested and enthusiastic observer of all facets of the world around him. As he journeyed to Mexico, he noted various flora, such as "the Copal varnish tree" growing in a "yard at Columbia" and palmettos, pomegranates, and a "cabbage palm." He also picked "whortleberries" along the way, reserving some to eat with his supper one evening, and ate blackberries he found growing along the side of the road. Through every town he appraised the architecture and layout of the streets. Clearly, he had been looking forward to seeing Florida and the wildlife for which it was known. He finally "saw the first alligator running wild and was brutal enough to kill it." The creature was only "about 3 feet long," but he seemed to derive pleasure from getting in touch with his primal instincts.[23]

Taking a steamer across the Gulf of Mexico from Pensacola, Greenhow finally arrived in Mexico, where he gauged the first official he met "to be a good natured silly old man," whose "quarters were in a little tavern." Obviously, he possessed some of the same cultural arrogance relative to Mexican citizens as did others in the United States. As he made his way through the country, he noted not only the terrain of the land and the currents of rivers but also the crime in the area and the relaxed style of Mexican dress.[24]

After delivering his official and unofficial messages, he hurried to leave for home, feeling "a large earthquake at Jalepa" just as he packed "to quit the place." Passing through Richmond, Greenhow then escorted his sister to Washington, at which point the trip from Richmond to Washington became her great adventure. Although not as exciting as Robert's trip south of the border, Mary Greenhow commented on "accidents . . . innumerable" that

22. RG; John Niven, *Martin Van Buren: The Romantic Age of American Politics* (New York: Oxford University Press, 1983), 443, 444; Paul A. Varg, *United States Foreign Relations, 1820–1860* (East Lansing: Michigan State University Press, 1979), 119.

23. RG, 3 (June 1, 1837), 6 (June 3, 1837), 7 (June 5, 1837), 9–10 (June 7, 1837), 11 (June 3, 1837).

24. Ibid., 40 (June 27, 1837), 46 (June 28, 1837), 52 (June 30, 1837); Varg, *United States Foreign Relations,* 170.

included the loss of some of her "banboxes," frightening sights such as "a man whose nose was tied up with a black ribbon," and intrigues that included "a runaway couple" onboard ship. They arrived safely on September 2, 1837, a week before her eighteenth birthday, and she began her whirlwind stay in the nation's capital.[25]

Robert had married Rose Maria O'Neal of Montgomery County, Maryland, a little over two years earlier, and by the time of Mary's visit, their family included a daughter, Florence, and at least three servants, Charles, Mary, and "Aunt Patty." "Brother" and "Sister," or "Miss Rose" as Mary sometimes referred to her, lived on the north side of K Street between Twelfth and Thirteenth, where Mary had her own room and a "sky parlour."[26]

Mary enjoyed a comfortable and affectionate relationship with her brother. He seemed to share many of her interests; they fueled each other's passion for knowledge. She respected him for his accomplishments and his "perfect knowledge of Paris," but it is evident that they were on an equal footing with each other despite an age difference of nineteen years. They spent time reading to each other from *Blackwood's Edinburgh Magazine*, a journal that focused on history, both ancient and recent, and current events. When Robert "commenced writing his book on Mexico," he asked Mary Jane to help him keep his papers in order. While in Mexico, he had ordered wax Mexican figures to be sent to him in Washington. They arrived broken, forcing him to endure his sister's laughter as he attempted "mend[ing] his babies, putting a leg here, a hand there."[27]

During the winter of 1837–38, Robert introduced his sister to the inner workings of the national government, seeming to both understand her curiosity and to share it. Possibly he renewed his enthusiasm for the federal hub by seeing it again through Mary's eyes. For instance, on September 21, 1837, he interrupted her while she was putting her "hair in papers" by rushing in to ask if she wanted to go with him to witness Cherokee Indians signing a treaty. Infected by his enthusiasm, she pulled a bonnet over the papers "and was dressed in two minutes," ready to leave. She needed to stand on a bench in order to witness "thirty [Cherokee] chieftains in their high day dresses, with their faces painted in the most horrible manner," smoke the calumet.

25. RG, 62 (Aug. 2, 1837); MJCG/MHS, 1 (Sept. 4, 1837).

26. *Richmond Enquirer*, June 2, 1835; MJCG/MHS, 22 (Oct. 16, 1837), 29 (Nov. 4, 1837), 34 (Nov. 19, 1837), 38 (Nov. 28, 1837), 44 (Dec. 14, 1837), 46 (Dec. 24, 1837), 75 (Mar. 25, 1838), 38 (Nov. 29, 1837); *The Washington Directory, and Governmental Register, for 1843* (Washington, D.C.: Anthony Reintze, 1843), 35, LOV, microfilm.

27. MJCG/MHS, 2 (Sept. 6, 1837), 51 (Jan. 3, 1838), 43 (Dec. 10, 1837), 41 (Dec. 6, 1837).

After Secretary of War Poinsett addressed the Indians, Mary heard "the deep grunt by which they signified their assent to his propositions . . . to send them [to] the other side of the Mississippi." As young as she was, Mary suspected that the "poor wretches," as she called them, would "be cheated out of their lands by *the great father*, for they will receive one-tenth . . . [the] value of their hunting grounds." Mary Jane Greenhow's strength of character had already developed to such an extent that she was flustered by neither her appearance in curling papers nor that of an Indian chief in only "a very short hunting shirt" and "leggings . . . to his knees," with the space between them "being perfectly bare." More important to her was the significance of the occasion and its consequences for the Indians.[28]

Robert also saw to it that his sister watched the legislature in action. Women had been allowed in the galleries of Congress since the time Rep. Fisher Ames arranged for a female acquaintance to watch him give a speech. There had been no written rules against it, just an assumption that women would not be interested. Mary Jane Greenhow was interested. She visited the Capitol at least three times during her visit to Washington, once specifically "to hear Mr. [Henry] Clay" speak. It is apparent that the relationship between Mary and Robert was based on mutual values and interests. Mary's feelings about her other brother, James Washington "Wash" Greenhow, though, bordered on hero worship.[29]

Mary Jane and Wash, a lawyer in Richmond, were close. Although only two years older than Mary, Wash exhibited paternal instincts toward her that she accepted. Gender rather than a difference in age accounted for his attitude. In protecting, advising, and spoiling her, he imitated the behavior he had witnessed among other males in his family, and she seemed to abide his dominant attitude. A letter from Wash put Mary "in fine spirits." Word that a visit from him would be delayed prompted her to label him "provoking" or herself "ready to cry with vexation" and disappointment. In the process of undressing one evening when he arrived for one of his short visits to Washington that winter, she "heard a carriage at the door" and looked to see Wash getting out of it, threw her "robe de cambre [*sic*] on in a second and ran to meet him," then sat up with him until two o'clock in the morning, catching

28. Ibid., 10 (Sept. 21, 1837, emphasis hers).
29. Ibid., 20 (Oct. 8, 1837), 46 (Dec. 24, 1837), 64 (Feb. 20, 1838); William E. Ames, *A History of the National Intelligencer* (Chapel Hill: University of North Carolina Press, 1972), 260–61.

up on his news. During another of his arrivals, she "nearly broke [her] neck running downstairs . . . to see him."[30]

Washington Greenhow spoiled his sister. She knew, for instance, that "he would not dare to come without bringing [her] something pretty," and he did not disappoint her, bringing her "beautiful dresses" and "a diamond ring." He also escorted her "on the avenue" when she asked. She allowed him to exchange a walking dress for her, "which he thought too light," because she had "great confidence in his taste." And when he disapproved of an accessory, he did not merely suggest but strongly stated that she would not wear it. Mary complied. Regarding Wash, she stated, "I believe he loves me dearly," and she loved him in return. The name "Washington Greenhow," she would say years later, "thrills my heart." To her, he was "a statesman" with a strong passion for his "calling."[31]

Brother Robert was old enough to be Mary's father, yet their relationship seems to have resembled a close friendship. But Washington, though equal to her in age, sometimes acted out the role of father toward her. Part of the explanation for this could be innate personality differences or, in Robert's case, the mellowing of age. It could also reflect the contrast between their father's relationships with his two wives. The models of adult gender interaction had been different for the two men: the first, a couple of equal age, openly affectionate and sharing common interests; the second, a union of vast age difference and disparate experiences. Whatever the reasons for their dissimilar attitudes toward their sister, the Greenhow brothers clearly loved her. In return, although a spirited young woman, Mary Jane Greenhow tried to maintain good behavior and an even temper for her brothers, appreciating both their protection and friendship.[32]

In Robert's wife, Rose, Mary found an affectionate sister, a kindred spirit, and a spirited opponent all in one. Just two years apart in age, they could be content to stay home together and spend the evening sewing, talking, and laughing. But they could become quickly frustrated with each other. Mary called Rose "impudent" for telling a friend that she had "designs" on her husband, and Rose scolded Mary when she exhibited questionable manners with

30. MJCG/MHS, 66 (Feb. 28, 1838), 48 (Dec. 26, 1837), 58 (Jan. 23, 1838), 59 (Jan. 30, 1838), 14–15 (Sept. 29, 1837), 72 (Mar. 18, 1838).

31. Ibid., 57 (Jan. 17, 1838), 14 (Sept. 29, 1837), 9 (Sept. 20, 1837), 73–74 (Mar. 21, 1838), 15 (Sept. 29, 1837); MGL, 831 (June 2, 1865).

32. See Nancy J. Chodorow, *Feminism and Psychoanalytic Theory* (New Haven: Yale University Press, 1989), 49–55.

men who were pursuing her. When Mary "merely bid good morning" to a suitor as she breezed past him, "Miss Rose glared." Although the two women enjoyed an open and friendly relationship, their spirited personalities, attractive to the Greenhow men, could cause mild sparks when face to face in open conflict.[33]

The most serious arguments between them ignited over the rigid and vigorous visiting schedule that Washington high society demanded of people such as the Greenhows. Nineteenth-century etiquette books laid out the ground rules for *visiting*. Only when two people had been introduced by someone well known to each did either secure the right to drop by for a *visit*. More often than not, the *visit* meant merely dropping off a calling card and leaving. It was considered a breach of etiquette to do even this, however, if not first introduced to the hostess or host by a third party. The custom depended upon respect people held for each other but, more important, ensured that no one within the circle would have their reputation tainted by socializing indiscriminately. Being *visitable* meant that a person had achieved recognition in society as someone with whom others in this network would be comfortable, someone who shared common interests and values.[34]

The special society Washington offered, in which the politically powerful met by day to administer the country's business and then dined and danced by night to underscore their prestige and importance, was, for the most part, something that Mary enjoyed. She merely endured morning visits, however, because she was "compelled to do" them. Actually, morning visits were between the hours of twelve and three in the afternoon. During these hours, the women of the house were required to be dressed and ready to receive their visitors without delay or send word by their servant that they were "not at home," meaning that they were otherwise occupied.[35]

The simple act of leaving calling cards carried myriad social connotations, especially a conspicuously absent return card. For a very potent example, when Peggy Eaton, wife of Sen. John Eaton of Tennessee, arrived at the

33. Louis A. Sigaud, "Mrs. Greenhow and the Rebel Spy Ring," *Maryland Historical Magazine* 41, no. 3 (Sept. 1946): 175; MJCG/MHS, 34 (Nov. 15, 1837), 43 (Dec. 12, 1837), 65 (Feb. 24, 1838).

34. *Etiquette at Washington*, 45–50.

35. *A Full Directory, for Washington City, Georgetown, and Alexandria* (Washington, [D.C.]: E. A. Cohen, 1834), LOV, microfilm; MJCG/MHS, 24 (Oct. 17, 1837), 32 (Nov. 9, 1837), 45 (Dec. 19, 1837), 52 (Jan. 4, 1838), 53 (Jan. 5, 1838), 54 (Jan. 9, 1838), 60 (Feb. 3, 1838), 62 (Feb. 12, 1838), 32 (Nov. 9, 1837), 45 (Dec. 19, 1837), 52 (Jan. 4, 1838), 53 (Jan. 5, 1838), 59 (Jan. 31, 1838), 60 (Feb. 3, 1838), 62 (Feb. 12, 1838); *Etiquette at Washington*, 45.

home of Vice President John C. Calhoun in 1829, Floride Calhoun was "not at home" to her, and the absence of Mrs. Calhoun's card on the tray inside Mrs. Eaton's front door told the tale. The vice president's wife, first hostess in Washington after the death of President Andrew Jackson's wife, Rachel, officially snubbed Peggy Eaton, letting her know that the daughter of a tavern keeper was not *visitable*. In fact, historian Kirsten Wood has argued that this particular incident shows that women's social power permeated the political world, for the "Eaton Affair" contributed to the dissolution of Jackson's cabinet.[36]

Mary Jane Greenhow's temper could be tested with the unpredictability of the custom. She complained that if she "dressed to receive visitors, none called." Or if she was not prepared and told the servants to announce her "not at home," then the visitor would be someone important to her, leaving her frustrated. "I was sorry when I found Geo. May's card on the table," she wrote of a prospective "handsome" beau. These rules of etiquette could cause dissension in the household. Mary and Rose "had quite a quarrel" one day about whether Mary "should see persons who called." Mary lost the argument and "dressed [her]self accordingly" but did not change her mind. She declared that it was "the greatest relief in the world to . . . hear the servant say '*not at home*.'" She hated being "dressed up in furs & feathers and visiting from morning to night." At times, to guard against possibly long visits, she met her visitors with her "bonnet on," letting them think she was on her way out. In the end, however, she forced herself into the regimen because, as she stated, "when you are in Turkey, you must do as the Turkeys."[37]

Nothing annoyed Mary Greenhow more in the visiting rounds than a poor conversationalist. "Keeping up the ball of conversation" was an art that Mary had learned well, and she did not appreciate people who could "say yes and no as well as any body" but added little else to the discussion. Yet she grew equally weary of a man who would "not let anyone talk but himself," which was an etiquette infraction. According to an etiquette guide of the time, men were "fonder of giving their own suggestions than of listening to those of others" and were admonished to let "the ladies" select the topics of discussion "in order to prevent the selection of subjects beyond the depth of" women's knowledge. Although expected to be the most skilled conversationalists, some

36. Frank, *Justice Daniel Dissenting*, 95, 96; Kirsten E. Wood, "'One Woman So Dangerous to Public Morals': Gender and Power in the Eaton Affair," *Journal of the Early Republic* 17, no. 2 (summer 1997): 237–75.

37. MJCG/MHS, 53 (Jan. 6, 1838), 57 (Jan. 22, 1838), 29 (Nov. 4, 1837), 11 (Sept. 21, 1837, emphasis hers), 29 (Oct. 28, 1837), 5 (Sept. 18, 1837).

men evidently felt limited, for on one occasion Mary and Rose "peeped through the door" before greeting their visitor in the parlor and caught him "rehearsing" his conversation "before the glass."[38]

Although visiting wore on her, there were exceptions, such as her visits with Dolley Madison, widow of the ex-president, who lived on Lafayette Square. Rose's sister, Ellen, married Dolley Madison's nephew, James Madison Cutts, and Rose accepted many invitations to Madison's home. Mary seemed taken by the "dear old lady," who enjoyed the company of young people. Dolley Madison was somewhat sensitive about her advancing age, yet she retained an out-of-fashion wardrobe of gown and turban that only served to date her more firmly in the past, prompting Mary to call her "a tragedy queen." But upon longer acquaintance and a deeper understanding of Dolley Madison's character, Mary Greenhow believed her to be "a beautiful woman" who was "affectionate in her manners" to the point that she insisted upon kissing Mary whenever she saw her.[39]

Even with all of its rules and expectations, Mary Jane Greenhow felt fully confident in her performance before Washington society. During her stay with Robert in 1837–38, her life was filled with parties, attending nearly forty in six months, two at the White House, where she "had the pleasure of shaking hands" with President Van Buren. The Greenhows were also invited to parties at cabinet members' homes, such as that of Secretary of State John Forsyth, whom Mary enjoyed because the family was southern and "free from anything like pride or hautiness [sic]," but found their parties too crowded since "everyone who chooses to leave a card is invited." Secretary of War Poinsett and his wife also entertained large parties. Guests at these gatherings savored elaborate displays of treats: molded ice cream and sculpted castles made of sugar-glazed fruits. Intimate sociables, such as those at Senate Secretary Asbury Dickens's home, were more in keeping with Mary's tastes. Co-owners of the *National Intelligencer* Joseph Gales Jr. and William Winston Seaton entertained in very different fashions, neither of which earned Mary

38. Ibid., 12 (Sept. 23, 1837), 43 (Dec. 10, 1837), 71 (Mar. 12, 1838); *Etiquette at Washington*, 103, 99.

39. *Washington Directory* (1843), 55; Ames, *National Intelligencer*, 253, 256; MJCG/MHS, 30 (Nov. 5, 1837), 36 (Nov. 25, 1837), 28 (Oct. 25, 1837), 47 (Dec. 25, 1837); Sigaud, "Mrs. Greenhow and the Rebel Spy Ring," 184–85; Rose Greenhow to Dolley Madison, Mar. 4 (year unknown), Dolley Madison Papers, LC; Frances Cutts to Ellen E. Cutts, Aug. 7, 1833, Cutts Family Papers, LC. James Madison Cutts was son of Richard and Anna Payne Cutts, Dolley Madison's sister.

Greenhow's approbation. While Sarah Seaton, sister to Gales, extended invitations to large numbers for parties at their home on E Street, Sarah Gales preferred small soirees on Friday evenings.[40]

Mary Greenhow felt "perfectly at ease" among the "elite of the elite" at these social functions. She arrived with her family dressed in "Indian muslin . . . trimmed with pink rosettes," and her hair curled in "ringlets each side" with a "demi wreath of roses" on her head, looking the part of a romantic belle. Or she might choose black crepe for dramatic effect. She usually arrived ready for fun and frolic and, indeed, often found it. One reason she preferred small gatherings was that she wanted plenty of room for dancing, especially favoring the Virginia Reel, "danced with . . . spirit." If Mary Greenhow could dance, play cards, and have "real old-fashioned fun," she considered the party a success. Often, however, she endured "stiff" gatherings of "crowd[s] of stupid people" or a set of "old codgers." As a young woman of marriageable age, Mary Jane Greenhow deemed parties at which "there were not beaux enough" crashing disappointments, even though hostesses typically judged the success of these affairs by the number of women present.[41]

Added to the parties and the self-imposed vigorous visiting schedule were the excursions "on the avenue." Through all of these events, Mary Greenhow collected "beaux." Flirtations awakened her to the milestone she was approaching. She felt a heightened sense of power mixed with mild concerns for her future. Although she flirted lightly with a married man and one who was engaged, she also fell "half in love" with a few who were eligible. Richard Cutts, another of Dolley Madison's nephews, briefly caught her attention. Others she found "very handsome and very agreeable" but then mentioned little else about them. John Randolph, a friend from Richmond, claimed her for a dance, during which she "had great difficulty making him behave himself." Martin Van Buren Jr. presented her with a rose, which she appreciated enough to underline the fact in her journal, but she often referred to him as

40. MJCG/MHS, 51 (Jan. 2, 1838), 14 (Sept. 29, 1837), 54 (Jan. 9, 1838), 60 (Feb. 3, 1838), 64 (Feb. 20, 1838); Niven, *Martin Van Buren*, 405, 408; list of parties, MJCG/LC; *Full Directory, for Washington City* (1834), 7; *Washington Directory* (1843), 21; Ames, *National Intelligencer*, 87, 107, 108. See also Clement Eaton, "Winifred and Joseph Gales, Liberals in the Old South," *Journal of Southern History* 10, no. 4 (Nov. 1944): 461–74.

41. MJCG/MHS, 13 (Sept. 25, 1837), 31 (Nov. 9, 1837), 51 (Jan. 2, 1838), 24 (Oct. 18, 1837), 54 (Jan. 9, 1838), 62 (Feb. 12, 1838), 65 (Feb. 21, 1838), 62 (Feb. 16, 1838), 45 (Dec. 19, 1837), 51 (Jan. 2, 1838), 45 (Dec. 19, 1837); Ames, *National Intelligencer*, 107.

"little Martin" and found it more fun to tease him than to take him seriously as a suitor.[42]

She especially liked men in uniform and was "crazy for an invitation" to a "party at the barracks," but she never received one. Robert Rodgers, son of Commodore John Rodgers and Minerva Denison Rodgers, occupied a great deal of Mary Greenhow's time. She enjoyed the company of this "gentlemanly young man" but found him "rather stupid." At first blush, she found herself "half in love" with Alexander Macomb, a general's son, and called him her "pet" but, upon longer acquaintance, decided he did not have "quite enough life" for her. The reverse might have also been true since later Mary found Macomb in the back room of a store, flirting "with a pretty little French girl."[43]

The young men endured this behavior because, during courtship, they suspected it was more drama than substance. Robert Rodgers, the young man Mary found "rather stupid," wrote of one of her friends that she was "very much employed in acting the part of an anxious lover" for a suitor who had gone to sea for the navy, even though she had "so many strings in her bow." He reported to his brother, John, that Washington was "gay," that "squeezes" were "in vogue," and that "the young ladies enjoy themselves, which constitutes the gaiety," implying that he endured the parties merely for the sake of "the young ladies."[44]

Clearly, Mary Greenhow was more interested in flirting and testing her powers of attraction than in taking any of her beaus seriously for long. She thought Edwin Dickens was "a handsome little fellow," then reminded herself that "he was a Dickens." She disconcerted her suitors by "always quizzing them" or laughing when they tried to read poetry to her. Unless a man could keep up with her in conversation, or even take "command," she lost interest. Mary wanted a suitor who exhibited "the boldness of a man" within the limits of genteel behavior.[45]

42. MJCG/MHS, 24 (Oct. 18, 1837), 38 (Nov. 28, 1837), 48 (Dec. 27, 1837), 49 (Dec. 28, 1837), 50 (Dec. 30, 1837), 51 (Jan. 2, 1838), 55 (Jan. 14, 1838), 56 (Jan. 14, 1838), 60 (Feb. 1–3, 1838), 65 (Feb. 21, 1838), 56 (Mar. 2, 1838), 68 (Mar. 5, 1838), 74 (Mar. 22, 1838), 75 (Mar. 25, 1838).

43. Ibid., 36 (Nov. 21, 1837). 24 (Oct. 18, 1837), 26 (Oct. 19, 1837), 29 (Oct. 28, 1837), 30 (Oct. 31, 1837), 33 (Nov. 15, 1837), 39 (Dec. 1, 1837), 43 (Dec. 12, 1837), 51 (Jan. 2, 1838), 62 (Feb. 12, 1838), 64 (Feb. 20, 1838), 65 (Feb. 21, 1838), 66 (Feb. 28, 1838). Information on John Rodgers and on the Macomb family comes from the Rodgers Family Papers, LC.

44. Robert Rodgers to John Rodgers, Jan. 21, 1837, Rodgers Family Papers.

45. MJCG/MHS, 15 (Sept. 29, 1837), 43 (Dec. 12, 1837), 61 (Feb. 6, 1838), 67 (Mar. 2, 1838), 68 (Mar. 5, 1837).

Wondering if "Cupid" would ever make her blind enough to commit her life to one man, Mary Jane watched as two of her friends married that winter, then slept on pieces of their wedding cakes and bid dreams of her future husband to come to her in her sleep. None did. Clearly, she was not ready for marriage but suffered from what historian Nancy Cott has identified as "marriage trauma," symptomatic of young marriageable women during this period, arising in part from the conflict they sensed between the drive for romance and the practical necessity of an economically secure future. It also developed in young belles who realized the added responsibilities and the restrictions on their freedoms that marriage would bring. Mary Jane Greenhow marveled that her friends talked freely about their impending marriages and were "as unembarrassed as if it were an everyday affair." One of the women passed through the ordeal "collected and composed as if she had been married 6 years instead of six days." But her other friend finally began showing signs of fear, and Mary chalked it up to the fact that she had "only a few days grace." Before long, however, even this nervous bride had "settled down into a quiet little married woman," a condition Mary Greenhow judged bleak.[46]

While she enjoyed the attention paid to her by the young gentlemen of Washington, Mary Greenhow much preferred spending time with women. She especially missed her best friend, Edmonia "Eddie" Christian, from Henrico County, just outside Richmond. To her journal she confessed, "I would give anything . . . if Eddie was but here; all the girls here love gentlemen so much that I, who am not *very* fond of them, feel lonesome; I had so much rather talk to Eddie than any of the men I have seen yet." In fact, she started her Washington journal, "for Eddie's amusement during the long winter nights [she] hope[d] to spend with her ere three moons [were] accomplished." Eddie had qualities Mary looked for in a friend: trust, equality, and sincerity, which to Mary was as important as "a looking glass . . . in which you can see your blemishes." There were times when Mary wrote of her in the homoerotic language identified for women of the Victorian age, when women were increasingly set apart from men and not expected to express themselves openly or intellectually in mixed company. At the end of her first journal entry, Mary wrote, "Good night Eddie, I should like to know if you think of me as much as I do you." A "beautiful night" would remind her of the night she and "Eddie . . . kept watch together in the window." She pouted if she

---

46. Ibid., 32 (Nov. 12, 1837), 38 (Nov. 28, 1837), 41 (Dec. 6, 1837), 43 (Dec. 12, 1837), 70 (Mar. 10, 1838), 78 (Mar. 28, 1838); Cott, *Bonds of Womanhood*, 80–83.

did not hear from her friend often, scolding her, and wondering if "Eddie has forgotten me." When a letter did arrive, Greenhow was ecstatic.[47]

Without Eddie in Washington, Mary was forced to form new friendships. When Eliza "Liz" O'Neal, a relative of Rose, stayed at the Greenhows' for a short time, Mary first believed her to be "a sweet girl" who could possibly make her stay "more pleasant." When she caught "Lizzy and Martin Van Buren [Jr.] fighting over a bottle of wine," however, she decided that she liked "her very much." Liz O'Neal became Mary Greenhow's partner in rebellion against the stress and boredom of polite society. One evening, while at home without supervision, the young women "amused" themselves by "burning sugar in the candle, imitating the looks & gestures of some . . . friends, and finally, by hiding behind the window curtains," spying on Robert and Rose as they arrived home. On another evening alone they "ran romping about the house like two tomboys."[48]

Henrietta Henly also helped ease her boredom. With bright moonlight to guide them, they "ran on at a wild rate, dancing and singing and . . . waltz[ing]" from one door to the other "on the pavement" or "amused" themselves "smoking cigars" when left to their own devices. Even Rose, the one who insisted that Mary follow all of society's rules, had her moments. So much alike in temperament, and both destined to become "outrageous rebels," they found themselves "in a frolicsome humour" one night. "Wrapped up in sheets," they went next door to the Wadsworths' and "threw the door open, . . . much to" their neighbors' "astonishment." When freed from the visiting schedule, she and her friends walked up Pennsylvania Avenue to shop at Madam Bihler's Fancy Store, Savage's, or Claggett's, then stopped at Kinchey's, one block down, for ice cream.[49]

Mary Greenhow could have quieter moments, however, in which she played with baby Florence, sewed, or read. In fact, while in Washington that

47. MJCG/MHS, 24 (Oct. 17, 1837, emphasis hers), 1 (Sept. 4, 1837), 30 (Oct. 28, 1837), 5 (Sept. 15, 1837), 4 (Sept. 11, 1837); Carroll Smith-Rosenberg, "The Female World of Love and Ritual: Relations between Women in Nineteenth-Century America," *Signs: Journal of Women in Culture and Society* 1 (1975): 1–30; MJCG/MHS, 1 (Sept. 4, 1837), 4 (Sept. 11, 1837), 22 (Oct. 16, 1837), 35 (Nov. 19, 1837), 38 (Nov. 28, 1837), 46 (Dec. 24, 1837), 58–59 (Jan. 22, 1838), 73 (Mar. 18, 1838).

48. MJCG/MHS, 55 (Jan. 14, 1838), 58 (Jan. 28, 1838), 71 (Mar. 12, 1838), 75 (Mar. 25, 1838).

49. Ibid., 32 (Nov. 10, 1837), 42 (Dec. 8, 1837), 47–58 (Dec. 25, 1837–Jan. 23, 1838), 9 (Sept. 20, 1837), 29 (Oct. 28, 1837), 71 (Mar. 12, 1838), 72 (Mar. 15, 1838), 73 (Mar. 21, 1838), 75 (Mar. 25, 1838), 76 (Mar. 25, 1838); *Full Directory, for Washington City* (1834), 31; *Washington Directory* (1843), 6, 15, 188, 191.

winter of 1837–38, she read more than twenty books, either alone in her room or aloud with the family. Some of her favorite times were with family, and as the winter continued, she became increasingly anxious to get back home to Richmond. Although she had enjoyed her "wild kicks" in Washington, she wrote, "there is a magic in *home* which no pleasure, no occupation can obliterate." When Wash came to escort her home in April 1838, she quit her diary by writing, "and here endeth my adventures."[50]

Within two years her life changed dramatically. She returned to Robert's house when her father, realizing that "his age and growing infirmities" would hamper his business management, moved his wife and daughter to his son's home in Washington. There he intended to live out the rest of his life. He died on Tuesday, June 30, 1840, "at the residence of his son, in the city of Washington." With the death of her father began two decades of loss in Mary Greenhow's life, forcing her to draw upon all of the spirit and fire her character could provide.[51]

50. MJCG/MHS, 34 (Nov. 15, 1837), 38 (Nov. 28, 1837), 45–46 (Dec. 19, 1837), 2 (Sept. 6, 1837), 3 (Sept. 9, 1837), 6 (Sept. 23, 1837), 7 (Sept. 23, 1837), 18 (Oct. 6, 1837), 21 (Oct. 10, 1837), 26 (Oct. 20, 1837), 29 (Oct. 25, 1837), 30 (Nov. 4, 1837), 33 (Nov. 12, 1837), 36 (Nov. 25, 1837), 38 (Nov. 29, 1837), 40 (Dec. 3, 1837), 45 (Dec. 19, 1837), 46 (Dec. 24, 1837), 48 (Dec. 26, 1837), 51 (Jan. 3, 1838), 57 (Jan. 17, 1837), 64 (Feb. 20, 1838), 67 (Mar. 1, 1838), 68–69 (Mar. 6, 1838), 57 (Mar. 25, 1838), 78 (Apr. 10, 1838), 9 (Sept. 20, 1837, emphasis hers), 75 (Mar. 22, 1838), 79 (Apr. 10, 1838). Some of the books she read during this period were *Venetia, Ivanhoe, The Pickwick Club, Victims of Society, Scourge of the Ocean,* and *Robinson Crusoe.*

51. Richmond Hustings Court Book 40:482–83, LOV; *Richmond Enquirer,* July 3, 1840.

3

"In the Palm Days of Old Winchester"

The Environment of Mary Greenhow Lee's
Transformation to Responsibility

Mary Jane Greenhow's life underwent dramatic changes in the two decades between her father's death in 1840 and the Civil War. From a young woman whose "wild kicks" were tolerated by her family, she became a wife and adopted a new family and town. In Winchester, Virginia, she threaded together new filaments of her *connexion*, enjoying and participating in her husband's success and the activities of the town. But before the war removed her from Winchester, she lost her closest family members, took on the responsibility of mothering her husband's nieces and nephews in 1848, lost her husband in 1856, and assumed the role of widow. In the meantime, her strong love of family and the value she placed on environment enabled her to appreciate the time she spent in "the palm days of old Winchester." Her strength of character and intelligence would see her through when the "palm days" ended and a more difficult era began.

Robert Greenhow's family brought his remains back to Richmond by train on July 1, 1840, and buried him the next day at Shockoe Cemetery. Publicly, his obituary stated that he required no eulogy because he had an "unimpeachable and spotless character." The emotional reaction his family may have had is unknown, but clearly they had practical matters to face. Greenhow's real property in Richmond had been gradually diminishing. The values of his properties relative to the aggregate of land assessed in Richmond had ranged as high as 1.57 percent of the total property in the city in 1829. By 1840, his land taxes had fallen to 0.74 percent of the aggregate collected for the city, the result of selling off his holdings.[1]

In his will, written nearly a year before his death, Greenhow appointed son Robert his executor and required him to have the estate appraised, then to sell at public auction specific properties and slaves to satisfy outstanding debts. To his wife, Mary Lorraine, he left three slaves, Patty, Caroline, and his "good and trusty servant Robert," as long as she remained unmarried. His widow received the silver plate purchased during their marriage and any furniture from the household and books from the library that she wanted. Additionally, as long as she remained his widow, she would be allowed use of his pew at Monumental Church. All of his estate taken by his widow, however, would revert to "daughter Mary Jane" at her mother's death or in the event she remarried.[2]

Mary Jane Greenhow received the family's piano and all of her father's tenements and property located on the north corner of E and Twelfth Streets, with the requirement that she pay five thousand dollars out of her real-property value to her brother James Washington Greenhow to equalize his portion of the estate. Should the sale of his estate not cover his debts, however, this property would be sold as well. Robert Jr. received two properties; the silver owned by his father and his mother, Mary Ann Greenhow; the silver inherited from John Greenhow; and silver bequeathed to Greenhow by his "respected friend Robert Saunders" of Williamsburg. James Washington received any books from the library not selected by his mother, and his father's watch, "mathematical instruments, . . . globes and maps."[3]

Until and if it was sold, however, rents from the property were to be divided equally among all three of his children. Although the value of each child's portion remained equal, given the fact that Mary Jane was required to give Washington five thousand dollars from her portion to make it so, it is significant that Robert Greenhow left his youngest son no real property. The bequest of personal items signifying an interest in the larger world could be

1. *Richmond Enquirer*, July 3, 1840; A. Bohmer Rudd, ed., *Shockoe Hill Cemetery, Richmond, Virginia, Register of Interments, Apr. 10, 1822–Dec. 31, 1950* (Washington, D.C.: A. Bohmer Rudd, n.d.), 20; Richmond Land Tax Registers, 1819, 1825–40, LOV.

2. "Will and Codicil of Robert Greenhow Sr.," Richmond Hustings Court Book 8:263, LOV.

3. Ibid.

evidence that Washington's father saw a restless spirit in him, a spirit that would keep him from planting firm roots. Indeed, when Washington died nine years later, he was far from home in Clarksville, Tennessee.[4]

When the estate was finally settled in September 1840, Robert Jr.'s portion of the properties was valued at $18,130. Mary Jane retained the property located at the corner of E and Twelfth Streets and the adjoining house and lot on E Street, the combined value of both listed at $17,873. Interestingly, the Greenhow heirs settled the rest of the property differently than their father had specified. Instead of merely paying Washington the $5,000 from Mary Jane's portion of the properties, she granted to him, "in consideration of natural love and affection," the remainder of the properties bequeathed to her, valued at $8,500. Additionally, both Robert Jr. and Mary Jane granted to Washington ownership of the slaves George, Racha, Eliza, and Agnes, their value estimated at $1,550.[5]

Once they gained property from his estate, Robert Greenhow's children became tangled in the same web of property-based debt their father had participated in, though the senior Greenhow had most often held the position of creditor in life. Indeed, debt in myriad forms was one of the significant things binding his cohort of Virginia elite together. From a dizzying array of deeds of trust, at least one thing is clear: those who owned property probably owed money to their friends, their brothers, or their in-laws. George, Robert, Samuel, and John Greenhow held deeds of trust for each other and, in a few instances, foreclosed on each other as well. More often than not, Robert Greenhow ended up with property another brother had encumbered or was holding in trust for someone else. Other men who knitted themselves to Greenhow through debt were Peter V. Daniel, James Rawlings, Alexander Duval, Gordon Bacchus, Rev. Richard Channing Moore, Thomas R. Price, brothers Samuel G. and John Adams, and William, Robert, and Alexander McKim, all of whom were civic or economic leaders in Richmond. It is conceivable that turning to each other for financial support was natural because

4. "Genealogical Notes," Tyler Family Papers (Women of Virginia Project Records), CWM.

5. "Division of the Estate of Robert Greenhow, Senior," Richmond Hustings Court Book 41:438–43; Richmond Hustings Court Book 50:614–15; Mary Wingfield Scott, *Houses*, 59–60. The Greenhow children sold their family home on Capitol and Tenth Streets to Mann Valentine and William Breedon in 1846 for $8,600; they in turn sold to Hugh W. Fry and Sons, Grocers and Commission Merchants, in 1851. Various other owners took possession through the years until, in 1883, the city purchased the lot and tore down the house to make room for a new city hall. See Richmond Hustings Court Book 50:614–15; and Mary Wingfield Scott, *Houses*, 59–60.

they moved in the same circles, trusted each other, and had the property and assets to supply the need. And each time they signed their names to another deed of trust, it tightened their *connexion*, whether done consciously or not.[6]

According to historian Daniel P. Jordan, this "network of indebtedness" was not all that unusual for Virginians and was the result of the economic changes facing these southerners during the years of the early Republic. This intricate web of debt, however, could have a lighter side. In 1824 George Greenhow was indebted to Robert for combined bonds amounting to $7,000, against which Thomas Diddep held in trust "property to wit one brindle cow, a small sow and two pigs, a bank of corn in said Ro. Greenhow's barn, . . . one wheel barrow with all poultry which . . . Thos. Diddep may and shall whensoever required to sell at public auction" to go toward paying this debt. Whether or not the wording of this deed of trust was meant to show that Robert Greenhow had little intention of forcing his brother to repay this debt, it does prove that the brothers enjoyed a sense of humor.[7]

Greenhow's heirs also contracted with their father's generation and some of their own in the *connexion* in an ever expanding web of debt. Mary Jane put her inherited property on the line almost immediately. On January 1, 1841, John D. Munford began holding in trust the four-story brick building on Twelfth Street for Robert Saunders, who loaned Mary Jane $7,200. That summer Washington borrowed $2,300 from James A. Seddon on the Twelfth Street property he had acquired in the settlement between himself and the other heirs. This property included a three-story brick building and a two-story brick house with a barber shop located in the front. He sold part of the property the next year for $5,200 and also bought three acres of land in Henrico County on the stage road at Bottoms Bridge. Robert Jr., still residing in "the City of Washington," borrowed $1,500 from Wellington Goddin in 1850, with his father's friend Gustavus A. Myers holding the deed of trust on the Main Street property left to him by his father until three months later, when he paid off the obligation. Although on a smaller scale and on the debtor end, the Greenhow children followed their father's example of tying themselves to the *connexion* through debt.[8]

Mary Jane Greenhow also reaffirmed her ties to the *connexion* through

6. Henrico County Deed Books 4:673, 5:719, 26:4, 75–76, LOV; Richmond Hustings Court Books 10:350–54, 18:255–60, 383–87, 22:202–4, 26:75–76, 40:218, 42:259–61; Sheldon, *Richmond, Virginia*, 119, 120, 128; Danforth and Claiborne, *Historical Sketch*, 127.

7. See Jordan, *Political Leadership*, 28; Henrico County Deed Book 26:75–76.

8. Richmond Hustings Court Books 42:515–16, 530–31, 43:463–65, 57:98–101, 515–16; Henrico County Land Tax Registers, 1841–45, LOV.

marriage. The next important phase in her life began on May 18, 1843, the day she married Hugh Holmes Lee, a twenty-nine-year-old lawyer from Winchester, Virginia, and her distant cousin. The Greenhows and Lees had been connected not only by kinship through the years but also, quite possibly, by the threads of the urban *connexion*.[9]

This urban *connexion* began in the colonial period. "Urban" might seem an exaggeration when referring to towns like Williamsburg or Winchester in the nineteenth century, for they fell far short of the populations of cities such as Philadelphia or New York. By 1810, however, Virginia had several former villages that fulfilled the types of services normally associated with urban centers, such as providing transportation links and supplying goods and services for outlying areas. Size is especially not important in reference to western towns like Winchester, which by 1800 was larger than Lexington, Kentucky, or Pittsburgh, Pennsylvania.[10]

Besides the Chesapeake link between Virginia's Tidewater and Maryland's planters, the ports in Norfolk and Baltimore linked these areas for other trade as well. Political office was yet another strand of the web, bringing together men from all over Virginia in Richmond. The Episcopal Church, of which the Greenhows were active members, served as another link. Yearly conventions met each May in alternating towns, bringing Episcopalians throughout the diocese to places such as Winchester, Staunton, Wheeling, Charlottesville, and Richmond.[11]

Certainly, many of these members were already acquainted with each other, even related, as families had dispersed westward in the eighteenth cen-

9. *Genealogies of Virginia Families*, 4:13, 15–16; *William and Mary Quarterly*, 1st ser., 7 (1898–99): 17; "Genealogical Notes," Tyler Family Papers. Two of the children of Joseph and Margaret Davenport in Williamsburg were Elizabeth and Judith. Elizabeth married Anthony Hay; their daughter Sarah Elizabeth married Henry Nicholson; their daughter Elizabeth married Daniel Lee; and their son Hugh Holmes Lee married Mary Greenhow. Judith Davenport married John Greenhow, and their son Robert, with wife Mary Lorraine Charlton Greenhow, had Mary Jane Greenhow, who married Hugh Holmes Lee. Therefore, Mary's great-grandparents were Hugh's great-great-grandparents. Another connection between the two is historic. Henry Nicholson, Hugh's grandfather, and Robert Greenhow, Mary's father, both participated in the young men's military unit in Williamsburg that attempted to guard the magazine at the start of the Revolution.

10. See Ann Morgan Smart, "The Urban/Rural Dichotomy of Status Consumption: Tidewater Virginia, 1815" (master's thesis, College of William and Mary, 1986), 18–20; Robert D. Mitchell, *Commercialism and Frontier: Perspectives on the Early Shenandoah Valley* (Charlottesville: University Press of Virginia, 1977), 198–201.

11. George D. Fisher, *Monumental Church*, 73, 88, 105, 112, 120, 130, 163, 169, 180, 191, 241, 246, 249, 255, 374; Censer, *North Carolina Planters*, 6, 8.

tury. Besides young men just starting out and looking for land, established planters extended themselves west as well. By 1740, over 470,000 acres of the lower Shenandoah Valley had been acquired from Lord Fairfax by men from the eastern areas of Virginia. Most of them used these lands merely for speculative ventures, but some settled there, while others added to their already large holdings in the East through development and tobacco agriculture. Robert Carter of Nomini Hall began developing his lands in Frederick County around 1770, and by 1790, he was operating six plantations there with the help of tenants and as many as 124 slaves. By 1800, Nathaniel Burwell had transferred around 250 slaves to his holdings in Frederick County. Carter and Burwell grew tobacco both in the Tidewater and in Frederick County simultaneously, influencing the economies in both areas and introducing citizens from these sections to each other in the process.[12]

People who feel more comfortable with each other and share common values and interests are also more likely to make up the pool of possible marriage partners. In this way the *connexion* maintained its exclusivity, for certainly parents wanted to ensure that potential mates met criteria of eligibility before giving their blessings to a match. Yet, for any group, the more instances of contact, the higher the probability of interest, affection, love, and marriage arising for couples within it. So it was natural for young people within the *connexion* to be more likely to marry one another.[13]

Mary Greenhow spent time visiting friends and relatives in both Williamsburg and Winchester between the time of her father's death in 1840 and her marriage to Hugh Holmes Lee in 1843. Hugh's sister, Antoinette ("Nettie"), and Mary visited together at Carter's Grove, the Burwell family plantation outside of Williamsburg, in the spring of 1842. At that point, Carters Grove was home to another of Hugh's sisters, Susan, then married to Philip Carter Lewis Burwell ("P.C.L."), heir of the plantation. The Burwells had been married since 1836, and in 1842 their fourth child was born, which might have occasioned the visit by family members. In any event, Mary and Nettie did not remain at "the Grove" the whole time but spent March 16–May 2 in Williamsburg, enjoying "the gay scenes" of the town and flirting with many of the eligible young men attending the College of William and Mary.[14]

Mary Greenhow clearly enjoyed her stay in Williamsburg and the atten-

12. Mitchell, *Commercialism and Frontier*, 30, 120, 127–28, 178–79, 181.

13. Censer, *North Carolina Planters*, 65, 84–86; Schlotterbeck, *Plantation and Farm*, 243; Cecil-Fronsman, *Common Whites*, 3.

14. MGL, 501 (Oct. 25, 1863); MCS; George Harrison Burwell III, "Sketch of Carter Burwell (1715–1756)," 1961, CWF, 70–71.

tion of the men. During the courting phase of a young nineteenth-century woman's life, while in the process of connecting her family to another, she had greater autonomy than at any other time; young Victorian women were not as chaperoned or restricted as once believed. Mary Greenhow's experience bears this out. While in Williamsburg for those two and one-half months, she kept a record of her visitors, which, when tallied, amounted to 329, at least half of them men. She underlined the names of men who made the best impression on her; only a few received that distinction. One was Robert Ould, a law student at William and Mary who hailed from the Georgetown section of Washington. In fact, he was one of her first visitors— and her last. In the diary she kept through her visit, she jotted down for the final Williamsburg entry: "came home with Ould & had a long talk about two or three things."[15]

Quite possibly, a romance had begun between Mary Greenhow and Robert Ould. If so, he was not the only suitor who attracted her interest. She had a lively time on her visit to her father's hometown and seemed to wield a great deal of power as she met, danced with, and entertained the men in her *connexion*. Evidence of her sense of power also appears in the "mock chevalier society" she formed. Calling it the "Cerulean Society," the constitutional rules she laid out for the group called for meetings every Tuesday evening and stated that it was a "secret society" but that the secret was that there was "no secret." Membership included the "Cerulean Trio": Mary Greenhow, "Miss Lee," and "Miss Blair." The word "cerulean," according to the *Oxford Dictionary*, means "the color of the clear sky," or a "deep clear blue." But it also has a humorous meaning, referring to literary or learned women or a bluestocking. Which meaning Mary Greenhow had in mind when she named her club is uncertain, but given her wit and ability to laugh at herself, it is not beyond possibility that, in naming her "mock chevalier society," she was also mocking her own intellectual strengths. Men numbered about seven by the time the group disbanded near the end of April 1842, Robert Ould among them. Mary Greenhow was elected—or possibly self-appointed since the record does not reveal the procedure—"Presidentress" (and evidently the secretary as well since the minutes are written in her hand).[16]

It is clear from the record that the society was formed in part to facilitate flirtation. The men were termed "Knights" and were required to wear

15. Degler, *At Odds*, 19–20; MCS, May 2, 1842.

16. MGL, 501 (Oct. 25, 1863); MCS, Apr. 5, 1842. It is difficult to identify the "Miss Blair" in the group, but "Miss Lee" was Antoinette Lee, Mary's cousin and future sister-in-law.

badges. If the "Knights" had to be absent from a meeting, their excuses were to be written "in the form of a poem." At each meeting one "Knight," chosen the week before, read "a thesis on his own topic." Only a few of these offerings are in the record, but they covered subjects such as "the Philosophy of the Ball Room" and the industriousness of "Yankees." The only piece offered by Ould is his "Farewell," in which he assures Mary Greenhow, "if ever in future we should meet, a look, a nod of yours, shall exact the deepest homage of one who is proud to be your most faithful & obedient Knight." Although probably offered lightly, exacting this type of chivalry from her suitors can be interpreted to mean she perceived that she held a degree of power over them.[17]

Mary Greenhow favored the "Knights" with a poem as well. After chastising them for a disturbance they had engaged in and telling "them that they'd best avoid all duellings [sic], cards & dice," she bid them "a long & sad adieu." In a spurt of sectional pride, she also reminded them:

> Virginia's sons must bear in mind
> That on them rides the fate
> Of what we're taught to hold most dear
> Our own, our native state.
> We trust our Knights from southern climes
> Will not too soon forget
> Society nights in Williamsburg
> And those with whom they met.[18]

This passage has both regional and gender significance. Mary Greenhow is, on the one hand, revealing her allegiance to Virginia and her belief in the heritage that the citizens of the state should preserve. On the other hand, she is also exhibiting female influence over male behavior by drawing the men in her circle back to their heritage, reminding them of the role they were raised to assume, in order to guide their conduct.[19]

17. MCS, Apr. 5, 16, 23, 1842. See also MGL, 501 (Oct. 25, 1863).

18. MCS, 22–23 (undated poem). For the historic significance of gaming in the South, see Isaac, *Transformation of Virginia*, 5, 101; and T. H. Breen, "Horses and Gentlemen: The Cultural Significance of Gambling among the Gentry of Virginia," *William and Mary Quarterly*, 3d ser., 34, no. 2 (Apr. 1977): 239–41.

19. See Wyatt-Brown, *Southern Honor*. Wyatt-Brown argues that women's weakness stood as the reason for males to assert their power and that protecting women both physically and socially became the basis of the "Code of Southern Honor." Included in that protection of women was the protection of their community's reputation.

Besides entertaining visitors and presiding over Cerulean meetings, Mary Greenhow "played whist" and attended lectures, parties, and church. Although the entries in her diary for this period are brief, it appears that she maintained control in her numerous social activities. When "Ned" walked with her to a lecture, she "gave him a slap for . . . his impudence" but did not record the specifics of his cheeky behavior. The young people seem to have been left unchaperoned quite often, especially if they were merely "walking in the garden" or horseback riding. In this last activity Mary Greenhow ventured fairly far and exhibited a fearlessness that suggests a good deal of experience. On one occasion a group that included one married woman, a "Mrs. Saunders" (possibly Robert Saunders's wife), rode on horseback and in buggies to the Yorktown battlefield. Mary Greenhow rode horseback on the trip out but returned in a buggy, leaving one of the men to ride her "horse sideways" for the return trip, presumably because the animal still bore her saddle. During another ride, her horse "ran away" with her, but she did not record any special concern. She reported that it finally "carried [her] into a blacksmith's yard & then behaved very well" for the rest of her ride. The experience could have been frightening, but she did not embellish her report of the incident, suggesting that the drama amused rather than alarmed her. The rest of the journey was "a charming ride." Where another young woman might have ended the day at the blacksmith's yard, Mary Greenhow trusted her own skills and fortunes to handle the horse for the rest of the ride. In fact, the incident probably fed her spirit of adventure.[20]

Horseback riding occupied her time while visiting in Winchester the following fall as well. Her record for this visit is even more abbreviated than the one for Williamsburg yet is important because it reveals that, when she moved to Winchester as a young wife, she already had a comfortable knowledge of the town and the members of her *connexion* there. If her surroundings and the people she spent time with had been new to her, she would have recorded descriptions and her impressions. For the most part, however, she referred to people merely by their initials and mentioned intimate place names as though they were familiar to her, suggesting that this was not her first trip to the town. It would definitely not be her last.

During this visit, Mary Greenhow began a serious courtship that would

20. MCS, Mar. 23, Apr. 6, 7, 2, 21, May 2, 1842. See "Will and Codicil of Robert Greenhow Sr.," Richmond Hustings Court Book 8:263. Greenhow left silver to Robert Jr. that had been given to him by his "respected friend Robert Saunders" of Williamsburg. This may be the Saunders family Mary Greenhow spent time with on her visit in 1842.

lead to her marriage to Hugh Holmes Lee the next spring. Unfortunately, the more personal and profound Mary Greenhow's feelings, in all of the sources available, the less she wrote. The more important an event was to her personally, the less inclined she was to record her deepest impressions. For instance, in her 1837–38 diary, when she had "heard some news," she became "so distressed" that she did not feel like going out of the house; but "some news" is the only description she gave, refusing to reveal what had touched her so deeply. Later, during the war, the "death of a friend" pained her to a depth that froze her words before they reached the page. Obviously influenced by the romanticism of the age, which restricted her from expounding on specifics, she merely admitted that she could not write her feelings because they were "too sacred."[21]

For this reason, what Mary Greenhow wrote about Hugh Holmes Lee in the diary she kept during their courtship is significant for what she did not say as well as what she did. They spent a lot of time together, horseback riding, dancing, reading from Dickens, eating oysters, playing whist, sleighing, and "making faces." Through it all, she merely referred to him as "H.L." but eventually granted him the honor of "H.L." and, finally, "H.L.," signifying in her own shorthand that he was becoming very important to her. For a period of about ten days, she did not even write his initials and seemed to be in a bad humor, deeming an "evening at Dr. Maguire's . . . *especially* stupid," for instance, and noting her daily activities even more tersely than earlier. During this period, she did cryptically note "Female client" without explaining the significance of her comment; it could be that she attributed Hugh's absence from her social activities to legal work he was performing for a woman Mary believed to be a rival.[22]

In any event, when Hugh again appears in her daily record, it is as "H.L.—afternoon—charming walk at night." Her last Winchester entry ends, "H.L. so kind & agreeable." Her next entry, written on December 17, 1842, finds her back home in Richmond, "end[ing] three of the happiest months of" her life. The only other notation written by Mary Greenhow in this diary is dated January 29, 1843. In it she wrote: "Will the dreams of perfect happiness in which I now indulge ever be realized? I fear not." If she was referring to marriage with Hugh Holmes Lee, she was wrong. Within four months, they were married.[23]

21. MJCG/MHS, 66–67 (Mar. 1838); MGL, 463 (Aug. 22, 1863).
22. MCS, Oct. 14, 22, Nov. 6, 15, 19 (emphasis hers), 21 (emphasis hers), Dec. 1–11, 1842.
23. Ibid., Dec. 11, 16, 17, 1842, Jan. 29, 1843.

On the evening of May 18, 1843, a Reverend Norwood joined Mary Jane Charlton Greenhow and Hugh Holmes Lee in marriage at Monumental Church in Richmond. She later remembered that on that day, "peace, love & joy filled" her heart, and friends and family filled the pews of the church. At the time, the Episcopal Diocese of Virginia was holding their annual convention in Richmond, evidently presenting a double incentive for family and friends throughout the *connexion* to travel to the city. As an example of the joy prompted by the occasion, one friend left her pew and "interrupted the procession" as Mary and Hugh left the altar to start their new life. Mary Greenhow Lee, no longer a young Richmond belle, began her life as a responsible Winchester citizen.[24]

Present-day Winchester is located approximately twenty-five miles from Maryland and only ten miles from West Virginia on land originally belonging to Lord Thomas Fairfax, heir and proprietor of the Northern Neck of Virginia. Its first white inhabitants probably arrived no earlier than 1732, after German immigrant Jost Hite and his Scots-Irish partner Robert McKay obtained a 100,000-acre grant from Lt. Gov. William Gooch. With this the two were to act as agents for the colony to encourage settlement here as a buffer against Ohio Valley Indians. Col. James Wood is considered Winchester's founder. Born in Winchester, England, in 1707, Wood ultimately settled in Virginia and earned surveying credentials at the College of William and Mary in 1734. After surveying several tracts in the Shenandoah Valley, he finally settled down in the area that is now Winchester. The Virginia legislature established the town in 1752 after being presented with a survey by Wood for "twenty-six lots, of half an acre each, with streets for a town, by the name of Winchester," in Frederick County.[25]

By the first years of the nineteenth century, Winchester had all of the amenities expected of an urban area, if on a smaller scale. For one thing, the town

24. "Genealogical Notes," Tyler Family Papers; MGL, 104 (May 18, 1862), 382 (May 18, 1863), 872 (Sept. 24, 1865).

25. Oren Frederic Morton, *The Story of Winchester in Virginia: The Oldest Town in the Shenandoah Valley* (Strasburg, Va.: Shenandoah, 1925), 40, 29, 28, 59–60, 47; Warren R. Hofstra, "Land, Ethnicity, and Community at the Opequon Settlement, Virginia, 1730–1800," *Virginia Magazine of History and Biography* 98 (1990): 424–27; Richard L. Morton, *Colonial Virginia: Vol. II, Westward Expansion and Prelude to Revolution, 1710–1763* (Chapel Hill: University of North Carolina Press, 1960), 544, 545; Mary Tucker Magill, *Women; or, Chronicles of the Late War* (Baltimore: Turnbull Brothers, 1871), 3–4; Samuel Kercheval, *A History of the Valley of Virginia*, 4th ed. (Strasburg, Va.: Shenandoah, 1925), 175–76.

had become a supply center for migrants moving farther west. For another, its distance from Baltimore and Washington made it a good marketing nexus for farmers and customers in the Shenandoah Valley. As the county seat, Winchester developed as many other towns did in the nineteenth century, in a grid pattern that would make it familiar to most travelers. In addition, towns in the Upper South, as a mix of urban areas servicing rural surroundings, "gentrified," with the elite of the town driving further development of public space to reflect the separation of classes in the public spaces.[26]

The courthouse, enclosed in a "square" of rail fences and standing as a symbol of a well-ordered society, had in its yard a whipping post, dubbed "Black Betty," and two pillories placed on platforms. On the other end of the block stood the economic symbol of the town: Market House. Built of stone, two stories high, and taking up the better portion of the block, Market House sported six stone arches and housed a vegetable market and butchers' stalls in a brick addition on the south end. On the second floor, approached by steps attached to the outside of the building, was the Masonic Lodge room, approximately seventy feet long, with plastered walls and a fireplace on each end. Besides meeting space for the Masons, the room became an occasional concert hall, a public meeting room, or the setting for performances put on by the town's thespian society. On the north end of the building was another brick addition that housed town government offices. The street outside could be treacherous, with either boulders poking through the surface or hollows made by horse hooves filing up with water in bad weather, and the slope of the street made it necessary to chock the wheels of wagons parked there to keep them in place.[27]

This was the Winchester of Hugh Lee's parents' day. They moved to the town from Shenandoah County sometime between 1803 and 1805. Hugh's father, Daniel Lee, was clerk of the Chancery Court for Frederick County and president of Farmers Bank. One of his copying clerks described Daniel Lee as "a tall, high-featured, black-eyed man of elegant address, and uniform

26. Hofstra, "Land, Ethnicity, and Community," 444; *Winchester Virginian*, Apr. 22, 1840; David Holmes Conrad, "Early History of Winchester," in *Annual Papers of Winchester Virginia Historical Society*, Winchester–Frederick County Historical Society, vol. 1 (Winchester, Va.: Winchester–Frederick County Historical Society, 1931), 174; Lisa C. Tolbert, *Constructing Townscapes: Space and Society in Antebellum Tennessee* (Chapel Hill: University of North Carolina Press, 1999), 31, 39, 46, 97–98, 115.

27. Garland R. Quarles and Lewis N. Barton, eds., *What I Know about Winchester: Recollections of William Greenway Russell, 1800–1891*, vol. 2 (reprinted from *The Winchester News*, Winchester–Frederick County Historical Society; Staunton, Va.: McClure, 1953), 71, 99, 160.

politeness" who "sat as straight as an Indian over his writing, . . . took snuff like Bonaparte, and kept his papers as if they were bank notes."[28]

Daniel and Elizabeth Nicholson Lee raised their family in a large stone house on a two-acre tract along Washington Street. Surrounding the house were gardens and in the back was a stable. Furnishings inside the home signified both good taste and good fortune. The dining table, card tables, and settee were made, at least in part, of mahogany, and twenty chairs were ornamented with gold or silver gilt. A mahogany bookcase held works of such notables as Homer, Jonathan Swift, Adam Smith, Livy, Edmund Burke, Jean-Jacques Rousseau, and the histories of Rome, Greece, and the French Revolution. To help take care of all this, the family owned five slaves. In addition to the town property, Lee owned approximately four hundred acres in the county. To this property, Lee invited friends and family to celebrate the Fourth of July with barbecue dinners, Italian bands, formal toasts, and "thimble rigging" (a shell game).[29]

One of the Lees' friends (and a future friend of Mary Greenhow Lee), James Murray Mason, brought his bride, Eliza Margaretta Chew Mason, from her home in Philadelphia to Winchester soon after they married in 1822. Two years earlier, soon after he completed the study of law at William and Mary, Mason had chosen Winchester as his home and the location of his new law practice. On his first trip into Winchester, he rode into town on horseback, seated on his saddle-bags, and stopped in front of a tavern to seek

28. Winchester Personal Property Tax List, 1805, LOV; gravestone, Daniel Lee, Hebron Cemetery; David Holmes Conrad, "Early History of Winchester," 223; Shenandoah County Deed Book N:241, LOV. The later source records the sale of almost four hundred acres in Shenandoah County by Daniel Lee and shows him living in Woodstock in April 1803. The first year he is found paying personal property taxes in Winchester is 1805.

29. Winchester Personal Property Tax Lists, 1815, 1831; Garland R. Quarles, *The Churches of Winchester, Virginia: A Brief History of Those Established Prior to 1825* (Winchester, Va.: Farmers and Merchants National Bank, 1960), 204; "Appraisement of Daniel Lee's Estate," 1833, Frederick County Will Book 18:383–86, Frederick County Courthouse, Winchester, Va.; Quarles and Barton, *What I Know about Winchester*, 2:154, 179; Frederick County Land Tax Registers, 1827, 1832, 1833, LOV. Mary's mother-in-law, Elizabeth Lee, was the daughter of Henry Nicholson. When her parents died, she was adopted by her mother's brother, George Hay, who lived in Richmond and was attorney general of Virginia, a U.S. district judge, and son-in-law of President James Monroe. Hugh Lee's siblings were Lucy Peachy Powell (wife of William A. Powell of Loudoun County, Va.), Judge George Hay Lee (Charles Town, Va.), Mrs. Chaplain Hodges (New Orleans), Rev. Henry Lightfoot Lee (New Orleans, then Baltimore), Elizabeth Cabell (wife of Patrick Henry Cabell of Winchester, Va.), Laura Lee, and Marie Antoinette Lee. *Genealogies of Virginia Families*, 4:12–13.

lodging. In front of the tavern, he noticed a large group of men seated in chairs arranged in a semicircle jutting out into the street. Mason's approach stopped their conversation until he introduced himself to the landlord and made arrangements for a room. When the landlord, in turn, introduced him to the group of Winchester citizens, they welcomed him warmly. At this point Mason began his Winchester *connexion*.[30]

Eliza Mason also experienced a warm reception and settled right in to the small-town society, so different from life in Philadelphia. In a letter to her family, she wrote, "Winchester is the place for the enjoyment of society without display." She related that wives from "half a dozen families, who are closely connected and who like each other vastly," met each afternoon at two o'clock, at one house or another, and visited or did "parlour work" for an hour until their husbands joined them for "most excellent dinners . . . without any parade or ostentation." Families represented in the group were those of Henry St. George Tucker, Alexander Tidball, Alfred H. Powell, Daniel Lee, and younger men in the *connexion*, brothers Robert Y. and Holmes Conrad.[31]

Their early years in Winchester were a struggle for the Masons in terms of both finances and supplies. James, on a number of occasions, was forced to write his family for a loan of money or simply for "Nachitoches snuff" from his favorite store in Georgetown. By 1828, though, Mason had become relatively successful, enabling him to purchase a large stone house, built in 1813 for Judge Dabney Carr, about a mile west of town. Mason named his new home "Selma." Although not furnished with the contemporary signs of style and fashion, such as mahogany chairs or Brussels carpets, the Masons made their home comfortable and pleasant for visitors. The rooms at Selma were smaller than those in more prominent houses, yet Eliza Mason decorated the rooms in a style that their budget could afford, using pieces she had brought with her from home as well. They did not acquire a sideboard or tea table right away, but card tables covered with green cloth served double duty

---

30. Garland R. Quarles, *Some Worthy Lives: Mini-Biographies, Winchester and Frederick County* (Winchester, Va.: Winchester–Frederick County Historical Society, 1988), 172–73; Virginius Cornick Hall Jr., *Portraits in the Collection of the Virginia Historical Society: A Catalogue* (Charlottesville: University Press of Virginia, 1981), 21; James M. Mason, *The Public Life and Diplomatic Correspondence of James M. Mason, with some Personal History*, ed. Virginia Mason (New York: Neale, 1906), 10, 12, 13, 14, 15. Mason was son of John and Anna Maria Murray Mason of Fairfax County and grandson of George Mason of Gunston Hall.

31. Mason, *Public Life*, 10, 14, 15.

when needed. They also displayed a piano and Japanese desk, and the rooms were accented with chess pieces, books, and a "phrenological skull," of interest to James if not to his wife.[32]

Mason's welcome to the community was cemented by 1826, when he began representing Frederick County in the Virginia House of Delegates. After one term in the U.S. House of Representatives, he was elected to the Senate in 1839, beginning a long run as a U.S. senator that lasted until Virginia seceded from the Union. In the meantime, his family grew with the addition of three daughters and three sons. The Winchester community celebrated each child's arrival and watched over the children when their parents were out of town, with "Mrs. Lee" and "Mrs. Tidball" stopping by to check on them.[33]

The Mason family, along with others in the Winchester *connexion*, apparently gave Mary Greenhow Lee a similar welcome when she adopted the hometown of her new husband. Lee had a successful law practice in Winchester, which he had operated from a second-floor office in a yellow building in Courthouse Square since 1840. By 1848, he was serving as receiver of the Circuit Court of Law and Chancery for Clark, the county adjoining Frederick. In 1853 he advertised that he would be practicing "in the Circuit Court of Clarke [*sic*], and give his attention to the collection practice generally, in Frederick and the surrounding counties." His collection activities extended farther than the local area, however. As with politics, economics, and religious associations, lawyers connected urban areas through legal tangles, and Hugh Lee was no exception. In a case involving his client and the client's debtor in Richmond, Lee maintained a correspondence over a period of three years with the Richmond firm of Griswold and Claiborne for purposes of securing the debt. The significance of this thread of the urban *connexion* is that the Richmond firm's office was located on the corner of Eleventh and Capitol Streets, one block from Mary Greenhow Lee's family home. Additionally, the Claiborne and Greenhow families had been connected through debt,

32. James Murray Mason to John Mason, May 20, 1821, Apr. 17, Sept. 1, 1823, Mason Correspondence, James and John Murray Mason Papers (No. 5036), UVA; Mason to "Eilbach," n.d., ibid.; Mason, *Public Life*, 29, 16; Quarles, *Some Worthy Lives*, 172.

33. Quarles, *Some Worthy Lives*, 172; U.S. Bureau of the Census, Eighth U.S. Census, LOV, microfilm; Kate, Anna, and Benjamin Mason to Eliza Chew Mason, June 2, 1840, Ida Mason Dorsey Brown Papers (Mss1B8134a), VHS; Eliza Chew Mason, Commonplace Book, ibid. Two of the Mason children, Ida and Virginia, grew especially close to Mary Greenhow Lee when she joined the community. In fact, it was to Virginia ("Jeannie") that Lee directed her Civil War journal when she first began writing it in March 1862.

friendship, and the church for at least one generation. Besides gaining a wife of wit, intelligence, and proficiency in the social graces, Hugh Lee also gained business connections.[34]

But Lee was more than a lawyer to his wife and to his town. According to Mary Greenhow Lee, he had a "natural fondness for military pursuits." In 1837, when Lee was only twenty-three years old, he had become captain of the Highland Blues Light Infantry Company of the 31st Regiment in Frederick County. Their uniforms were blue-and-buff-colored coats modeled in the colonial fashion, with "yellow buckskin knee breeches." In 1849 Lee, as colonel of the militia, ordered the 31st and 51st Regiments to a three-day officers-training session in Winchester, which would end with a "parade on Market St." at eleven o'clock on the morning of May 17. The significance of this event could not have been lost on his wife since it would mark the eve of their sixth wedding anniversary. To watch her "military hero," as she remembered him, marching his regiment past their house was probably, in part, a gift to her from her husband. During the Civil War, she would watch similar events against the backdrop of serious military conflict. On this occasion in 1849, however, Mary Greenhow Lee was still living in the "palm days of old Winchester."[35]

Although no surviving sources clearly reveal the character of Hugh and Mary Lee's life together, they probably enjoyed a companionate marriage as the form matured through the nineteenth century, defined as a partnership, although still assigning distinct roles to both husband and wife by gender ideology. We know from what she did not like about the young men who flirted with her in Washington that Lee would have been intelligent, witty, schooled in the social graces, and probably a good dancer, or Mary would not have joined her life to his. From the references she made of him through the filter of grief after his death, they were happily married. She thought of him as

34. *Winchester Virginian*, Feb. 5, 1840; indenture of James Markham Marshall, Nov. 21, 1848, James Marshall Papers (Mss2 M35638b), VHS; *Winchester Virginian*, Sept. 21, 1853, Mar. 15, 1854; Hugh Holmes Lee to Griswold and Claiborne, Richmond, Oct. 31, 1848, Oct. 4, 11, 1851, Claiborne Family Papers, VHS; *Ellyson's Business Directory, and Almanac, for the Year 1845* (Richmond, Va.: H. K. Ellyson, 1845), 16; Richmond Hustings Court Book 78B:26–27. See also Danforth and Claiborne, *Historical Sketch;* and *Genealogies of Virginia Families: From the Virginia Magazine of History and Biography*, vol. 3 (Baltimore: Genealogical Publishing, 1981), 959–60.

35. MGL, 313 (Feb. 14, 1863), 831 (June 2, 1865); "Ben Ritter, Miscellaneous Notes," pt. 6, May 29, 1984, Ben Ritter Collection (12 WFCHS), HL; Cornelia A. McDonald, *Diary with Reminiscences of the War*, ed. Hunter McDonald (Nashville: Cellom and Glertner, 1934), 87 n; MGL, 530 (Dec. 17, 1863); *Winchester Virginian*, May 2, 1849; MGL, 734 (Dec. 8, 1864), 748–49 (Dec. 26–28, 1864).

"my darling" and wondered, during her most difficult decisions, if he would approve, seeming to miss his guidance in her life. The fact that she maintained the forms of deep mourning, even down to the black-edged stationery she used as late as ten years after his death, suggests that she missed both her husband and her marriage.[36]

The historiographical emphasis on "separate spheres" for nineteenth-century women portrays households in which wives, as "True Women," remained subordinate to their men, charged with maintenance of the private. The public sphere of men's dominance was assumed to have been the most important and more powerful. While it might be true that power within marriage was unequal and that men maintained the advantage when it came to decisions relative to finances, we might want to consider separating the concept of power into public and private spheres of influence.[37]

We tend to think of power in terms of the ability to control others, whether in the corporate or the political realm, or in terms of strength over weakness. But its strict definition is the ability to influence behavior. From this perspective, then, physical strength, economic capacity, and voting rights are simply examples of the tools of influence, not the proof of power. Therefore, although nineteenth-century men had more of the tools of influence, that does not necessarily mean they had most or all of the power. Within the home, women's influence often controlled behavior, and this can be seen as a sign of at least private power for nineteenth-century women. Although they could not go to the polls at this time, women were not without political influence. In fact, as partisanship became essential to politics in the 1840s, men began drawing women into the political debate for purposes of moral persuasion and agitation to action.[38]

36. Jabour, *Marriage in the Early Republic*, 3–6, 9–10, 13, 27; MGL, 335 (Mar. 22, 1863), 614 (June 4, 1864), 865 (Sept. 5, 1865), 878 (Dec. 10, 1865); Mary Greenhow Lee to Mary Williams, June 7, 1866, Philip Williams Family Papers (172 WFCHS), HL.

37. Gary K. Bertsch, Robert P. Clark, and David M. Wood, *Comparing Political Systems: Power and Policy in Three Worlds* (New York: Macmillan, 1986), xxii. For regional variations on the nineteenth-century "Cult of True Womanhood," see Jacquelyn Dowd Hall, "Partial Truths: Writing Southern Women's History," in *Southern Women: Histories and Identities*, ed. Virginia Berhard et al. (Columbia: University of Missouri Press, 1992), 11–29; Elizabeth Fox-Genovese, *Within the Plantation Household: Black and White Women of the Old South* (Chapel Hill: University of North Carolina Press, 1988); and Suzanne Lebsock, *The Free Women of Petersburg: Status and Culture in a Southern Town, 1784–1860* (New York: W. W. Norton, 1984).

38. Elizabeth R. Varon, *"We Mean to Be Counted": White Women and Politics in Antebellum Virginia* (Chapel Hill: University of North Carolina Press, 1998), 1–3, 71–102; Cynthia A. Kierner, "Genteel Balls and Republican Parades: Gender and Early Southern Civic Rituals, 1677–1826," *Virginia Magazine of History and Biography* 104, no. 2 (spring 1996): 185–210; Mary

Additionally, although the social construction of middle-class women's roles seems to have consigned them to domestic space, women were also promised increased influence in their families the more effectively they managed them. As historian Bonnie G. Smith has argued, we should look at the construction of spheres not as "evidence for a conspiracy theory of women's history," but as something women themselves helped develop. Women were not merely acted upon—they participated in the construction of their roles. Within the home, they became keepers of tradition based on natural time rather than on the rhythms of the marketplace. Natural time applies to the gender in charge of reproduction rather than production, time that includes menstruation, childbirth, lactation, and menopause individually, and meals, anniversaries, illnesses, and death socially. By maintaining the natural rhythms of life, nineteenth-century women had a great deal of private power. Whether or not later generations find private power of less value than public power, in an age of transition, when industrial capitalism was dehumanizing labor, the home was essential for reemphasizing the intrinsic worth of humanity and for nurturing those values.[39]

In fact, although women's place might have shifted to the private sphere in the nineteenth century, it does not necessarily imply a loss of influence. When Hugh Lee, at twenty-nine years of age and already established in his law practice, chose Mary Greenhow as his wife, it is obvious that he did not select a weak woman. Her personality does not fit the term "subordinate." Intellectually strong, quick witted, and opinionated, Greenhow might have entered her marriage knowing that, to the outside world, she would be considered subordinate to her husband. She accepted that. Within their union, however, she became a partner, assuming the duties of maintaining their home while Hugh sustained the administration of their business affairs. Mary Greenhow Lee later asserted that "husbands replace the world," not that husbands took away the world. She willingly took on the duties of wife as they were described in her era. It would have been uncharacteristic of her to do so if she had not believed she would contribute to that partnership equally. Considering how much Mary Greenhow Lee had appreciated the intellectual challenges provided by men in her immediate family and later by the men in her life as a widow, it is clear that her happiness with her husband came in

P. Ryan, *Women in Public: Between Banners and Ballots, 1825–1885* (Baltimore: Johns Hopkins University Press, 1990), 133–38.

39. Newton, *Learning to Behave*, 92–93; Bonnie G. Smith, *Ladies of the Leisure Class: The Bourgeoisies of Northern France in the Nineteenth Century* (Princeton, N.J.: Princeton University Press, 1981), 17, 14, 47, 49, 65.

part from his treatment of her as an equal and contributing partner in their life, not as his subordinate.[40]

The Lees resided in a brown wood-frame house, purchased from David L. Danner in May 1845, on a large lot along Market Street, just a block away from the Market House. A large structure, it had two floors, an "attic chamber," cellar, office, storeroom, and porches facing both streets. The house was so close to the streets that, on one porch, "a parapet" touched the sidewalk. On the grounds were stables, vegetable and flower gardens, and raspberry bushes. The Lee's home was necessarily large. Hugh's father had died in 1833, and Hugh had taken over responsibility for his mother and his two unmarried sisters, Laura "Lal" Lee and Antoinette "Nettie" Lee, all of whom lived with them. Depending on the specific year, the Lees owned as many as four slaves, also members of their "household."[41]

Except for personal-property tax lists, there are few sources giving evidence for the furnishings inside the house. The year they purchased the house, the Lees paid taxes on a piano, which Mary had inherited. From her listings of housework in later years, it appears that Mary Greenhow Lee took pride in the home she established with Hugh, which would have given her both a sense of identity as a good homemaker and pleasure in displaying evidence of their success. As Bonnie Smith argues, the nineteenth-century home did not stand as "the opposite of the market world but as its complement; one, the world of consumption, the other of production." Smith also points out that the way a wife decorated and arranged her living space was an articulation of what she wanted the world to think about her—a "linguistic system" of draperies, ruffles, and domestic arrangements that said she was "important to an industrial society."[42]

When Mary Greenhow Lee moved there, Winchester had a population of over 650 adult white males, over 300 slaves, 260 horses, nine attorneys, five doctors, two newspapers, and one dentist. It also boasted of having the Win-

40. Degler, *At Odds*, 26–29, 36–37; MGL, 865 (Sept. 5, 1865).

41. Quarles, *Occupied Winchester*, 15; Quarles, *One Hundred Old Homes*, 99; Winchester Deed Book 8:487–88, 9:148, Frederick County Courthouse; MGL, 74 (Apr. 21, 1862), 109 (May 22, 1862), 281 (Dec. 25, 1862), 336 (Mar. 24, 1863), 356 (Apr. 13, 1863), 368 (Apr. 27, 1863), 424 (June 26, 1863), 445 (July 27, 1863), 513 (Nov. 14, 1863), 569 (Mar. 17, 1864), 570 (Mar. 18, 1864), 584 (Apr. 26, 1864), 666 (Aug. 17, 1864); Winchester Personal Property Tax Lists, 1843–55.

42. Bonnie G. Smith, *Ladies of the Leisure Class*, 54, 85, 87, 88, 91; MGL, 220 (Sept. 3, 1862), 227 (Sept. 8, 1862), 361 (Mar. 18, 1863), 379 (May 13, 1863), 384 (May 21, 1863), 396 (June 5, 1863), 424 (June 26, 1863), 430 (July 6, 1863).

chester and Potomac Railroad Company, although the corporation was "not in a very prosperous condition." Eventually, the railroad became more financially sound but never became a boon to its stockholders. It did create a new threat to children, forcing the company's agent to put notices in the newspaper "request[ing] . . . parents and guardians to prevent their children from running at large at the Depot and on the tracks of the Rail Road."[43]

For visitors to the town who arrived by rail, carriage, horse, or stage, there were at least four hotels at which to lodge, the Eagle, the Union, the Taylor, and the American. Each offered stabling for horses of the guests and a "Table . . . furnished with all the varieties which the season and market afford, and . . . Bar supplied with the choicest of liquors." For protection, the town had three fire engines, the "Union," "Sarah Zane," and "Friendship." The Winchester Academy, run by John Peyton Clark, provided the rudiments of education for young boys in the area, and the first medical college in the state, the Medical School of the Valley of Virginia, was opened in the city in 1826 by Dr. Hugh Holmes McGuire.[44]

Winters were dull in Winchester; summer was the "gay season." For fun, boys played bandy, a game resembling field hockey that became so dangerous to "heads and shins" that schoolmaster Clark bought the boys a (round) football but could not interest them in the game. Winchester firemen began the tradition of honoring themselves with "a ball" to break the tedium. Outsiders brought excitement to town as well. "Bear-baiting" filled the streets with "country folk," and a "balloon ascension [sic]" made the young people "crazy to go up in it." For more productive entertainment, the women of the Lees' church put on fairs and public dinners to contribute financially to physical improvements at Christ Church, on the corner of Boscowen and Washington Streets. Built in 1828, Winchester's Episcopal church became almost as important to Mary Greenhow Lee as did her home, so it is probable that when the "ladies" offered a "supper to build a bell tower" in 1854, she had a hand in the activity. In any event, they were successful—the tower was added to the building the next year.[45]

43. Winchester Personal Property Tax Lists, 1843, 1849; *Winchester Virginian*, Sept. 13, 1954.

44. *Winchester Virginian*, Aug. 5, 1846, July 25, 1849, Jan. 23, 1850, Sept. 13, 1854, June 4, 1856; Quarles and Barton, *What I Know about Winchester*, 2:161; St. George Tucker Brooke, "Autobiography of St. George Tucker Brooke Written for His Children," 1907, VHS, 13, typescript; Quarles, *Some Worthy Lives*, 158.

45. Brooke, "Autobiography," 13; Robert Y. Conrad to Kate Conrad, Nov. 10, 1852, Robert Y. Conrad Papers (Mss1C7638a), VHS; Robert Y. Conrad to Robert Y. Conrad Jr., Nov. 1,

Religion, imparted to Mary Greenhow Lee from childhood as an essential part of her life, became even more important to her in the decade before the war. In those ten years death claimed her natal family, a sister-in-law, her mother-in-law, and her husband. On July 2, 1848, Hugh's sister, Susan Burwell, died. Philip Carter Lewis Burwell sold his Carters Grove plantation in James City County and brought his four children back to Winchester to live. From that point on, Burwell's children considered the Lee home theirs. Louisa, Lewis, Laura, and Robert moved into Mary and Hugh's house on Market Street, already so full of family members.[46]

In September the next year, Mary's brother, Washington Greenhow, died in Clarksburg, Tennessee. Although her immediate reaction to his death is lost to the record, it must have been difficult for her to accept, given their closeness in both age and affections. The next loss to the family occurred in 1853 when Hugh's mother, Elizabeth Lee, died at seventy years of age. On her gravestone her family had chiseled in the granite that she had been a "woman of glory," who had found "the way of Righteousness." The following year Mary Greenhow Lee lost her remaining sibling, Robert. He had retired from the State Department in 1850 and moved his family to San Francisco, California, where he continued to work on his history of Mexico and became an agent for the Land Commission for the new state. Although he survived the fire that gutted much of downtown San Francisco in May 1850 just after he had arrived, an accident claimed his life in 1854. He lived just long enough to sign a brief will, leaving all of his "estate both real and personal" to Rose, his "beloved wife." Although he had named a friend in California as his executor, Hugh Lee became the administrator of Robert's estate. Still reeling from Robert's death, Mary then lost her mother, Mary Lorraine, the following year. She and Hugh buried her near Hugh's parents in the family plot at Mount Hebron Cemetery in Winchester. Through all of these losses, Mary Greenhow Lee's faith in God and her husband helped her cope with the grief. But on October 10, 1856, Hugh Lee died as well.[47]

1856, ibid.; Robert Y. Conrad to Powell Conrad, Feb. 22, 1854, Holmes Conrad Papers (Mss1C7637b), VHS; *Winchester Virginian*, Nov. 22, 1854; Quarles and Barton, *What I Know about Winchester*, 2:28. Lee's influence in the church is evident during the Civil War years, when she took charge of arranging the rectory for a new visiting rector and when men in the church came to her for advice about continuing services during the winter months of the war when fuel was at a premium. See MGL, 581 (Apr. 16, 1864), 721 (Nov. 14, 1864).

46. Gravestone, Susan Lee, Mount Hebron Cemetery, Winchester, Va.; Burwell, "Sketch of Carter Burwell," 72; Bureau of the Census, Seventh Census, LOV, microfilm.

47. "Genealogical Notes," Tyler Family Papers; gravestone, Elizabeth Lee, Mount Hebron Cemetery, Winchester, Va.; Rose O'Neal Greenhow to John Y. Mason, May 8, 1850, John Y. Mason Correspondence (No. 496), Eastern Shore of Virginia Historical Society (photocopy,

Virginia statutes did not require the registration of cause of death until 1912, and no known sources reveal how Hugh Lee died, but it was probably brought on by an illness of a chronic nature. Although there were several severe cases of typhoid fever in Winchester at the time, Lee's health could have been failing for some time, for Mary Greenhow Lee mentioned later, "sometimes I fancy . . . his health would have been restored by the change in his mode of life." This statement was in reference to her belief that "had he lived," Hugh Lee would have been militarily active in the Confederate cause during the war; but it also suggests that a long-term, active lifestyle would have had a beneficial effect on his health, evidence that his health problems had been chronic.[48]

Whatever the cause, Mary Greenhow Lee became a widow that October day, one she remembered later as "the darkest day of [her] existence," a time when "iron . . . entered her heart," and she "commenced to live alone in this world." The next day her friend and neighbor Robert Young Conrad wrote to his son Robert Jr. simply: "Col. H. H. Lee died yesterday morning. He was a worthy and useful man." Mary Greenhow Lee thought her husband was more than that. She had a monument placed over his grave that reads: "Mark the perfect man and behold the upright for the end of that man is peace."[49]

SHC); Barbee, "Robert Greenhow," 182; "Will of Robert Greenhow," Richmond Circuit Court Book 1:166, "Inventory," 184, "Settlement," 334, LOV; gravestone, Mary Lorraine Greenhow, Mount Hebron Cemetery, Winchester, Va.; *Winchester Virginian*, Oct. 15, 1856. In 1865 a former acquaintance of Washington Greenhow encountered Mary as she was visiting in Richmond and mentioned her brother's name. She recorded her reaction to this meeting in her journal. "How little those around me realize how that name [Washington Greenhow] thrills my heart," she wrote. "I have lived over during this war what his course and my husband's would have been; the one as a statesman, the other as a military hero, each one carrying out with pure patriotism the natural bent of their strong passion for those two callings." MGL, 831 (June 2, 1865). Although Hugh Lee became the administrator of Robert Greenhow's estate, Hugh's death in 1856 left the job to Mary; in the final disposition of Robert's estate, "Mary Jane Lee" is named as the administrator. An obituary of Hugh would have been helpful in gaining more information about him for this biography, such as where he had been educated and how he died; one was not uncovered. In the issue of the *Winchester Virginian* dated October 15, 1856, along with his death notice is the promise that his obituary would appear the following week. Unfortunately, no copy of the October 22 edition of the *Winchester Virginian* exists as far as the indexes of extant newspapers reflect. For this reason, among others, Mary Greenhow Lee's husband remains a rather shadowy figure in her biography.

48. Blanton, *Medicine in Virginia*, 269; Robert Y. Conrad to Robert Y. Conrad Jr., Nov. 1, 1856, Robert Y. Conrad Papers; MGL, 313 (Feb. 14, 1863).

49. MGL, 173 (July 14, 1862), 240 (Oct. 10, 1862), 491 (Oct. 10, 1863); Robert Y. Conrad to Robert Y. Conrad Jr., Oct. 11, 1856, Robert Y. Conrad Papers; gravestone, Hugh Holmes Lee, Mount Hebron Cemetery, Winchester, Va.

Hugh Lee may have rested in peace, but he left his wife's world in turmoil. Although a lawyer with obvious health problems, he did not leave a will. His family members, "in consideration of the love and affection" for her, eventually deeded the house to Mary in a life estate, but she was also left with the care of his nieces and nephews, still living with them, and her two sisters-in-law. Added to that were other legal matters to deal with, among them the final settlement of her brother Robert's estate, for which she took over as administrator. Hugh did leave her with income from railroad stock and, evidently, some land upon which she had wheat grown for sale; but some of these sources were part of Daniel Lee's estate, which Hugh had been administering, and would eventually draw Mary Greenhow Lee into a lawsuit that would not be settled until after her death.[50]

In a series of letters she wrote in an effort to collect a debt owed to her husband, however, the iron strength of the new widow becomes evident. John Y. Mason, at that time the U.S. minister plenipotentiary to France, and his son, Lewis E. Mason, of Richmond, owed Hugh Lee $1,540 plus interest. The first letters Mary Greenhow Lee wrote to Lewis Mason in February 1857 were written in the third person, as if she were merely copying the words written for her by someone else, presumably Philip Williams, her lawyer in Winchester. Although the letters are all written in a respectful tone, the first are almost pleading. They begin with a request, asking if "Mr. Mason will oblige Mrs. Hugh H. Lee very much, by letting her know the exact time" he could "pay her the balance of the money due." She also explained that she would not bother him but that "she may miss the opportunity of making a favourable investment" on time. She wrote her next letter in the first person and was more forceful, stating, "it would put me to the greatest inconvenience to wait longer than the 1st of July."[51]

By July 13, 1858, she still had not received the money, and Lewis Mason had decided, "for fear of disappointing" her further, to "make no further promise" but that he would "settle the debt . . . as soon as possible." Lee's response to these assurances, though polite, clearly show that she had begun to lose patience. She wrote, "it would be very painful to me, to resort to any

50. MGL, 479 (Sept. 19, 1863), 519 (Nov. 23, 1863), 525 (Dec. 5, 1863), 576 (Apr. 5, 1864), 614 (June 4, 1864), 704 (Oct. 11, 1864), 744 (Dec. 22, 1864), 766 (Jan. 18, 1865); Winchester Deed Book 13:275–77, 283–84, Frederick County Courthouse; "Settlement of Robert Greenhow's Estate," Richmond Circuit Court Book 1:334.

51. Mary Greenhow Lee to Roscoe Heath, Feb. 17, 1857, Mason Family Papers; Mary Greenhow Lee to Lewis E. Mason, Mar. 24, Mar. 30, July 9, ibid.; Virginius Cornick Hall Jr., *Portraits*, 163–64.

measures which might force a payment." Then she ended the letter with both sugar and vinegar, telling Mason that, although she regretted the tone of her letter, "necessity compels me to be firm." By August, she had the money, and Lee sent a final letter stating, "nothing but necessity would have made me hurry you in making this final payment." If she had been able to secure the money "from various other sources," Lee wrote, she "would not have called on" Mason until "it suited" his "convenience." These letters show that, although Mary may have assumed the subordinate position of wife in marriage, she was perfectly capable and willing to take care of her own affairs, both public and private, as a widow.[52]

For Mary Greenhow Lee, the "palm days of old Winchester" were now over and a new, more turbulent time just beginning. Her strength of character, however, added to the wit and intelligence fostered by her father, and the respect and trust she had gained from her new community as Hugh Lee's wife would see her through her most difficult times.

52. Mary Greenhow Lee to Lewis E. Mason, July 16, Aug. 3, 23, 1858, Mason Family Papers; Lewis E. Mason to Mary Greenhow Lee, July 13, 1858, ibid.

Mary Greenhow Lee

Courtesy Winchester–Frederick County Historical Society

Edmond Randolph House, purchased by Robert Greenhow in 1811

Courtesy Valentine Richmond History Center

Mary Greenhow Lee's home at 132 North Market Street

Courtesy Ben Ritter, Winchester, Va.

Christ Episcopal Church on West Boscawen Street in Winchester

Courtesy Ben Ritter, Winchester, Va.

James Murray Mason

Courtesy Ben Ritter, Winchester, Va.

Robert Young Conrad

Courtesy Ben Ritter, Winchester, Va.

Cornelia P. McDonald

Courtesy Ben Ritter, Winchester, Va.

John Peyton Clark

Courtesy Ben Ritter, Winchester, Va.

York Hospital, 112 South Cameron (Market) Street

Courtesy Ben Ritter, Winchester, Va.

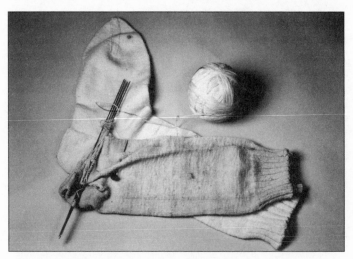

Stockings knitted by Mary Greenhow Lee during the Civil War

Courtesy The Museum of the Confederacy, Richmond

Frederick County Court House with Confederate prisoners taken in third battle of
Winchester in fenced yard

Sketch by James E. Taylor from *With Sheridan Up the Shenandoah Valley in 1864: Leaves from A
Special Artist's Sketchbook and Diary* (Cleveland: Western Reserve Historical Society, 1989).
Courtesy The Western Reserve Historical Society, Cleveland, Ohio.

Winchester Market House, 1864

Sketch by James E. Taylor from *With Sheridan Up the Shenandoah Valley in 1864.*
Courtesy The Western Reserve Historical Society, Cleveland, Ohio.

Rose O'Neal Greenhow and
daughter in Old Capitol Prison,
Washington, D.C.

Courtesy Library of Virginia

Graves of Hugh Holmes Lee and
Mary Greenhow Lee, Mount
Hebron Cemetery. Obelisk marks
Hugh's grave; small stone to right
marks Mary's. Flag beside Mary's
grave placed by Turner Ashby
Chapter, United Daughters of the
Confederacy.

Photo by the author, June 6, 1996

4

"Secesh Lives Here"

132 North Market Street

*A*hortly after Hugh Lee's death, the *Virginia Free Press* printed a letter written by Mary Greenhow Lee's good friend James Murray Mason. Fearing a Republican victory in the upcoming presidential election, Mason stated that, if such were to happen, the South would have but one course: "immediate, absolute, and eternal separation." Mason had been involved in sectional debates on behalf of the southern states, Virginia especially, since his election to the Senate in 1839. As author of the Fugitive Slave Act, he had a vested interest in the outcome of the Compromise of 1850. Then, in 1858 he took part in the heated debate over the admission of Kansas to the Union, an extreme arena of sectional conflict. Mason and all of Winchester were drawn further into the conflict the next year when John Brown conducted his raid at nearby Harpers Ferry. Mary Greenhow Lee's thoughts on these events are unknown. Although she did not begin her journal until the war was almost a year old, evidence suggests that she was a secessionist from the start of the conflict.[1]

1. *Virginia Free Press*, Oct. 30, 1856; Quarles, *Some Worthy Lives*, 172; U.S. Senate, *Speech of Hon. J. M. Mason, of Virginia, on the Admission of Kansas, Delivered in the Senate of the United States, Mar. 15, 1858* (Washington, D.C.: Geo. S. Gideon, 1858).

Both of Mary's brothers had been Democrats and had participated energetically in politics. Southern Republicans of Jefferson's day began forming a
new Democratic party under the expert manipulation of New York's Martin
Van Buren, who established a strong bond with the Richmond Junto, the lead
spokesman of which was Thomas Ritchie. In fact, it was the coalition of old
Republicans from the southern Atlantic states and Van Buren's New York
who helped elect Andrew Jackson to the presidency in 1828. The new generation of Virginia politicians were less affluent, less tied to the land, and less
agrarian than the Jeffersonians had been. While they looked forward to an
economically expansive era, they continually measured their performance by
the victories of the past. Therefore, their loyalty to the Republican ideals of
the Revolutionary generation remained constant, even though the means by
which they believed that ideal could be reached splintered in several directions.[2]

Robert Jr.'s political proclivities are evidenced in his appointment during
Jackson's administration and the special duties assigned by President Van
Buren, his entrance into the federal bureaucracy stemming from his association with leading Democrats. James Washington Greenhow's partisanship is
even more evident than his brother's. In 1843 the younger Greenhow worked
on the Virginia Democratic Committee under Chairman James A. Seddon in
preparation for the election of 1844. After Polk's victory, Washington
Greenhow communicated directly with the president on at least one issue.
He also fiercely protected Virginia's honor, as exhibited in both written communication and in his participation in at least one duel, fought over an insult
appearing in the Richmond papers. The young Greenhow served as second
for Thomas Ritchie Jr., who won the duel. Their opponent, John H. Pleas-
ants, lost both the duel and his life over his suggestion that Virginia should
abolish slavery. Had these men been alive during the secession crisis, they
undoubtedly would have argued for separation. Given Mary Greenhow Lee's
family background, her close ties to Mason, and her avid southern patriotism
during the war, it seems safe to conclude that she was not strongly opposed
to Virginia's ultimate secession.[3]

2. Niven, *Martin Van Buren*, 120; Richard P. McCormick, "New Perspectives on Jacksonian
Politics," *American Historical Review* 65, no. 2 (1960): 288–301; Jordan, *Political Leadership*, 31,
205, 209, 214; Wade Lee Shaffer, "The Richmond Junto and Politics in Jacksonian Virginia"
(Ph.D. diss., College of William and Mary, 1993), 2, 3, 14; Wilentz, "Society, Politics, and the
Market Revolution," 75.

3. Robert Mercer Taliaferro Hunter to [?], Feb. 20, 1843, Robert Mercer Taliaferro Hunter
Papers (Mss2H9185a1), VHS; Washington Greenhow to John Y. Mason, Nov. 22, 30, 1846,

Winchester's geographic location involved some of its citizens in the efforts to suppress John Brown's raid on the armory at Harpers Ferry on October 16, 1859. In a scheme to liberate slaves by arming them courtesy of the U.S. arsenal, Brown led seventeen men toward Harpers Ferry, cutting telegraph wires along the way. With little difficulty the men seized the armory after first killing a free black from Winchester, Heyward Shepherd, a baggage master for the Baltimore and Ohio Railroad, who failed to halt as the raiders made their way into town along the track. Around noon the next day, Lewis Telghman Moore of the 31st Virginia Militia, the man who had replaced Hugh Lee as colonel of the Morgan Continentals, received word from Col. Robert W. Baylor of Jefferson County to gather his forces and meet him at Harpers Ferry immediately. Within an hour Moore had 150 Frederick County volunteers riding the Winchester and Potomac Railroad on their way to help suppress the abolitionists.[4]

At Halltown, about four miles from their destination, the train was forced to stop; the men marched the remaining distance. As they made their way along the tracks, some of the volunteers, students at the medical school in Winchester, stumbled upon the body of a man they presumed to be a casualty of Brown's raid. After the surviving insurrectionists gave themselves up to Col. Robert E. Lee and Lt. J. E. B. Stuart later that night, the medical students packed the body in a wooden crate and sent it on to the Winchester school to be used as a cadaver. Upon examination of papers found in the dead man's pockets, they realized that he was John Brown's son, though they had little sympathy for "Massa Possumattamie," as a young local woman called him, referring to the killing of five men along Pottawatomie Creek in Kansas perpetrated by John Brown and seven other men in 1856 while associated with a free-state volunteer company in the territory. School officials removed the head and preserved the body for educational purposes.[5]

Mason Family Papers (Mss1M3816c/a), VHS; Washington Greenhow to Henry Alexander Wise, Feb. 5, 1844, Henry Alexander Wise Papers (No. 2380), Eastern Shore of Virginia Historical Society (photocopy, SHC); Thomas Ritchie Jr., *A Full Report, Embracing All the Evidence and Arguments in the Case of the Commonwealth of Virginia vs. Thomas Ritchie, Jr., Tried at the Spring Term of the Chesterfield Superior Court, 1846* (New York: Burgess, Stringer, 1846). For an explanation of the generational shift from Jeffersonian Republicans to Jacksonian Democrats, see Jordan, *Political Leadership*, 31, 205, 209, 214; Shaffer, "Richmond Junto," 2, 3, 14; and Wilentz, "Society, Politics, and the Market Revolution," 75.

4. David M. Potter, *The Impending Crisis: 1848–1861*, completed and ed. Don E. Fehrenbacher, New American Nation Series (New York: Harper and Row, 1976), 369–77; Delauter, *Winchester in the Civil War*, 1–2.

5. Delauter, *Winchester in the Civil War*, 1–2; Potter, *Impending Crisis*, 211–12, 370–77; Kate Sperry, "Surrender, Never Surrender!" Kate Sperry Papers (80 WFCHS), HL, 198–99, type-

A week after his capture, John Brown faced arraignment in the Jefferson County Circuit Court, presided over by another of Mary Greenhow Lee's Winchester friends, Judge Richard Parker, who later conducted Brown's trial. Parker's charge to the grand jury emphasized justice. He reminded them that they had sworn to make "diligent inquiry and calm investigation," and to go beyond that, he warned, to "act upon prejudice, or from excitement or passion," would do "wrong to that law" they had agreed to uphold. In fact, although Brown never evidenced signs of remorse for his actions, he believed his trial had been fair and stated, "considering the circumstances," the court's treatment of him had "been more generous" than he expected. Judge Parker sentenced Brown to hang on December 2, 1859.[6]

As northern abolitionists stepped up their pressure against the South's stubborn retention of slavery, rhetorical debates between the sections increasingly used feminine metaphors to tinge the opposing region with weakness. The South viewed northern abolitionists as unmanly, being led by female reformers who had turned from their proper private sphere to participate in public agitation. Historian Catherine Clinton interprets John Brown's raid as a sexual assault on a weakening South. Indeed, she asserts that the "sexualized language" adopted by the South to describe Brown's raid is evidence that southerners viewed his attack as a "figurative 'rape.'" In this context, Brown's raid constituted an insult to southern honor, and his execution was necessary to bring satisfaction to that insult.[7]

As historian David Potter has pointed out, while the political debates in Congress and between Illinois senatorial candidates Abraham Lincoln and Stephen Douglas had "caused a considerable part of the American public to think about the philosophical aspects of slavery, John Brown focused attention dramatically upon its emotional aspects." Southerners, and especially local Virginians, were alarmed to learn that, instead of voicing condemnation of Brown's actions, northerners cried out against his execution. Fearing that

---

script. Kate Sperry was seventeen years old when the war began. She lived with her grandfather, Peter Graves Sperry, and her aunt Mary W. Sperry. Kate eventually married Dr. E. N. Hunt of the 2d Mississippi Regiment and moved to a "plantation home" at Cedar Hill, near Ripley, Mississippi. She died in 1886. See the introduction to her typescript by her daughter, Lenoir Hunt.

6. Parker quoted in Quarles, *Some Worthy Lives*, 195; Brown quoted in Potter, *Impending Crisis*, 377; Delauter, *Winchester in the Civil War*, 4.

7. Catherine Clinton, "Sex and the Sectional Conflict," in *Taking Off the White Gloves: Southern Women and Women Historians*, ed. Michele Gillespie and Catherine Clinton (Columbia: University of Missouri Press, 1998), 43–63; Bertram Wyatt-Brown, *Yankee Saints and Southern Sinners* (Baton Rouge: Louisiana State University Press, 1985), 186–87.

misguided minds might plan his escape, Virginia governor Henry A. Wise ordered militia units to guard the condemned man until his hanging. On October 31 the Morgan Continentals once again left home and spent five weeks in Charles Town (now in West Virginia) on guard duty. Another local man and friend of Mary Greenhow Lee, Turner Ashby, quickly recruited a volunteer cavalry unit and rode to Charles Town for the purpose of guarding Brown until the execution, foreshadowing the service he would offer later during the war for the interests of his state.[8]

Suspicion of northern motives grew rapidly after Brown's execution. When Virginians learned that northern responses to the hanging included traditional rituals of national mourning, such as the tolling of bells, they became even more convinced that North and South were already separate countries emotionally. Fear of slave insurrections was something the North did not share with the South, and when southerners noted northern refusal to condemn Brown for plotting one, then even some of the staunchest southern Unionists began to reevaluate their sentiments. Editorials in Richmond newspapers predicted the results even before Lincoln's election, stating that Brown's actions had "advanced the cause of disunion more than any other" and that the Union's "days are numbered."[9]

After Lincoln's election, South Carolina's secession in late 1860 was the subject of intense scrutiny by the people of Winchester. Secession became the main topic of conversation in town. As Mary Greenhow Lee's friend Cornelia McDonald remembered, "whenever two people met, that was the subject discussed." Although some believed that secession was inevitable, others argued that once northerners realized the threat to their supply of cotton, they would be more conciliatory to the southern states. Still others, even those who hated slavery, refused to be dictated to by outsiders and preferred secession to northern interference. Cornelia McDonald thought, however, that "everybody seemed . . . bereft of their sober senses." She even argued with her husband, Angus, when he applauded South Carolina's actions, reminding him that there might be war. His answer was that "there will be no war" because the South would "have the world on [its] side, for the world will have cotton."[10]

In his study of secession, historian Steven Elliott Tripp found that the

8. Potter, *Impending Crisis*, 356, 4–5; Quarles, *Some Worthy Lives*, 5.
9. Quoted in Potter, *Impending Crisis*, 384.
10. Oren Frederic Morton, *Story of Winchester*, 146; McDonald, *Reminiscences of the War*, 11–13.

elites of Lynchburg, Virginia, did not favor war but wanted even less to lose their traditions and heritage. For them, as the decision grew nearer, remaining tied to the North and adjusting to the changes they feared from a Lincoln-led nation would be more radical than Virginian independence. The same could be said for conversations around Winchester dinner tables. Although it would appear to be a conservative stance to remain firm in the Union, conservation of southern tradition and institutions was a key secessionist motive. Southerners explained their movement toward disunion in terms of the American Revolution. They were not departing from their historical beliefs but ensuring they would not lose them.[11]

On February 4, 1861, Winchester citizens elected delegates to Virginia's secession convention, which would begin the following week. All four of the candidates were members of Mary Greenhow Lee's social circle, two running as secession candidates, Frederick W. M. Holliday and William L. Clark Sr., and two as Union men, Robert Y. Conrad and James Marshall. The Union candidates won by more than a two-to-one margin, 3,188 votes to 1,473, suggesting that Winchester had a typically western bias to remain in the Union. Historiography has described Conrad, an active Whig, as the conservative leader of the convention due to his firm resolve to keep Virginia in the Union. Early on, nothing would have pleased him more; newspapers condemned him after secession, stating that he had "voted to the last against the second Declaration of Independence, and for continued subjection to the power of the Federal government." His efforts at the convention went toward helping "Virginia present an undivided front," to maintain equilibrium, and at times, such as after speaking for one and a half hours and straining his voice "almost to cracking," he felt his work was bearing fruit.[12]

Later, however, he became less certain, noting that "the agitation

11. Steven Elliott Tripp, *Yankee Town, Southern City: Race and Class Relations in Civil War Lynchburg* (New York: New York University Press, 1997), 2, 87; Drew Gilpin Faust, *The Creation of Confederate Nationalism: Ideology and Identity in the Civil War South* (Baton Rouge: Louisiana State University Press, 1988), 14, 21.

12. Delauter, *Winchester in the Civil War*, 6–7; Garland R. Quarles, Lewis N. Barton, C. Vernon Eddy, Mildred Lee Grove, eds., *Diaries, Letters, and Recollections of the War between the States* (Winchester, Va.: Winchester–Frederick County Historical Society, 1955), 14–16; Oren Frederic Morton, *Story of Winchester*, 147; Henry T. Shanks, *The Secession Movement in Virginia, 1847–1861* (Richmond, Va.: Garrett and Massie, 1937), 160, 183, 189; Beverley B. Munford, *Virginia's Attitude toward Slavery and Secession* (New York: Longmans, Green, 1910), 277; unidentified newspaper clipping, Scrapbook of Mrs. Holmes Conrad, Scrapbook Collections, ESB; Robert Y. Conrad to wife, Elizabeth Whiting Powell Conrad, Mar. 15, 1861, Robert Y. Conrad Papers (Mss1C7638a), VHS.

throughout" the eastern portion of the state was "gaining apparent strength to the secessionists," even though "their whole position," to Conrad, was "so untenable and . . . absurd that it must in the end be abandoned." What has not been emphasized, however, is that Conrad began losing his own belief in the desirability of Virginia remaining in the Union. He wrote to his wife that the "black-republican party" was deluded if they believed they could "safely maintain a party upon anti-slavery principles," thinking that "Virginia and the middle states will . . . acquiesce." To the contrary, if the North did not accept the "propositions" put forth by Conrad and the others on his committee, he wrote, "certain it is that we must at once make open war upon Federal authority, and proceed at once . . . to the effort of constructing for ourselves, and all the States that will unite with us, a new confederation." Conrad was a Unionist, though not to the point of losing Virginia's "interests and respectability." Unfortunately, his secessionist friends and neighbors back home, including Mary Greenhow Lee, remained unaware of his conditional national loyalty. He cautioned his wife, "do not shew [sic] my letters to any but the family."[13]

Another member of Mary Greenhow Lee's *connexion*, Alexander Hugh Holmes Stuart of Staunton, also "voted to the last against" secession. Stuart was a member of the committee charged with hand delivering a resolution dated April 8, 1861, to President Abraham Lincoln. In this resolution the Virginia delegates cautioned Lincoln that coercion of the seceded states would only cause further "disturbance of the public peace" and asked him to inform them of his intentions.[14]

Lincoln had read a newspaper account of the Virginia delegates' intention to meet with him and had prepared a written response. Therein, the president reminded them that he had previously outlined his policy on this matter

13. Robert Y. Conrad to wife, Elizabeth Whiting Powell Conrad, Apr. 3, 1861, Robert Y. Conrad Papers.

14. Alexander F. Robertson, *Alexander Hugh Holmes Stuart, 1807–1891: A Biography* (Richmond, Va.: William Byrd, 1925), 184–99; Scrapbook of Mrs. Holmes Conrad; MGL, 846 (July 17, 1865), 857 (Aug. 17, 1865). Born in 1807 in Staunton, Virginia, the son of Archibald Stuart, Alexander H. H. Stuart was educated at the College of William and Mary and studied law at the University of Virginia, graduating in 1828. His mother was Eleanor Briscoe Stuart, sister to Elizabeth, wife of Judge Hugh Holmes of Winchester. Hugh Holmes and Archibald Stuart were both justices in the General Court of Virginia and married to sisters from Winchester. This family is an example of the urban *connexion*'s ties by kinship and marriage. See Barringer et al., *University of Virginia*, 334–35; Quarles, *One Hundred Old Homes*, 56–57; Oren Frederic Morton, *Story of Winchester*, 147; Shanks, *Secession Movement*,, 160, 183, 189; Beverley B. Munford, *Virginia's Attitude*, 277.

and would not give up U.S. property no matter where it was located. By this time, Fort Sumter had fallen to the South Carolinians, and Stuart suggested to the president that, since forts such as Sumter were used for local protection, they could be abandoned easily once the need for that defense was gone, which was now the case in South Carolina. Lincoln was unconvinced. Stuart left with the delegation, finding the president's answer to them "highly unsatisfactory" but believing that, although Lincoln stated that he had the power to recapture public property and discontinue mail service to the seceded states, he did not believe the president indicated any resolve to make use of that power.[15]

By the time the delegates returned to the Virginia convention with the reply, however, Lincoln had announced his proclamation calling for 75,000 troops. Conrad's letters to his wife continued even more pessimistically afterward. The call for armed forces "and the apparent disposition of the Northern people," he wrote, "indicate a civil war." Conrad was uncertain that Lincoln would go that far, believing that he was merely trying "to satisfy his party," that "unless a madman," Lincoln was only trying to threaten the South, not start a war. The specter of war was the main reason Conrad and Stuart "voted to the last against" secession. As Conrad described his feelings to his wife, "never before have I felt such a weight upon my brain and my heart." Trying to sustain a moderate position at the convention after Lincoln's call for troops was a losing proposition. He realized that with "the danger . . . so imminent, and the minds of all on both sides . . . so much excited, that" they had by that point "only to consider . . . . defense."[16]

Stuart implored his fellow delegates to think what secession would do to Virginia. With the conflict at that point in "the extreme southern part of our Atlantic coast," secession of Virginia would then "transfer the seat of war to this fertile and salubrious country." Even worse, if the other Border States remained in the Union, it would leave Virginia surrounded by enemies, not merely the northernmost defense line of the southern states. Stuart reminded the convention that it was not courageous or chivalrous to rush in unprepared for war, only foolhardy. The state was nearly bankrupt and had very little in the way of ordnance. Stuart was not alone in his opinion. Contrary to an earlier view of the wealthy planter class solidly leading the way to secession, more recent studies have revealed that the elite were divided over the issue.

15. Alexander F. Robertson, *Alexander Hugh Holmes Stuart*, 184–99.

16. Robert Y. Conrad to Elizabeth Whiting Powell Conrad, Apr. 16, 17, 1861, Robert Y. Conrad Papers.

Besides the practical considerations of secession, there were those southern men of honor who believed honor was earned through calm and deliberative responses to threats against their community, making decisions based upon reason rather than emotion. If their community formed a consensus contrary to their opinion, however, these men would not press their stand further. On April 17, 1861, the Virginia convention voted eighty-eight to fifty-five for their state to follow the Lower South out of the Union.[17]

By the end of May, Virginia's secession had been ratified by the people, and Jefferson Davis reported to the Provisional Congress of the Confederate States of America, in Montgomery, Alabama, that Virginia, "that honored Commonwealth," had "united her power and her fortunes with ours and become one of us." Once the decision was made, Stuart and Conrad threw their support behind their state. Stuart was reported in the *New York Times* as having "addressed the people of Augusta [County] on May 27, urging them to make every sacrifice towards defending their rights." Conrad's position still remained suspicious to his Winchester neighbors, however. Although he thoroughly supported Virginia's defense "against the unjust and unholy war which Lincoln and his party had declared," until the secession vote had come in from the populace, he decided "to give no advice upon the subject" and "did not even appear at the polls to vote for or against secession." In his caution against lending undue influence, Conrad appeared to his neighbors to be lukewarm in his patriotism. Criticism forced him to publicly declare his position, stating that the "malignant and insane war" breaking out against his state came from "the miserable pretext that Virginia is in insurrection against Abraham Lincoln" and that the "Northern people" were standing by and allowing a "public servant of a free people" to become "a military despot."[18]

Whether or not Mary Greenhow Lee read Conrad's statement, for nearly a year thereafter she "rather doubted" his patriotism. During Winchester's first Union occupation in March 1862, she reported with pleasure that Conrad had been seen walking on the street one day when he encountered a noted Unionist, Boyd Pendleton, who "offered to shake hands." Conrad "put his hands in his pockets, . . . and walked on," at which point Lee became "quite

17. Wyatt-Brown, *Yankee Saints*, 184–89, 204–9; Stuart quoted in Alexander F. Robertson, *Alexander Hugh Holmes Stuart*, 195–99; Beverley B. Munford, *Virginia's Attitude*, 278–79, 281.

18. Dabney, *Virginia*, 294; Jefferson Davis, *The Messages and Papers of Jefferson Davis and the Confederacy, Including Diplomatic Correspondence, 1861–1865*, vol. 1, ed. James D. Richardson (New York: Chelsea House, Robert Hector, 1966), 77; *New York Times*, June 5, 1861; *Richmond Enquirer*, June 7, 1861.

pleased with" him again, suggesting that his moderate stance during the secession debate had not pleased her.[19]

Winchester was both geographically and politically linked to the western counties that eventually formed the Union state of West Virginia. When the citizens of Winchester heard of the events at Fort Sumter and Lincoln's call for troops, however, most, though not all, switched positions, aligning themselves with the South. Although some of the residents remained staunch Unionists, most of them enthusiastically prepared for war. Mary Greenhow Lee took part in these activities by joining both the County Society and the Harmon Society, organized by the women of the town to sew uniforms and put together supplies for the army. Although there is no record that she invited soldiers into her home during these preparations, her willingness to do so once fighting commenced suggests that she probably did. It would certainly have suited her personality to have become caught up in the carnival atmosphere of the town at the outset of war.[20]

Winchester had experienced a long history of conflict. George Washington, as commander of Virginia forces charged with guarding the frontier during the French and Indian War, chose Winchester as his headquarters. In April 1756 he requested of the House of Burgesses that "a strong Fort [be] erected at this place, for a general Receptacle of all the Stores, &c. and a place of Residence for the Commanding Officers." He reasoned that Winchester's location, "lying directly on the Road to Fort Duquisne [sic]," made "this very Town at present the outmost Frontiers . . . of the utmost importance; as it commands the communication from East to West, as well as from North to South." The House of Burgesses approved Washington's request, and by May 23, 1756, Fort Loudoun was under construction on Main Street about two hundred yards from the edge of town, with Washington himself supervising the construction and lending the use of his own Mount Vernon blacksmith for some of the work.[21]

Washington's relations with Winchester residents during the war were not easy. He found that they were unwilling to give up their wagons, horses, or supplies to defend the frontier unless served with a warrant, and he com-

19. MGL, 12 (Mar. 14, 1862), 15 (Mar. 16, 1862), 544 (Jan. 23, 1864), 733 (Dec. 7, 1864), 747 (Dec. 25, 1864), 621 (June 16, 1864).

20. Shanks, *Secession Movement*, 199; Oren Frederic Morton, *Story of Winchester*, 147; MGL, 47 (Apr. 1, 1862).

21. Oren Frederic Morton, *Story of Winchester*, 65; Magill, *Women*, 3–4; George Washington, *The Papers of George Washington*, ed. W. W. Abbot, Colonial Series, vol. 3, Apr.–Nov. 1756 (Charlottesville: University Press of Virginia, 1983), 49–50, 62 n.

plained that "people here in general are very selfish," that the "Tippling Houses" in Winchester were "a great grievance," and that all of his "efforts . . . to raise the militia" there had "proved ineffectual."[22]

In contrast to Washington's experiences with eighteenth-century Winchester's reluctant citizens, most residents in April 1861 joined in the exuberant southern patriotism spreading across the state. In Richmond the Confederate flag appeared on the state capitol even before secession had been ratified, and Robert Conrad reported to his wife that the city was "filled with the signs and sounds of war," with "every young man . . . buckling on his armour." A young friend of Mary Greenhow Lee from the Baltimore branch of her *connexion*, Randolph "Ranny" Harrison McKim, was a student at the University of Virginia when war broke out. Excitement began on campus even before Virginia entered the conflict. Ranny joined with six other young conspirators, waiting until the middle of the night to saw their way through the roof of the rotunda to plant a homemade Confederate flag. In Winchester someone removed the "U" and "N" from the sign above the Union Hotel, rendering the name of the establishment—now the "Ion Hotel"—less meaningful yet more patriotic.[23]

With nearby Harpers Ferry deemed Virginia's first line of defense against northern invasion, local militia groups throughout the state began arriving in Winchester to lend support even before Virginia had officially seceded. As Col. James K. Edmondson of the 27th Regiment reported to his wife on April 21, Winchester was the town where "all forces are to be quartered for the present. Troops are concentrating very fast." The town almost doubled in population overnight. Men arrived with their companies, some of them bringing their own pistols or hunting rifles, but many without weapons of any kind. Frederick County quickly appropriated ten thousand dollars to equip many of these volunteers with arms and supplies, but in the meantime, citizens opened their doors to the young men, boarding them until the army could organize. Leading citizens of Winchester, Robert Conrad and James

22. Washington, *Papers*, 397; Richard L. Morton, *Colonial Virginia: Vol. II*, 646–47. During the War for Independence, Winchester was again a military headquarters, this time as a prisoner-of-war camp for as many as 1,600 British soldiers. Thus by 1860, Winchester's population of 4,400 citizens had a long history of strategic value. Oren Frederic Morton, *Story of Winchester*, 88–89, 145. Population figures include 655 freedmen and 708 slaves.

23. Dabney, *Virginia*, 294; Robert Y. Conrad to Elizabeth Whiting Powell Conrad, Apr. 19, 1861, Holmes Conrad Papers; Rev. Randolph Harrison McKim, *A Soldier's Recollections: Leaves from the Diary of a Young Confederate* (New York: Longmans, Green, 1911), 1–3, 7–9; JC, Feb. 9, 1862. Julia Chase's diary entry mentions the letters being restored to the hotel's sign.

Marshall among them, wrote to Robert E. Lee to see what was being done to arm the militia and prepare the area's defense. Lee responded that Col. Thomas Jonathan Jackson of Lexington would leave Richmond on April 28 "with orders to muster into service, at Harper's Ferry, the companies there ready; and that every effort" would "be made to supply them with batteries."[24]

James Murray Mason visited Jackson at Harpers Ferry and reported to General Lee that, from his observations, "all were in good hands under [Jackson's] command." Confederate general Joseph E. Johnston soon replaced Jackson at Harpers Ferry, however, and then abandoned the place for lack of defensibility, at which point Johnston located his Army of the Shenandoah just north of Winchester and made the Taylor Hotel his headquarters.[25]

Young women in town were delighted to see the army more permanently attached to Winchester. As young Emma Riely, a friend of Mary Greenhow Lee's nieces, recalled, "the girls all had a good time, for brass buttons and gold lace were very attractive." Mary Magill contrasted the excitement of war preparations with "the arrival of the daily mail," one of the former highlights of life in the sleepy town. Magill remembered the early part of the war as a time when "prancing steeds were seen coming and going in all directions," and the young people thrilled to see men such as Turner Ashby "mounted on a jet black horse." She noted that his "pallor was rendered more striking from the long black beard which swept to his waist, full moustache and jetty hair, . . . mingled with the sweeping black ostrich feather which drooped from his military cap." Colonel Jackson impressed the residents as well, though his appearance was less striking, his own style of riding "certainly not graceful."[26]

Winchester also filled with flags. Besides the homemade Confederate ban-

---

24. Gov. John Letcher to Maj. Gen. Robert E. Lee, Apr. 27, 1861, *OR* 2:784; Lee to Jackson, May 1, 1861, ibid., 793–94; Lee to Jackson, May 6, 1861, ibid., 806–7; *Richmond Enquirer*, Apr. 30, 1861; James K. Edmondson, *My Dear Emma: War Letters of Col. James K. Edmondson, 1861–1865*, ed. Charles W. Turner (Staunton, Va.: McClure, 1978), 3; Delauter, *Winchester in the Civil War*, 9; Mason, *Public Life*, 192–93; Robert E. Lee to Robert Y. Conrad, James Marshall, Edmund Pendleton, Hugh Nelson, and Alfred M. Barbour, Apr. 27, 1861, R. E. Lee Collection, ESB; JC, July 4, 1861.

25. Mason to Lee, May 15, 1861, *OR*, 2:848–50; Jackson to Col. R. S. Garnett, adjutant general, May 25, 1861, ibid., 877; reports of Gen. Joseph E. Johnston, May 23–July 22, Oct. 14, 1861, ibid., 470–78; Johnston to Gen. S. Cooper, adjutant and inspector general, June 24, 1861, ibid., 948–49; *Richmond Enquirer*, June 2, 1861; Delauter, *Winchester in the Civil War*, 10.

26. Emma Cassandra Riely Macon and Reuben Conway Macon, *Reminiscences of the Civil War* (privately printed, 1911), 11; William P. Parker, "Diary of a Surgeon of the 7th Tennessee Regiment in Virginia, May 20, 1861–May 21, 1862," Jan. 28, 29, 30, 1862, Special Collections, Leyburn Library, Washington and Lee University, Lexington, Va.; Magill, *Women*, 15, 25, 26.

ners floating from windows and off of housetops, militia groups from the Lower South began to arrive in town, blending in their own local colors to that of the town. The first regiment to arrive was from Alabama, then Georgia sent their military men, with banners of red and white silk displaying the state's insignia and bordered with a gold fringe. The Georgia regiment's uniforms of green and gold, when mixed with the gray and gold of the Virginia troops, added to the festive atmosphere.[27]

Not everyone in Winchester participated in the enthusiasm and excitement. Several citizens retained their Unionist sympathies throughout the war, among them Harriet Hollingsworth Griffith, a young Quaker woman, who recorded that her "loved and honored America, this our beautiful country, is now in arms. Brother warring against brother, and what for. . . . My heart is sad, very sad." Another Winchester Unionist, Julia Chase, reminded herself on July 4, 1861, that it was the anniversary of when "independence was declared by our forefathers. Into what a sad condition our beloved country has fallen."[28]

Cornelia McDonald, a secessionist whose husband commanded a Confederate cavalry unit, understood that war would not be entertaining for long. She watched the young soldiers play games and fill their time with fun and "gaiety" between drills, then contrasted the scenes with "the melancholy face of their commander," who looked at them with "a deep sadness . . . on his countenance." Clearly, although preparations for war seemed to breathe vibrancy into the formerly tranquil Valley village, more reflective residents grieved over the ugliness to come.[29]

Although Mary Greenhow Lee's Civil War journal does not begin until the following March, the "horrors" of war touched her earlier. When she learned that Richard Ashby had been seriously wounded at Kelly Island on June 26, 1861, she wrote to his brother, Turner, to "beg that as soon as your brother can bear the journey, you will bring him to my house & let my sisters & myself endeavor" to take care of him. She had been frustrated by "contradictory accounts" of Ashby's condition, the result of a saber cut on his

27. Magill, *Women*, 15; Mason, *Public Life*, 192; McDonald, *Reminiscences of the War*, 19; Delauter, *Winchester in the Civil War*, 8.

28. HHG, June 9, 1861; JC, July 4, 1861. Griffith was the daughter of Aaron Hackney Griffith and Mary Parkins Hollingsworth Griffith. Aaron and his brother Joseph, along with two nephews, founded the firm of Griffith, Hoge, and Company as well as the Friendly Grove Factory, one mile south of Winchester, where they manufactured textiles. Another factory founded by Aaron and Joseph later became the Brookland Woolen Mills.

29. McDonald, *Reminiscences of the War*, 19.

head, bullets through his arm and hand, and a bayonet shoved into his stomach, and asked Turner for a direct report on "Dick's" condition. She then ended her letter: "My sisters join me in . . . kindest remembrances to Dick, and the hope that he will trust himself to our nursing. We will promise to care for him, as if he were our brother."[30]

Richard Ashby died four days after Lee wrote her letter, so it is doubtful that he made the journey to her house for care. Soon, however, she had other casualties to concern her. The town quieted down on July 19 when the army left for Manassas. Citizens were cheered a few days later to learn that the Confederates had risen victorious in their first major confrontation against Federal forces two days later. The army's return, however, brought the realities of war within sight. The men entered the town absent the enthusiasm that had attended their earlier march out. They also brought with them wagons loaded with the severely wounded, who were quickly deposited in several makeshift hospitals in town, the first of several such scenes Lee would witness during the war. This was the pattern she would endure through the next four years: encouraging news, then devastation and frustration.[31]

Certainly, Mary Greenhow Lee must have been delighted and proud to learn that her good friend James Murray Mason had been selected as the Confederate emissary to England, along with John Slidell to France and Lucius Q. C. Lamar to Russia, to gain foreign recognition for Confederate independence. Yet when the captain of the USS *San Jacinto* seized Mason and Slidell from the *Trent*, a British Royal Mail steamer, as it left Havana, Cuba, for England in November, it is likely that she was as angry as the British. Also in November reorganization of the army created the Valley District within the Department of Northern Virginia, and Maj. Gen. Thomas J. Jackson, since Manassas known as "Stonewall," took charge of the newly created command, establishing his headquarters at the Taylor Hotel. Julia Chase wryly recorded of Jackson's entrance into town, "the citizens of Winchester feel perfectly safe now, I suppose." Mary Greenhow Lee's reaction to Jackson's arrival in town in November is not recorded. Her dread at his leaving the

30. MGL, 646 (July 21, 1864); Mary Greenhow Lee to Turner Ashby, June 30, 1861, Turner Ashby Papers (Mss1As346a), VHS; Quarles et al., *Diaries, Letters, and Recollections*, 16–19; Quarles, *Some Worthy Lives*, 4–5. Lee's letter refers to a time that she and her family had spent at the Ashby home in Fauquier County, suggesting that her offer of help was not based merely on patriotism but also on their *connexion*.

31. Quarles et al., *Diaries, Letters, and Recollections*, 16–19; Quarles, *Some Worthy Lives*, 4–5; JC, July 23, 1861; Delauter, *Winchester in the Civil War*, 11–12.

next spring, however, prompted her to begin her extensive Civil War journal.[32]

On February 27, 1862, Maj. Gen. Nathaniel P. Banks, commander of the Union district that encompassed the Shenandoah Valley, crossed the Potomac at Harpers Ferry via a pontoon bridge and placed his 38,000 troops on the south side of the river, within reach of Winchester. Lincoln wanted the town. Jackson had 4,600 men at his disposal and knew he was no match for Banks in terms of numbers, but his objective was not to attack and destroy; he merely intended to complicate Federal ambitions. Union general George B. McClellan, camped with 200,000 troops near Washington, waited for spring, when he could move on Gen. Joseph Johnston's troops at Centreville. Jackson's mission was to cause enough alarm in Washington to prevent McClellan from moving away from the capital. Furthermore, considering his relatively small number of troops, Jackson needed to avoid a general engagement.[33]

To accomplish this, the Confederates had to evacuate Winchester and place themselves in a more defensive position. Banks's cavalry waited just outside of town, and the citizens knew it. They had become accustomed to the security of Jackson's army, and his decision to leave with the enemy close by made them aware of their vulnerability. The majority of Jackson's force consisted of Valley men. When his army left, so did fathers, husbands, brothers, and sons. The Confederates marched out of Winchester on March 11, 1862; Banks entered uncontested the next day. At the same time, Mary Greenhow Lee began her Civil War journal.[34]

When Banks seized Winchester, Mary noted with sorrow in the first entry of her journal "the Yankee flag waving over the Court House & Hotel." Less than a year before, the "Yankee" flag flying above the city's courthouse had been the symbol of her nation. Her national identity, however, had changed

32. Davis, *Messages and Papers*, 141–42, 311–12; Joseph H. Lehmann, *The Model Major-General: A Biography of Field-Marshal Lord Wolseley* (Cambridge, U.K.: Riverside; Boston: Houghton Mifflin, 1964), 114–15; Clement Eaton, *A History of the Southern Confederacy* (New York: Free Press, 1954), 70; *OR*, 5:909; Benjamin to Jackson, Oct. 21, 1861, ibid., 938; Special Orders No. 206, Nov. 5, 1861, ibid.; McDonald, *Reminiscences of the War*, 49 n; Delauter, *Winchester in the Civil War*, 13; JC, Nov. 9, 1861.

33. T. K. Cartmell, *Shenandoah Valley Pioneers and Their Descendants: A History of Frederick County, Virginia* (Berryville, Va.: Chesapeake, 1909), 328; Col. G. F. R. Henderson, *Stonewall Jackson and the American Civil War* (1898; reprint, 2 vols. in 1, New York: Longmans, Green, 1949), 164–67; Fred Harvey Harrington, *Fighting Politician: Major General N. P. Banks* (Westport, Conn.: Greenwood, 1970).

34. Cartmell, *Shenandoah Valley Pioneers*, 328.

in the span of months. Now a citizen of the Confederate States of America, Lee saw the Union flag symbolizing foreign invasion and occupation. Lee's identity as a southern woman had merged with the identity of a Confederate national, specifically a "Secesh," the name Union soldiers gave to disloyal citizens in occupied zones. This extension to her personality was born at the onset of war, grew during the first Union occupation, and matured as she waged her own style of warfare throughout the contest. The core of her identity, her southernness, gave her reference points by which to judge the rightness of her actions. The war exercised that southern spirit. Lee's journal helped her make sense of the changes in her life.[35]

Confederate nationalism was present at the time of secession; a nationalistic impulse presided in the Lee home on North Market Street in Winchester too. Mary Lee's Confederate identity was not new at war's end, when she was associated with other Secessionists in defeat. It was born at the beginning, when President Lincoln denied the South's right to secede. More important, her journal also provided Lee with a mirror in which she could watch her nationalism mature.

On May 4, 1862, with less than a month of Union occupation behind her, Lee wrote in her journal: "I never felt more confident, of the final & speedy success of the cause, than now, though we are passing through our dark days." On April 16, 1865, even after learning of Gen. Robert E. Lee's surrender at Appomattox, she recorded: "I do not despair even yet [and] I shall not give up till terms of peace have been accepted by the whole Confederacy." Her identity as a Confederate had not altered, unless possibly strengthened, over time. This is not to say that she had been free of external pressures. In fact, the conditions of her life during the war had made routine the exception and disruption the rule. Before the fighting ended, military control of Winchester changed officially thirteen times, but the town also suffered minor raids during periods when neither army held the town. Through it all Mary Greenhow Lee remained constant in her belief in southern independence.[36]

---

35. MGL, 4–5 (Mar. 12, 1862); Philip Gleason, "Identifying Identity: A Semantic History," *The Journal of American History* 69, no. 4 (Mar. 1983): 911, 914, 918; Erik H. Erikson, "Ego Development and Historical Change," *Psychoanalytic Study of the Child* 2 (1946): 393.

36. MGL, 89 (Apr. 4, 1862), 815 (Apr. 16, 1865), 544 (Jan. 1864); Margaretta Barton Colt, *Defend the Valley: A Shenandoah Family in the Civil War* (New York: Crown, 1994), 9–10. Colt's numbers regarding the military occupation of Winchester is probably the best assessment to date. Local historians have set the number of times "Winchester changed hands" during the war as high as seventy, but as Colt wisely points out, many of these "occupations" were merely raids through town that, though not official military takeovers, did cause life in the town to remain unsettled for the war's duration.

Mary survived the emotional trauma that upheaval can initiate by consistently reaffirming her identity in her journal while denying her enemies theirs. Early on she reported gleefully that "regiment after regiment [of the Union forces] pass every day *but not a face do they see,* at our house or our whole square. They gaze at the windows as they pass, while we, unseen, enjoy their mortification." This was during a time of occupation. During one of the many Union retreats, however, she reported, "we went to watch the faces of the Yankees when driven through town. I came back to our own porch and pavement *where I could be seen there.*" Although Lee may not have been conscious of it, she knew intuitively that reactions of the "others," her enemy, were important to her analysis of the war she waged against them. She also knew that depriving them of *her* reactions would deny her enemies of *their* identity: a conquering army. She refused to participate, especially when she felt that her doing so would benefit the enemy.[37]

By April, Mary had formulated a structure for her journal. It was to be "one of events, not of feelings." After September 4, 1862, when she sent her first installment to friend Virginia "Jeannie" Mason, daughter of James Murray Mason, Lee continued to keep her journal, no longer sure she would send it out but writing from "habit." By March 1, 1864, after dispatching the third installment, she had realized the importance of the journal in her life: "What I shall write now is merely for myself." By the end of the fourth volume, it had become "a companion." It had also, quite probably, become her way of maintaining the most important part of her identity: a Secesh woman of Winchester. On March 17, 1862, five days into Winchester's first Union occupation, northern peddlers came to Lee's door to sell her "their cheap goods . . . , which I was too patriotic to buy." As they left her door, she heard one of them say, "Secesh lives here." Mary Greenhow Lee embraced that notion. To be identified as Secesh became her goal for the remainder of the war.[38]

Being a Secesh became a thread of continuity. Psychologists often advise those undergoing a series of ruptures in their lives to keep a journal. One goal of this is to create a narrative that links change to something familiar. The account can then connect the events of chaos to the core of the identity, producing some semblance of order by maintaining the one constant a person can cling to: the "Self." Additionally, the more extensive one's vocabulary, especially the more skilled one is in variation and grammar usage, the easier it is to personify the "Self" one wants to portray in difficult situations. Mary

37. MGL, 18 (Mar. 1862), 652 (July 24, 1864, emphasis added).
38. Ibid., 73 (Apr. 20, 1862), 224 (Sept. 4, 1862), 564 (Mar. 1, 1864), 17 (Mar. 17, 1862).

Greenhow Lee's education had been extensive. She peppered her journal with French phrases and had definite opinions on everything from politics to society. To pass the time, she and her family read to each other from classics such as *King Lear*, which they did by each speaking the lines of the various characters, and from current works such as *Les Miserables*, which Lee deemed "a stupid book." It is not surprising then that she was equipped to use her journal as a canvas for portraying her "Self" as a Secesh, especially as she perceived how the "Other," her enemies, viewed her.[39]

While Lee cited Confederate leaders and soldiers as "God-fearing," "God-trusting," and "noble," she always referred to Union soldiers as "Yankees." She at times stripped them of manliness, at least in her view, by calling them "dandies." They were "vile wretches" to her, merely "creatures," the "vilest race under the sun." Sister-in-law Laura Lee used similar metaphors in her descriptions of Union troops. The soldiers had taken over one of the houses in town as both a barracks and a stable. In describing the arrangement, she wrote, "the horses . . . quartered on the first floor, the other brutes above." Mary Lee's observations of officers were just as harsh: Maj. Gens. Philip Sheridan and George Custer were both "common looking vulgarians" in her opinion.[40]

Lee gives clues to why she thought of these men in such terms. During the first occupation of Winchester, she quickly developed an attitude by which she could exist within a society where the rules had suddenly changed. A slaveowner and notable member of Winchester society, Mary was not accustomed to feelings of insecurity and oppression. Her world had turned upside down, and she felt herself subject to the whims of people who neither recognized her nation nor her own place in it. By labeling the invaders in terms that questioned not only their authority but also their very humanity, she used a defensive mechanism to protect herself from the shifting of social place she sensed around her. "I cannot get up a feeling of fear for the Yankees; I have such a thorough contempt for them that I do not realize they are human beings & I feel able to protect myself from them." Yet epithets coming at her from the other side merely reinforced her goal to create and maintain an identity of opposition. She referred to herself as a "Confederate," "rebel,"

39. Nelson N. Foote, "Identification as the Basis for a Theory of Motivation," *American Sociological Review* 16 (Feb. 1951): 15–16, 18; Paul Rock, *The Making of Symbolic Interactionism* (Totowa, N.J.: Rowman and Littlefield, 1979), 111–15; MGL, 301 (Jan. 1863), 587 (May 1864).

40. MGL, 564 (Mar. 1863), 10–11 (Mar. 1862), 654 (July 1864), 54 (Apr. 1862), 747 (Dec. 25, 1864), 754 (Jan. 2, 1865), 765 (Jan. 17, 1865); LL, Apr. 19, 1862.

"Secessionist," and "true Southerner." She also told her opponents openly that she "was their enemy."[41]

Always conscious of how she appeared to her enemies, Lee jotted down their reactions to her. It was a way of checking her role, the expectations she had of her "Self," and her influence on the "Other." The more convinced a person is of the role that he or she should play in an unfamiliar scene, the more confidence they feel. Of course, it took both Confederates and Federals in her environment to help Lee create her Confederate "Self." Writing in her journal provided her with briefing and debriefing periods to plan her behavior, assess its results, and measure her status in the group by the reactions of the opposition. Then her perceived success rate gave her confidence for the next series of encounters.[42]

In Lee's view there must have been something lacking in northern citizens that would cause them to disregard a state's right to form a new government. Only the unenlightened and uncivilized would pursue the horrors of war in an attempt to prohibit a just separation. The South had history on its side for this argument, a history that the North should have remembered. In January 1861 an article appeared in *DeBow's Review*, an agrarian and sectional journal of the South, arguing that the United States had been from the beginning two distinct sections, artificially yoked together by a constitution that deprived the South of two-thirds of its representation, its pride, and its spirit. "Loss of independence," according to the article, and "extinction of nationality" would be far worse than civil war.[43]

The ideal of "a nation" can precede classic commonalities normally ascribed to it (that is, geography, language, history, race, or a combination thereof). The historic construction of a "nation" arises from the assumption that loyalty to it replaces all others. The transformation into a nation, however, requires a central loyalty, eliminating other objects of patriotism and filling the void with new symbols that evoke a patriotic response. Citizenship in the new nation is made from a sense of obligation, such as military service, and symbols that represent distinctions from other nations. Such a symbol for the South was the Confederate flag.[44]

41. MGL, 30 (Mar. 25, 1862), 290 (Jan. 4, 1863), 62 (Apr. 1862).

42. Foote, "Identification," 15–16, 17–19, 20.

43. "National Characteristics: The Issue of the Day," *DeBow's Review* 30 (Jan. 1861): 45, 43, 46, 52.

44. Eric Hobsbawm, "Some Reflections on Nationalism," in *Imagination and Precision in the Social Sciences: Essays in Memory of Peter Nettl*, ed. T. J. Nossiter, A. H. Hanson, and Stein Rokkan (London: Faber and Faber, 1972), 386, 388, 389, 392, 393.

When southerners watched the Stars and Stripes lowered for what they believed to be the last time, many were subdued and somber. That flag had signified their history, their traditions, and their national pride. It is not surprising then that, in a contest to create the Confederate flag, hundreds of citizens entered designs very similar to Old Glory. Unfortunately, the design officially chosen, the Stars and Bars, was not distinctive enough from the Union flag to readily be recognized in battle. A battle flag was quickly designed, which is now known as the "Rebel Battle Flag," or "Southern Cross," a red square field with a blue saltier (cross) containing thirteen white stars. Never officially adopted by the Confederacy, it was, however, the flag under which southern troops most widely fought. With the two extra stars, the flag reflected the optimism for (though not the reality of) Missouri and Kentucky joining the other seceded states. Testimony to the success of this "unofficial" battle flag of the Confederacy is given by the fact that it is still used as a regional symbol in the South.[45]

Mary Greenhow Lee spent quite a bit of space in her diary describing the adventures of her own flag. She hid it on March 11, 1862, just before Federals occupied the town. When Union soldiers came to her door on the thirteenth demanding her "secession flag," she told them she had sent it to a "place of safety." Doubting her, they demanded to search her house. Standing her ground, she informed them it would require higher rank than theirs to force her to allow them into her home. Asked again the next day, she again denied having a flag. She admitted to her journal, however, that "our bonny red flag shall yet wave over us." Even as late as February 1864 the banner was a source of intrigue. The flag still remained elusive. During this latter search, one of Lee's nieces was "wearing" it under her clothes.[46]

When Cornelia McDonald's house was taken over as a Federal headquarters, she somehow managed to withstand the strain of caring for her family amid the enemy. One intrusion galled her enough to complain, however. She informed the officer in charge that, as long as the Union flag flew over her front door, she would be forced to use the back one. "In the afternoon I noticed the flag had been removed and floated some distance from the house," she remembered. Kate Sperry, a younger Winchester Secesh, reported that

45. Boleslaw D'Otrange Mastai and Marie-Louise D'Otrange Mastai, *The Stars and the Stripes: The American Flag as Art and as History from the Birth of the Republic to the Present* (New York: Alfred A. Knopf, 1973), 124, 130; Faust, *Creation of Confederate Nationalism*, 8; David Eggenberger, *Flags of the U.S.A.* (New York: Thomas Y. Crowell, 1959), 141–42.

46. MGL, 1, 6, 7, 9, 11 (Mar. 1862), 554 (Feb. 9, 1864).

she and her friends angered the occupying troops by refusing to walk under the Union flag. Instead, they purposefully left the sidewalk and proceeded through the mud; when a large Union flag was suspended across the street, they circled to the back of the building. The Confederate flag had become a signal to these women of patriotism; the Union flag now represented the enemy.[47]

Allegiance to a flag, however, is an outward observance; it does not explain deeper foundations of nationalism. The debate among southern historians over the existence of Confederate nationalism has varied, from those who propose the South lost the war because it had little or no nationalistic base to others who assert that the ideology that forced the split is still present today. On one side of the debate are those who believe southern cohesion stemmed from emotionalism rather than nationalism. They argue that mistrust of the North and fear of slave insurrections made southern whites feel not only isolated but also defensive and that southern political unity came from a sense that congressional power was shifting away from them. Hysteria after Lincoln's election rather than firm ideological convictions impelled the South into war. Still others argue that, although the main difference between the North and South was its peculiar institution, slavery had become so charged an issue that it appeared as a distinct ideology.[48]

On the other side of the debate are historians who assert that southern culture was distinctive even at the time of the Constitutional Convention. James Madison noted even then that complications surfaced from dissimilarities between regions as much as between large and small states. Thomas Jefferson acknowledged southern distinctiveness in his *Notes on the State of Virginia*. To the question of what "particular customs and manners . . . may happen to be received in [your] state," Jefferson chose slavery as a custom unique to his "nation." He recognized that slavery necessarily created a different character in the inhabitants exposed to it and believed that, when children witness their parents treating other humans in a despotic way, there can be a certain detrimental effect on their manners. But Jefferson also believed

47. McDonald, *Reminiscences of the War*, 45; Sperry, "Surrender, Never Surrender!" 146–48.

48. C. Vann Woodward, *The Burden of Southern History*, rev. ed. (Baton Rouge: Louisiana State University Press, 1968), 62; Potter, *Impending Crisis*, 471–72, 461, 469; Kenneth M. Stampp, *The Imperiled Union: Essays on the Background of the Civil War* (New York: Oxford University Press, 1980), 252, 255, 258; John McCardell, *The Idea of a Southern Nation: Southern Nationalists and Southern Nationalism, 1830–1860* (New York: W. W. Norton, 1979), 3.

that southerners would view these manners as normal after several generations.[49]

One can argue that, if slavery was the only unifying force in the South, the institution was at least a uniquely southern problem that northerners did not share. Whether united in defense of it or from fear of its repercussions, slavery was a southern characteristic. Jefferson's hint at behavioral distinctions within a slave society adds weight to the argument. In fact, white southerners, whether slaveholder or not, unified in whiteness under the slave society, with many nonslaveholders merely waiting their turn to own a slave or two. If nations are aware of homogeneity in their numbers, then generations of slaveowners and those wishing to become ones might have evolved into a distinctive people.[50]

On March 22, 1862, the Lees' slave Evans ran off, as did several others in town. Laura Lee was in "shock" from disappointment and had to lie down; she had been sure he would be "faithful." Mary Lee, however, was not surprised. She wrote, "I have never had the least confidence in any negro" and considered him "ungrateful." On April 5 Mary noted that she "miss[ed] Evans . . . every hour" and that she had heard he was having problems with his leg. "If so, I know he has often wished he was at home, where he was as carefully nursed as any other member of the family."[51]

Neither of these women could realize that if Evans had felt like "any other member of the family," he would not have left. But their lives had always included people they both shackled and sheltered. That Mary used the word "ungrateful" means she thought of herself as Evans's protector as well as his owner. And Laura's use of the word "faithful" also suggests a connection based on more than ownership, possibly even friendship. This complex relationship between the races was very much a uniquely southern characteristic but not necessarily a Confederate one. In Winchester at least, slavery and the fear of slave revolts do not explain Confederate nationalism. Granted, Mary Greenhow Lee scorned emancipation, dreaded manual labor when the "servants" were gone, and "was near fainting and more unnerved than by any sight I have seen since the war" started when she encountered a Union "company of negro Infantry" in April 1864. These were not, however, uniquely Confederate fears.[52]

49. Carl N. Degler, *Place over Time: The Continuity of Southern Distinctiveness* (Baton Rouge: Louisiana State University Press, 1977), 9–10; Thomas Jefferson, *Notes on the State of Virginia*, ed. William Peden (New York: W. W. Norton, 1982), 162–63.

50. Degler, *Place over Time*, 73, 81.

51. LL, Mar 22, 1862; MGL, 26 (Mar. 22, 1862), 53 (Apr. 5, 1862).

52. MGL, 21 (Mar. 19, 1862), 262 (Nov. 24, 1862), 575 (Apr. 3, 1864).

Unionist Julia Chase and Secesh Mary Greenhow Lee had been on opposite sides of disunion and were not on friendly terms during the war. These two women did have one thing in common, however. Chase was fond of neither abolitionists nor of Lincoln's Emancipation Proclamation. Even when the Union army had finally taken charge of Winchester, she could not be content, for along with the army came abolitionists. She believed that the town's first Union commander, General Banks, "ought to be strung up" because he had made it his business to liberate slaves in the area. At the time, Chase wished that all of the abolitionists, even Banks, were "tied up in a bag and made way with." Further, she was as apprehensive about the appearance of the black regiment in 1864 as Lee. When she learned that such soldiers were in Winchester to "conscript all the able-bodied negro men in the County," she wrote: "I don't know how we are to get along. [We] shall have no one to do anything for us." On this, Julia Chase and Mary Greenhow Lee were in agreement. Lee reported in 1862 that "this emancipation bill in Congress is furthering our party in all the border states, where the Union men own slaves." Slavery might have been a regional problem, but racism remained a national one. At the same time, loyalty to nation or region could not have rested on the issue of southern retention of its peculiar institution.[53]

There are two problems with trying to identify distinctions in another culture. Members of any given culture are too familiar with their own customs to name them, and those who are studying it from outside often lack sufficient understanding to take the distinction seriously. For instance, when asked by the secretary of the French legation at Philadelphia, Francois Marbois, what were "the particular customs and manners" of Virginia, Thomas Jefferson

---

53. JC, May 26, 1862; Julia Chase, diary, Oct. 19, 1862, Apr. 3, 1863, quoted in Quarles, *Occupied Winchester*, 41, 43; MGL, 57–58 (Apr. 8, 1862); David M. Potter, *The South and the Sectional Conflict* (Baton Rouge: Louisiana State University Press, 1968), 75. See also John David Smith and William Cooper Jr., eds., *A Union Woman in Civil War Kentucky: The Diary of Frances Peter* (Lexington: University Press of Kentucky, 2000), 93, 118, 143; Drew Gilpin Faust, "The Peculiar South Revisited: White Society, Culture, and Politics in the Antebellum Period, 1800–1860," in *Interpreting Southern History: Historiographical Essays in Honor of Sanford W. Higginbotham*, ed. John B. Boles and Evelyn Thomas Nolen (Baton Rouge: Louisiana State University Press, 1987), 79–81, 86; Jeremy Atack and Peter Passell, "Slavery and Southern Development," chap. 11 of *A New Economic View of American History from Colonial Times to 1940*, 2d ed. (New York: W. W. Norton, 1994); Edward Pessen, "How Different from Each Other Were the Antebellum North and South?" *American Historical Review* 85 (Dec. 1980): 1119–49; Gavin Wright, "The Efficiency of Slavery: Another Interpretation," *American Economic Review* 69 (Mar. 1979): 219–26; and Fred Bateman and Thomas Weiss, *A Deplorable Scarcity: The Failure of Industrialization in the Slave Economy* (Chapel Hill: University of North Carolina Press, 1981), 163.

named slavery as one distinction. He prefaced his answer, however, by stating that "it is difficult to determine on the standard by which the manners of a nation may be tried," adding that it "is more difficult for a native to bring to that standard the manners of his own nation, familiarized to him by habit." In other words, cultural distinctions are normally not apparent to the culture being asked. But outsiders studying a culture could be blinded by a lack of empathy toward its history. What a nation's citizens say about their own society does not always appear rational to those who harbor opposite values and beliefs, thus producing skepticism.[54]

This lengthy discussion about southern nationalism points to the complexity of the question. Whether historians approach the issue by studying unifying or dividing forces, loyalty to a nation, new or otherwise, depends upon many elements. The degree to which individuals are encouraged to be loyal to family and community conditions their fidelity to wider institutions. Loyalty alone, however, does not form a national bond. Common interests are also necessary for the cohesiveness of a community to allow the idea of a state to exercise sovereign power over it. While Mary Greenhow Lee's experiences cannot sort this out for all of the South, generalizations that attempt to portray the validity of southern nationalism do not demonstrate the responses of the individual southerner.[55]

After General Lee's surrender at Appomattox, Mary tested the idea of defeat on the pages of her journal, writing, "All the energy & enthusiasm of my nature . . . was warmed into full development for my country, my beloved southern Confederacy." Whether or not historians believe southern nationalism valid might depend upon whom they ask. If they ask Mary Greenhow Lee, she would give them little room for doubt. Much of her nationalistic spirit was grounded in a belief in Virginia's right to secede more than with climate, history, traditions, or proslavery arguments.[56]

Historian David Potter made the intriguing observation that "the United States is the only nation in history that for seven decades acted politically and culturally as a nation . . . before decisively answering the question of whether it was a nation at all." Since the issue of state sovereignty had been so divisive at the 1787 Constitutional Convention, it had been tabled indefinitely. "We the people" became sovereign, leaving the question open as to who the "peo-

54. Jefferson, *Notes on the State of Virginia*, 162; Hobsbawm, "Some Reflections on Nationalism," 385.
55. Potter, *The South and Sectional Conflict*, 37–43, 56–61, 69, 78–80.
56. MGL, 814 (Apr. 15, 1865).

ple" were. Potter reminds us that the "citizens of the Old South" had "never transferred the sovereignty itself" from the states to the nation. In fact, Virginia's ratification on June 27, 1788, specified that "the powers granted under the Constitution being derived from the people of the United States may be resumed by them whensoever the same shall be perverted to their injury or oppression."[57]

Mary Greenhow Lee probably understood the conditions Virginia set forth when joining the Union. Her friend James Mason had notified Congress in 1860 that the right of secession was "not an open question in Virginia," because his state had "maintained that our Federal system was a confederation of sovereign powers, not a consolidation of states into one people." Mason argued that if Virginia ever believed the "compact broken," then the state itself could decide "both the mode and measure of redress." It would be unusual if Lee and Mason had not discussed this issue, but even so, the culture in which Lee grew up and the independence at the core of her identity made her a believer in Virginia's right to leave the Union. On April 17, 1862, she noted that it was the anniversary of "dear old Virginia['s] secession." The war was brought on, in her opinion, by the Union's failure to recognize the state's right to leave: "The fault" for all the bloodshed "is theirs, not ours." Furthermore, she was unwilling for France or England to lend a hand in the war until the Confederacy had won spectacular victories on its own so that the new nation could be recognized by those foreign powers "as an equal, & not as a dependent inferior."[58]

Being thought of as inferior was new to Lee, and she allowed no one who did not recognize her status or regional allegiance to exercise power over her. At certain times under occupation, she was ordered not to wear a sunbonnet, not to sidestep around the Union flag, and not to go to the hospital to care for the Confederate wounded. She disobeyed all of these directives. She was also advised that she would have to give up some of her rooms as office space for Union commanders. She argued the advising officer out of the parlor he wanted and into a room in an addition of the house, the "wing," thus being able to truthfully state that Yankees had never been permitted to stay under her roof. If she had given in to these demands or had acknowledged at all the power the occupation government had over her, she would have felt that she was admitting the Union's right to prevent Virginia's secession.[59]

57. Potter, *Impending Crisis*, 479, 482 n.
58. Mason quoted in ibid., 483; MGL, 68, 67, 77 (Apr. 17, 16, 23, 1862).
59. MGL, 102 (May 1862), 314 (Feb. 15, 1863), 448 (July 31, 1863).

Mary Greenhow Lee was a southern national. Historians have argued that the South's only distinct history is one of defeat. Certainly, for many southern historians, distinctions arose at the end of the war, when the South lost, not at the beginning, but Lee's conception of the Confederacy began at secession. A Union surgeon asked her once what she felt to be the difference between the North and the South. She replied, "it was the difference between the oppressor and the oppressed." When southerners began moving toward secession, they carried out their debate in print and continued the written discussion after the war began, providing some explanations. Even as Mary explained herself to her "Self," she was a Secessionist. Both overtly and covertly she defiantly waged war by maintaining her personal independence from any foreign authority.[60]

60. C. Vann Woodward, "The Search for Southern Identity," *Virginia Quarterly Review* 3 (summer 1958), 333–35; Drew Gilpin Faust, "Altars of Sacrifice: Confederate Women and the Narratives of War," *The Journal of American History* 76, no. 4 (Mar. 1990):1228; MGL, 50 (Apr. 1862); Faust, *Creation of Confederate Nationalism*, 7, 84.

5

"Village on the Frontier"

Winchester, Virginia

The Civil War brought changes to each woman's life in the South. For Mary Greenhow Lee and her town, the only thing constant during the war years was change. Winchester was in, but not necessarily of, the Confederacy. Both Secessionists and Unionists resided there, provoking Lee to pepper her journal with complaints about former friends she now deemed traitors. By 1862, Winchester was no longer a community of likeminded citizens but a war zone. What did not change for Lee was her strong character and a determination to advance the cause of the Confederacy. In fact, the sustained turmoil of the war revived Lee into the lively, rebellious woman she had always been.

Located approximately twenty-five miles from Maryland, Winchester was both geographically and politically linked with Virginia's western counties (later West Virginia). In Mary Greenhow Lee's words, the town became a "village on the frontier" during the war because of its location, political sympathies, and practical advantages, changing hands—and flags—thirteen times. One advantage of the location was its accessibility, including nine macadamized roads running to or near Winchester. An added bonus was that the surrounding countryside could supply the armies with ample provisions. Thus, this southern town became the site of border warfare.[1]

Coveted by both sides, yet difficult for either to defend, Winchester sustained heavy casualties and damage during the war. Within four years, six battles raged in or near town. Besides human losses, many homes and businesses were destroyed. The 1865 land-tax assessment for Winchester lists $80,827 in devaluation of property, with ninety-eight buildings damaged and twenty-nine completely razed. Through it all, Mary Greenhow Lee watched and listened to the destruction, sometimes viewing the battles from the tops of her neighbors' houses. By the end of the war, the countryside had been laid a "barren waste," thanks to Union commander Ulysses S. Grant's order to Maj. Gen. Philip Sheridan to "do all the damage" to the Shenandoah Valley that he could. According to Sheridan, by the spring of 1865, his army had "destroyed the enemy's means of subsistence in quantities beyond computation," causing Mary to write in awe, "Sheridan—Sheridan, what demon of destruction has possessed you?"[2]

Winchester's wartime experiences were unique in that, once captured, the town did not long remain in Union hands. In cities such as Norfolk, Virginia, and New Orleans, southern citizens became accustomed to sustained occupation. To be sure, there were cities such as Galveston, Texas, that were eventually retaken by the Confederates and areas such as eastern Tennessee where military occupation fluctuated, but none with the frequency of Winchester. Southern citizens under permanent Union control, though restive and restricted, could fall into a rhythm of occupation. Winchester citizens could not. When Union general Nathaniel P. Banks arrived in New Orleans in January 1863, taking over for Benjamin Butler, he reported to his wife that "the

1. Colt, *Defend the Valley*, 9–10; MGL, 544 (Jan. 23, 1864); Oren Frederic Morton, *Story of Winchester*, 30, 147, 148. The roads leading to or near Winchester were the Valley Turnpike, running north and south (now Route 11), with the Cedar Creek Grade (now Route 622) and Middle Road (now Route 628) both connecting to the turnpike south of Winchester. On the east ran the Millwood Pike (now Route 50), running to Alexandria. Joining the Millwood Pike was the Front Royal Pike (now Route 522), leading to the Luray Valley. From the northeast was the Berryville Pike (now Route 7), which also terminated at Alexandria. On the west ran the Northwestern Turnpike (now Route 50), which stretched to the Ohio River, and the Pughtown Pike (also Route 50), running to Hancock, Maryland. See Delauter, *Winchester in the Civil War*, 2.

2. Winchester Land Tax Registers, 1865, LOV; James I. Robertson Jr., *Civil War Virginia: Battleground for a Nation* (Charlottesville: University Press of Virginia, 1991), 159; Philip Henry Sheridan, *Personal Memoirs of P. H. Sheridan, General, United States Army*, 2 vols. (New York: Charles L. Webster, 1888), 2:123; MGL, 408 (June 14, 1863), 790 (Feb. 26, 1865).

people are not hostile." Banks believed that peace was maintained in New Orleans in part from the conditioning an extended period of occupation afforded residents. Even though this is what he had expected in Winchester in March 1862, based on a report from Brig. Gen. W. A. Gorman that "the citizens of Winchester seem well disposed & . . . all pursuing their usual avocations," in reality, the atmosphere Banks found was to the contrary.³

Winchester was a border town not only because of geography but also due to sentiment. While opposing armies stayed busy reclaiming the town, the residents themselves remained divided over the secession issue. Mary Greenhow Lee's enemies were also her neighbors: Unionists such as the Charles Chase family, the Goldenbergs, the Hoovers, the Hennons, Bill Anders, and George and Kitty Miller. In naming these people in her journal, it was important to her to note which ones had "hung out Union flags" and those who had been "very attentive to the Yankees."⁴

Unionist Julia Chase's impressions of the Secessionists in Winchester are illustrative of the tensions in this border town. "The Secesh do not entertain very kind feelings to the Unionists," she wrote, "let them disguise the facts as they may." She called the Secessionists "demons" who were "terribly enraged against the Yankees" and stated they were "taunting in their remarks to the Unionists." Chase was correct. Mary Lee did not think highly of the Unionists, deeming them "fiend[s]" who were "worse than the Yankees."⁵

According to Chase, "the Secesh d[id] not always confine themselves to the truth," while Lee believed that the Unionists fabricated "the most outrageous stories." One day a friend brought Lee a letter found in the street.

3. Eaton, *Southern Confederacy*, 151–79; Noel C. Fisher, *War at Every Door: Partisan Politics and Guerrilla Violence in East Tennessee, 1860–1869* (Chapel Hill: University of North Carolina Press, 1997); Nathaniel P. Banks to wife, Jan. 15, 1863, Nathaniel P. Banks Papers, LC, typescript; W. A. Gorman to Nathaniel P. Banks, Mar. 12, 1862, ibid.; Faust, *Mothers of Invention*, 207–13. The turmoil in Winchester prior to secession was much the same as in Lynchburg, Virginia, at the time. Lynchburg did not suffer the same alternate occupation history, however, and the Unionists there never retained their strength in numbers or displayed any manifestation of their sentiments because they did not have the recurrent support of Union armies walking their streets. See Tripp, *Yankee Town, Southern City*, 89.

4. MGL, 5, 6, 8 (Mar. 1862); JPC, Mar. 12, 1862. Winchester was not the only border town where neighbors divided along sectional lines during the war. Lexington, Kentucky, citizens suffered similar conflicts. The diary of Frances Peter, a Unionist in Lexington, reveals the same animosity toward Secesh that Mary Greenhow Lee's journal exhibits against Unionists. Former friends down the block from the Peter home became the target of her worst criticisms during the war. See Smith and Cooper, *A Union Woman*, 3–4, 8–9, 22, 64, 66–68, 79–80, 87–88.

5. JC, July 25, May 25, 27, Sept. 3, 1862, May 8, 1863; MGL, 18 (Mar. 17, 1862), 21 (Mar. 20, 1862), 77 (Apr. 24, 1862), 82 (Apr. 28, 1862), 87 (May 2, 1862), 669 (Aug. 20, 1864).

Written by a "Yankee woman," the note stated that Lee was the "most prominent" Secessionist in Winchester and that Lee's servants reported her speaking out against Union officers to their faces, ranting that she hated them and
wishing that she "could kill them with [her] own hands." Lee called this "an
outrageous falsehood." Another letter charged that Lee "had carried on a
regular correspondence with the enemy, . . . was an outrageous rebel," and
deserved to be sent to Fort McHenry (in Baltimore). To Lee, these tales were
contrived as part of the process of war being waged against her personally.
She did not deny that she was a Rebel but simply preferred not to hear of her
enemies broadcasting the fact.[6]

It is interesting to note that Chase's diary is almost a mirror image of Lee's
journal. "Our troops" meant "Union" when coming from Chase; and her
"Glorious News!" was reported as "too terrible" by Lee. Of course, God received different pleas from each. More telling perhaps is that the "Yankee
flag" that upset Lee was, to Chase, a relief. "The glorious old flag is waving
over our town," Chase reported on the day of Winchester's first occupation
by Federal troops.[7]

Winchester was "our town" to both Lee and Chase, but war had changed
the meaning of "our" from community to contention. Chase asked in agony,
"Great God! Shall this thing always be?" Lee made a similar plea, "Where
will this all end?" Both of these remarks were made in the context of discord
between neighbors, not the provocations coming from opposing armies. The
character of this border town encompassed all the tensions and conflict of the
entire war, among both citizens and soldiers, though on a smaller scale.[8]

On January 23, 1864, Lee referred to her town as "a village on the frontier," a valid description. Winchester's position and importance to the two
armies kept it in turmoil throughout the war and placed it in a position much
like the "frontiers" of Europe, the border regions between nations. Citizens
never knew which force would have power over them. For instance, on December 2, 1862, Confederates again evacuated Winchester. Mayor J. B. T.
Reed received a message by flag of truce two days later from Union major
general John Geary, stating that he intended to move his forces in. "Unwilling to shed blood or destroy property unnecessarily," the general wrote, "I
demand an unconditional surrender of the city." Mayor Reed responded that

6. JC, June 16, 1863; MGL, 780 (Feb. 10, 1865), 597 (Apr. 11, 1864), 724 (Nov. 23, 1864).

7. MGL, 3 (Mar. 11, 1862), 5 (Mar. 12, 1862); Julia Chase, diary, Mar. 11, 12, 1862, quoted
in Quarles, *Occupied Winchester*, 40.

8. JC, May 8, 1863; MGL, 545 (Jan. 25, 1864).

"no resistance will be made." The Federals entered. Lee heard of the pro-
ceedings and recorded "that as the citizens could not defend the place," Winchester "was surrendered"; but she labeled the whole incident a "farce." After
dinner that evening she learned that the Yankees had left for Harpers Ferry,
and within a few hours she had the "pleasure of meeting squads of" her own
army returning to town. This frequency of change became commonplace for
the town.[9]

In fact, it was sometimes difficult to know which army at what hour might
be found in the streets. During September 1863, for instance, Winchester
endured no official occupation; but on nine days of the month, Federals appeared either on raids, brief stays, or to chase Confederate cavalry through
town. On February 5, 1864, Confederate cavalry entered in the morning,
then left, and Federals rode through later. Confederates raced in on April 8,
1864, followed by a Federal unit trying to catch them. Then shortly after,
the reverse transpired, with the southern unit chasing the northern one back
through town the other way.[10]

Lee became quite cynical about the changing military character of her
town. "Who will we belong to to-morrow," she would ask absentmindedly,
merely "curious to see which party" would "take possession" the next day.
One morning she awoke to the "clanking of sabres & dash of Cavalry" but
had become so inured to the unpredictability of war that she "did not get
up to see whether" Confederate or Federal soldiers were making the noise.
Instead, she went back to sleep. Lee had reached a saturation point and felt
little curiosity to see which army had possession because she knew it would
be only temporary. As Mary Magill recalled, Winchester "constituted the
shuttlecock in the great game . . . between the Federal and Confederate
armies."[11]

Residents became adept at recognizing the difference between mere raids
into town and signs of impending occupation; both began in a similar fashion.
Schoolmaster John Peyton Clark described the process of reoccupation. A
small body of cavalry would pass through, then another would enter from a
different direction, possibly leaving and setting up camp just outside of town.

9. MGL, 544 (Jan. 25, 1864); *OR*, 21:33; MGL, 268 (Dec. 4, 1862); Delauter, *Winchester
in the Civil War*, 111. Confederate units stayed until December 13, then evacuated once again,
leaving the town in the hands of civilians for ten days until the Federals returned once more, this
time for an official occupation.

10. Delauter, *Winchester in the Civil War*, 112–14.

11. MGL, 232 (Sept. 19, 1862), 430 (July 26, 1863), 454 (Aug. 8, 1863), 472 (Sept. 8, 1863);
Magill, *Women*, 201.

Later a larger force, as many as a thousand men, would enter, a sign to the citizens that the military was descending upon them for an extended stay. After the increase in military personnel, other physical signs appeared, such as telegraph posts and proclamations tacked to poles and doors to inform citizens of their position within the developing military post. Mary Magill noted that the arrival of "sutlers fill[ing] the stores with tempting goods" let residents know that they were under both military control and economic restrictions. The final indication of occupation was, as Lee complained, when the "captives" had to endure the "perpetual irritation" of a "cavalry soldier with drawn sabre" at every street corner.[12]

For Unionist Julia Chase, transference of military control was similarly frustrating. Her word choices describing the passages from one occupation to another implies growing impatience. She noted that when "our troops" evacuated the town, "the southern cavalry were ready to *hop in*," or she would state, "we pass from the U[nited] States into Dixie again" to mark their altered condition. When the town's status changed, her mood similarly reflected wry humor: "Since 4 o'clock this morning we have passed from Dixie into the U. States." Although Chase would have felt more comfortable in the latter circumstance than the former, her wording reflects neither anxiety nor excitement but rather ennui. Much like Lee, she knew that the situation was only temporary.[13]

With the town's population swelled to overflowing each time an army occupied it, housing shortages added another aspect to the turmoil. Most of the soldiers set up housekeeping in tents or makeshift shelters in the encampments outside of town, but Union officers appropriated residents' living and working space on demand. Although vexing enough for Secessionists to see the enemy walking the streets, it was even more so to pass them on the way to the kitchen.

In the nineteenth century, visitors followed protocol when approaching someone's home. Entrances were designed to subtly prepare visitors for the fact that they were entering private space as they ventured down walkways, past hedges, onto porches, and then sometimes into a vestibule. Most visitors were then greeted in the social zone of the house, the parlor typically or the dining room, if invited for a meal. Not even close personal friends would pre-

12. JPC, June 9, 1962; MGL, 72 (Apr. 19, 1862), 721 (Nov. 14, 1864), 770 (Jan. 25, 1865); Magill, *Women*, 117.

13. JC, Sept. 3, 1862, July 27, Aug. 17, 1863, July 21, 1864.

sume to enter the most intimate spaces of the house without being invited. War and overcrowding, however, greatly diminished respect for privacy in Winchester.[14]

Cornelia McDonald remembered that "every day would" bring "tales of the arrest of citizens, and occupation of houses belonging to them, while their families were obliged to seek quarters elsewhere." McDonald's first displacement came when New York cavalry officers quartered in her house. She and her family remained in the home but had to endure overcrowding and watching soldiers help themselves to milk from her cows, trample her flowers, and use "every conceivable utensil" in her kitchen.[15]

Forced into taking Union officers to board, Anne Tucker Magill fed Brig. Gen. James Shields at her dinner table while listening to his boasts that the South could never win the war. General Banks and his staff quartered at the Seever residence, and a Dr. Smith gave up his house for Federal offices. A General Hatch stayed with his men at Lloyd Logan's house, leaving only two rooms for the Logan family. Eventually, the Logans were completely removed from their home by Union general Robert Milroy. Mary Greenhow Lee believed that Milroy fabricated a reason to send the Logans south simply because "Mrs. Milroy [had] set her affections on" the Logan home, one of the most ostentatious dwellings in town.[16]

According to Lee, the Yankees were "behav[ing] outrageously" at the Sherrards' and Tidballs', "getting drunk & purposely annoying the family." Sitting and dining rooms, once used for receiving guests, became the sites of courts-martial. Some buildings and dwellings were transformed into stables. Dr. Fred Holliday, for example, had to endure horses housed on his first floor while he and his family lived upstairs. Mary Magill recalled that from windows and doors could "be seen peering the heads of mules and horses," with "people and animals living side by side . . . upon a social equality." The Ger-

---

14. Kasson, *Rudeness and Civility*, 170–73. For a study of the evolution of the trend of "privatization" of domestic space at the end of the eighteenth century, see also Isaac, *Transformation of Virginia*, 302–5.

15. McDonald, *Reminiscences of the War*, 43, 45–46, 63; MGL, 76 (Apr. 23, 1862).

16. MGL, 11 (Mar. 1, 1862), 140 (June 11, 1862), 347–50 (Apr. 1863); JPC, Mar. 14, 1862. Mary Magill found herself dislocated as a consequence of the Logan incident. She retold the story of Milroy's treatment of the Logans in a letter that fell into the general's hands, at which point he banished her. Ordered into a buggy, Magill was driven five miles outside Winchester, then left alongside the road with her luggage to wait for a traveler to offer her a ride. See Magill, *Women*, 214–20, 247; McDonald, *Reminiscences of the War*, 154.

man Reformed Church became, at various times, officer headquarters and a stable.[17]

The tone of Julia Chase's diary entries suggests that she accommodated both Union and Confederate troops without giving either an indication of her displeasure. Mary Greenhow Lee, however, did everything in her power to prevent Yankees from entering her home, a task requiring all of the mental and emotional strength she could muster. When almost two hundred Union cavalrymen arrived in town, several reined in their horses at the Lee house, and niece Louisa Burwell ran to shut the door, but the cavalrymen's "impertinent" looks frightened her until she backed away. Lee took charge; she "shut the door & bolted it." There were nights when she was awakened to "a thundering rap" on her cellar door and had to get up and inform the soldiers outside that her house was not a hotel, a restaurant, or a tavern.[18]

Lee used all of her ingenuity to keep the enemy from quartering at her home. During one attempt, they got no farther than her porches, where they spent the night. On another, when she feared that the dark windows of her office might lead military officers to assume that rooms were available, she "sat at the office door, constituting [her]self an army of occupation" for the evening to make it look as though the rooms were in use. To one officer demanding her office she reported that "the roof leaked." When that did not dampen his interest, she confided that the office door adjoined their sitting room, and she was certain that since "every word would be heard from one room to the other," it "would be mutually annoying" to everyone concerned, implying that she would be privy to sensitive information. He then departed, "apologizing for having intruded."[19]

In the end, Lee was not saved from quartering "Yankees." A Colonel Stanton demanded the wing of her house, and neighbors sent their slaves to help her reorganize her family's sleeping arrangements. She only had to give up her "dear old room" to the enemy for a few nights, however. Stanton was soon ordered to Baltimore and returned Lee's key to her with "thanks for the use of her room," for which she tagged him an "impertinent little dog." Cornelia McDonald recorded on April 14, 1863, that "a hospital steward and his wife are quartered on Mrs. Hugh Lee." Two days later Laura Lee wrote that, indeed, the provost sent word to Mary that she should prepare to receive "a

17. MGL, 72 (Apr. 19, 1862), 334 (Mar. 19–20, 1863), 337 (Mar. 24, 1863), 663 (Aug. 13, 1864); Magill, *Women*, 201.

18. MGL, 497 (Oct. 20, 1863), 549 (Feb. 1, 1864).

19. Ibid., 305 (Feb. 3, 1863), 398 (June 7, 1863), 754 (Jan. 2, 1865).

Mr. & Mrs. Clark." Mary confronted the provost on the issue, and he replied in a "jocular" manner that, since she had shown "so much delight when her other Yankees left [referring to Stanton], . . . he wanted to give her the opportunity to be delighted again." Mary recorded on April 19, "no Yankees have come & I earnestly hope the storm may have blown over." It is possible that the provost never intended quartering anyone on her but merely enjoyed goading "the most outrageous rebel in the town," who detested the idea of sheltering her enemies.[20]

The intrusion of enemy soldiers was galling enough to citizens, but stranger still were foreign military units and northerners who came to support the military or take advantage of chaos. Cornelia McDonald "hated the sight of the old town," encountering strangers "at every step, their eyes" revealing "curiosity or insolence." Dorothea Dix, Henry Ward Beecher, and Secretary of State William H. Seward, all high-profile individuals, intruded on Winchester's streets to remind the residents that life as they knew it would change, by force if necessary.[21]

One segment of the invading army that caused particular comment from the diarists was the foreign soldiers who comprised from 20 to 25 percent of Union forces, the largest portion recent German and Irish immigrants. Unable to make the distinction, citizens referred to some of the Germans as "Dutch," but the difference mattered little to a town under siege. The effect was the same; it merely underscored residents' awareness of a foreign invasion. According to Peyton Clark, who emphasized the force with a repetition of "8000 Dutch!" in his journal, the air was filled with "the smell of tobacco smoke and saur kraut [sic], a considerable cargo of the latter article" received recently by the "Yankee stores." Lee deemed "the Germans . . . a horrid looking set" who "filled . . . the air with their jargon & curses." Cornelia McDonald did not mind the noise and smells from the foreigners so much as their theft of her raspberries and potatoes. When she wrote to their colonel to complain about the invasion of her garden, however, her lack of sensitivity to their true nationality prompted an immediate and heated response. Col. Frederick G. D'Utassy of the Garibaldi Guard, 39th New York Volunteer Infantry, arrived at her door brandishing her note in his hand and spouting in broken English, "you call my men Dutchmen." His manner made her

20. Ibid., 329–33 (Mar. 1863), 336 (Mar. 24, 1863); McDonald, *Reminiscences of the War*, 156; LL, Apr. 16, 1863; MGL, 359–62 (Apr. 18–19, 1863).
21. McDonald, *Reminiscences of the War*, 42; JPC, Mar. 16, 29, Apr. 1, 1862; LL, Mar. 28, 1862.

laugh, which merely exacerbated his ire. She finally calmed him when she luckily guessed their true identity and said, "I should have taken you for a Hungarian." With that, the colonel settled down and assured her that he would keep his men from her garden. He did not, however, keep them from stealing her plums, even the green ones.[22]

Besides the sight of strangers and the smell of sauerkraut, the war brought new and sometimes disturbing sounds to town. When encampments covered the landscape surrounding Winchester, military drills sent "cannon shot . . . over the town" for days at a time. Neighbor warned neighbor of enemy searches and seizures by ringing bells of alarm. Noise became so commonplace that, at those times when the town was free of occupation, the silence could be almost more disturbing. Peyton Clark likened it to "the stillness of death."[23]

During occupations, military bands added to the noise. Lee complained of being "roused every morning at 6 o'clock by their reveille." Union bands harassed Secessionists with pieces such as "The Star Spangled Banner" and "Hail Columbia." Young Kate Sperry interrupted her journal writing for the day when the Federal band intruded on her reflections with their music. "Oh, deliver us," she wrote at the end, "they've turned off to 'Yankee Doodle.'" A northern band playing "Dixie," however, could be equally grating to the southerners. Of course, Union soldiers became just as annoyed when the residents sang their "infernal Secesh songs." Mary Greenhow Lee reported that, when she and her family were enjoying that very thing at the Sherrards' one evening, Federals retaliated immediately by climbing onto the Sherrards' roof and nailing a Union flag there.[24]

At times, military officials directed their bands to play in front of houses specifically identified as homes of loyal citizens. Unionist Harriet Griffith enjoyed the special attention her family received with this distinction, even though she could not remember who had directed it. "Major Somebody, Captain Somebody, and Doctor Somebody," she wrote, "brought the band and played for us." Lee relished good music too much not to give the Yankees their due. When northern musicians serenaded the Unionists, her ears caught strains flowing through town. "We have had the treat of most exqui-

22. Phillip Shaw Paludan, *"A People's Contest": The Union and Civil War, 1861–1865* (New York: Harper and Row, 1988), 281; JPC, Apr. 14, 18, 24, 1862; MGL, 75, 78 (Apr. 1862), 153–54 (June 23–24, 1862); McDonald, *Reminiscences of the War*, 74–75.

23. JPC, June 2, Sept. 1, 1862; JC, Jan. 18, 1864.

24. MGL, 24 (Mar. 21, 1862); McDonald, *Reminiscences of the War*, 56; Sperry, "Surrender!" HL, 158, typescript; MGL, 325 (Mar. 8, 1863).

site music," she admitted to her journal, even complimenting the "horrid Germans" for their "fine band[s] of music." She appreciated more, however, the serenades her house received from a "southern band," judging their performances "mediocre" while insisting that southern music played by southern men was "delightful to hear."[25]

The senses were bombarded when battles raged nearby with sounds that evoked even more emotion. Lee reported during the battle of Cedar Creek on October 19, 1864, "the Yankee bands have been playing all day; loudest when the cannonading was heaviest." The contrast of music over the sounds of fighting was abrasive, even when the band played "delightfully," because it meant that while she enjoyed the music, men were dying. One sound that both incited emotion and signified the rigors of combat was the "Rebel yell," music to the ears of Winchester Secessionists, the anthem of dread to Unionists. The first time the Rebel yell was heard in the Valley was during the first battle of Winchester in May 1862, but it would become a trademark of Confederate soldiers everywhere. Derived from southern hunting rituals, the battle cry was a piercing "Ah-e-e-e, ah-e-e-e." Confederate general Jubal A. Early characterized the sound as a "cheering peculiar to the Confederate soldier" and "never mistaken for the studied hurrahs of the Yankees." A psychological tool so penetrating it could be heard "above the storm of battle," the yell gave Confederate soldiers the confidence of group solidarity and Federal troops an eerie disquiet. For Unionists in Winchester, this peculiar southern sound, according to Julia Chase, filled them with "horror." For Secessionists such as young Emma Riely, however, a "volley of musketry in the street" heard simultaneously with the "famous 'Rebel yell'" signaled hope.[26]

Sounds of gunfire in the streets occurred not only when cavalry units chased each other through town but also when full-blown battles on the outskirts spilled over into Winchester. Wounded soldiers fell within sight of private homes. A "Lt. Col. Dorsey" of the 1st Maryland Regiment, a member of the Baltimore branch of Lee's *connexion*, was wounded near her house during the first battle of Winchester. Standing on her porch, she watched leaves fall from a maple tree in front of her house, cut down by random shots; heard another musket shot; and then saw Dorsey "riding slowly" to her house. She

25. HHG, Aug. 15, 1864; MGL, 83 (Apr. 28, 1862), 91 (May 7, 1862), 657 (Aug. 2, 1864), 777 (Feb. 5, 1865).

26. MGL, 708–9 (Oct. 19–20, 1864); "Rebel Yell" described in Stannard, *Richmond*, 170; report of Brig. Gen. Jubal A. Early, Dec. 27, 1862, *OR*, 21:663–67; McKim, *Soldier's Recollections*, 101; JC, May 25, 1862; Macon and Macon, *Reminiscences of the Civil War*, 21.

ran for Dr. Baldwin next door, and together they managed to get the officer situated inside and dressed his wounds.[27]

Battles in and around the Lee home became familiar to the family. The "rush of a cannon ball striking very near," for instance, roused Lee from sleep early one morning, though not enough for her to "get up to see." Of course, warfare in the streets could be dangerous. During the second battle of Kernstown, Lee not only watched men and ambulances passing but also experienced "balls whizzing by," one of them "striking the pavement" in front of her. When nephew Lewis Burwell came to check on her during the third battle of Winchester, the nearness of the fighting prompted him to beg the family to seek shelter in the cellar. By this time, however, the Lee women had become so accustomed to warfare that they "laughed at the idea" of running for safety.[28]

Lee never fled Winchester, but she did prepare for emergencies. Feeling at times as though she were sitting "on the edge of a burning volcano," she assessed news that Union armies were venturing close and determined whether or not to secrete away her valuables. Several times she sent her nieces, with the silver, "pistol, money, flag & other valuables," to hiding places she had secured around town. Before Confederates retook the town in May 1862, Julia Chase made similar preparations, hiding their silver and money and "keep[ing] the door and gate fastened all the time." During the first year of the war, while the town had been under the control of the southern army, Chase had not been fearful, even though her sympathies marked her as a Unionist. Between the first Confederate evacuation in March 1862 and their return in May, however, Chase came to realize that war was not simply cool, calculated maneuvers by opposing armies. To the contrary, it was a hotly contested rivalry in which both combatants and civilians fueled the bitterness that drove both sides. Much of the destruction in this old backcountry town was the result of emotional, not tactical, acts, recorded with equal dismay by Secesh and Unionist alike.[29]

By the end of May 1863, Mary Greenhow Lee doubted that "even a ghost" would have "the courage to visit such a dismal place as" Winchester. Confed-

27. JPC, May 26, 1862; MGL, 114 (Mar. 27, 1862).

28. MGL, 26 (Mar. 22, 1862), 206 (Aug. 19, 1862), 211 (Aug. 23, 1862), 410 (June 14, 1863), 481 (Sept. 20, 1863), 579 (Apr. 12, 1864), 642 (July 19, 1864), 625 (June 24, 1864), 685 (Sept. 19, 1864).

29. Ibid., 2 (Mar. 11, 1862), 151 (June 21, 1862), 267 (Dec. 2, 1862), 278 (Dec. 23, 1862), 305 (Feb. 3, 1863), 329 (Mar. 16, 1863), 349 (Apr. 9, 1863), 662 (Aug. 12, 1864); JC, May 25, 1862.

erate general Richard Ewell advised his future wife, Lizinka Brown, in Tennessee that she should not remain in the countryside, where there is "less restraint," but should return to Nashville because "in a city the enemy always are in organized bodies commanded by officers of rank who wish to conciliate" the residents. Winchester proved Ewell wrong. By the end of the war, with over $80,000 in recorded property damages, Lee's "poor old town" had not felt the kind hand of conciliation but rather the red-hot torch of retaliation.[30]

Union authorities devised various strategies to employ toward civilians during the war, depending upon the level of military action taking place. When the situation allowed, servicemen were to treat citizens with respect and provide for their basic needs and protection, expecting polite treatment in return. During hard fighting, when battles were the most pressing concern, what citizens could provide, and what restraints were necessary to keep them from interfering, were the highest, sometimes the only, considerations. Some generals even believed that treating southern citizens with respect and generosity would undermine the "tentative hold" southern political elites held over the population. The distance between policy and practice depended upon the personalities and patience of the individual officers and the level to which citizens pushed their own agendas.[31]

When Nathaniel Banks first occupied Winchester in March 1862, he issued an order that "all private property is to be respected." In reality, there was little he could do, or wanted to do, to save the property of "disloyal" citizens. When his cavalry unit needed horses, Secretary of War Edwin M. Stanton wrote to Banks to "levy upon the territory occupied . . . a military contribution of not less than fifteen hundred horses," but he directed that the burden of supplying horses was to "fall as far as possible upon those who have been . . . disloyal." These instructions commanded Banks to respect the property of Unionists more than Secessionists. Therefore, when he received a bill of $305.50 to repair a fence "destroyed by Federal Soldiers on the property of Col. Fauntleroy," a Confederate officer, the general replied that he could have stopped the destruction had he been notified of it while it was taking place but that "its restoration is a matter of more difficulty." When Mary Greenhow Lee's fence, and that of Dr. Baldwin's next door, were being torn

30. MGL, 393 (May 31, 1863); Richard Ewell to Lizinka Brown, Mar. 5, 1862, Confederate Military Leaders Collection, ESB.

31. Mark Grimsley, *The Hard Hand of War: Union Military Policy toward Southern Civilians, 1861–1865* (New York: Cambridge University Press, 1995), 2–4, 10.

down to feed the fires of soldiers camped on their lots, she sent a complaint to the Union commander immediately. A Major McGhee returned and "reprimanded the men strongly" but did not follow through. As far as protection of private property went, it made no difference how promptly citizens reported it. In this case, the soldiers' fires continued to burn, compliments of the Lee and Baldwin fences.[32]

Fences were not the only items lost to citizens. Soldiers stole spoons, tobacco, penknives, wine, whiskey, and money in great quantity. For officers' headquarters, they appropriated, by force, citizens' furniture. From Lee's cellar they "took milk, cream, butter, pickles, [and] tomatoes." Union soldiers did not merely steal from "disloyal" citizens, though. Lee reported that they "took $200" from "a strong Union man," being equally "odious to their friends as well as their foes." Several townspeople were awakened in the night by loud rapping on their doors and forced to give up blankets and pillows or face having the items taken from them personally by armed soldiers. Julia Chase complained about Confederate behavior as well. According to Chase, they cut down fences and spread "destruction wherever they" went, breaking into the Griffiths' house and threatening to "blow his daughter's brains out," stealing money, horses, and blankets. In Chase's estimation this was "a dreadful way of living." Some of the thefts were obviously driven by hunger or cold, but the effect of the whole made it seem to the residents that, rather than living under military rule, they were living under anarchy.[33]

Certainly, the explosions that awoke civilians in the night added to the fear that, as Cornelia McDonald expressed it, "the world was really in its last convulsion." A thirty-two-pound ball rudely roused the Conner family one night by crashing through the northwest corner of their house; flying through a closet, across the hallway, and into the room on the other side of the residence; ripping through the sheets on the bed; and then exiting out the south wall of the house, hitting the building across the street and finally landing in the gutter. No one was hurt, but at the very least, the Conners suffered jarred nerves.[34]

Whenever the Federal army made plans to leave Winchester, citizens looked for them to destroy the town on their way out as an act of vengeance

32. MGL, 18 (Mar. 17, 1862); Edwin M. Stanton to Maj. Gen. Nathaniel P. Banks, Apr. 9, 1862, Banks Papers; Gen. Nathaniel P. Banks to Mrs. M. S. Barnes, Mar. 22, 1862, ibid.; MGL, 308 (Feb. 6, 1863).

33. MGL, 7 (Mar. 1862), 130 (June 4, 1862), 137 (June 7, 1862), 498 (Oct. 22, 1862), 516 (Nov. 19, 1863), 69 (Apr. 17, 1862); JPC, Mar. 25, 1862; JC, Nov. 18, 1861, Jan. 18, 1864.

34. McDonald, *Reminiscences of the War*, 87; JPC, Aug. 18, 1862.

or simply to keep the Confederates from having use of it. Soldiers, possibly rankled by Secesh attitudes against them, spread the word that they planned "to burn the town before they left." Even Julia Chase knew that her own army had set fire to structures in several places and destroyed warehouses. Anticipating an evacuation, Mary Greenhow Lee predicted "our houses & everything we possess, may be blown up in a day or two" but later reported, "still here, neither burnt up, nor blown up." Relief was only temporary, however. Cornelia McDonald lay in bed one night when suddenly she felt the house shake, and glass from the windows shattered and fell around her on the bed. Her servant ran in screaming, "the town is on fire!" Lee, standing at the street corner near her home, also heard and felt the explosion, which "proved to be the powder magazine at the fortifications" on the outskirts of town. The Union army, upon orders to evacuate, had decided it more expedient to destroy their ammunition than move it. The result was a fire that engulfed the depot and several warehouses in town. Aside from the official destruction, soldiers also burned Peyton Clark's granary, woodhouse, and stables as they left. This act, Clark believed, was one of revenge, not military expediency.[35]

Wartime fires also claimed the town's post office, the "Baker & Bros. Store," Coontz's foundry, various warehouses, "Mr. Miller's Store in the centre of Main Street . . . where the houses are thickly built," and barns and crops outside of town. Some of these incidents were the effect of natural occurrences or accidents, and Lee gave Union officers credit on occasion for "making the Yankees work the engine till the fire was out." But other citizens were convinced that much of the destruction originated at the hands of Yankees, either in retaliation or out of military expediency, neither of which sat well with those who were left to protect their own property from blowing sparks or to assess their losses through smoke and ash.[36]

One such incendiary act left the medical college "burnt to the ground." Residents later learned that Federal soldiers set fire to the building, according to Peyton Clark, "in revenge for the fact that the body of old John Brown's son" had been "carried there as a subject for dissection." In reality, Mary Greenhow Lee knew that Oliver Brown's "bones" had been removed by Hunter McGuire, one of the teachers who at that point was serving under Stonewall Jackson as a surgeon. Although the medical school was lost, Lee

35. JPC, May 17, 1862; MGL, 103 (May 17, 1862), 113 (May 27, 1863). See also Sperry, "Surrender!" 195; JC, May 25, July 16, 1862; MGL, 170–71, 173 (July 11–13, 1862); McDonald, *Reminiscences of the War*, 87; MGL, 220 (Sept. 3, 1862); JC, Sept. 3, 1862; JPC, Sept. 8, 1862.

36. MGL, 113 (May 27, 1862), 141 (June 12, 1862), 669 (Aug. 20, 1864), 691 (Sept. 24, 1864); Sperry, "Surrender!" 195.

found some satisfaction in the fact that the absence of Brown's remains had foiled the Federals' "malicious design."[37]

Military commanders caught the retaliation frenzy as well. Stonewall Jackson "sent a flag of truce" to General Banks during the first Union occupation, saying that "if any more incendiary acts were committed" in Winchester, "he would retaliate on the prisoners he held." Banks replied "that death shall be the penalty of any such act." As the war ground on, the feelings of resentment built until the officers were sending threats to the citizens themselves. General Milroy let the townspeople know by an "oft repeated threat" that if Confederate "infantry enter town," he would "shell it." Confederate soldiers responded that "if a shell is fired into Winchester, Milroy & his infernal rascals shall be hung." In effect, residents were being drawn into the resentments growing out of the prolonged war. Only by a democratic process was the town saved from total destruction. Union officers met to discuss the question of whether or not to burn Winchester. According to Lee, "71 were in favor of burning, 100 against it and they decided they would only burn a few [buildings]. Whether we are of the honored number, I know not." She did not state whether or not the "honor" would have been in the burning or in the reprieve.[38]

Adding to the bitterness was a rash of civilian arrests. In the fall of 1861, immediately after Jackson set up his headquarters in Winchester, he ordered the arrest of Samuel A. Pancoast on charges of keeping carrier pigeons. Lee's friend Joseph H. Sherrard had informed Jackson about the pigeons, suspected, according to Julia Chase, of being used to send "messages to the injury of the southern Confederacy." George Pancoast, Samuel's son, wrote to Confederate officials on his father's behalf that Sherrard had made the charge "from personal enmity alone" and that his father had merely bought the pigeons "to mate some he had at home," not for purposes of covert operations. Nonetheless, Jackson sent Pancoast first to the guard house and then to Richmond.[39]

As time went on, arrests of civilians seemed to be made with even less foundation for cause. Before Jackson evacuated the town on March 11, 1862, he ordered the arrests of several Union sympathizers. Harriet Griffith, a young Quaker woman, recorded, "they say they intend to take all the Union

37. JPC, May 17, 1862; MGL, 103 (May 17, 1862), 113 (May 27, 1863). See also Sperry, "Surrender!" 195.

38. MGL, 144–45 (June 1862), 408–9 (June 14, 1863), 663 (Aug. 13, 1864).

39. JC, Nov. 15, 25, 1861; George L. Pancoast to Hon. Charles J. Faulkner, Dec. 19, 1861, OR, ser. 2, 2:1534.

men—Oh, I don't want Father to go." After listing those already removed to the guard house, Julia Chase wrote, "we are expecting nothing else but [that] Father will be arrested, as we learn the secessionists have 150 names down of Union people." The next day, as Jackson prepared to leave, Charles Chase was arrested, leaving Julia Chase feeling "indignant . . . towards the whole town." Her resentment began at this time and grew throughout the war. "To take an old man lying sick on the sofa," she wrote, "is outrageous." The arrests, whatever their purpose, fueled the growing bitterness between the town's factions.[40]

Military leaders, though supposedly dispassionate commanders abiding by the rules of warfare, fed and participated in the growing rancor. A group of Secessionist citizens circulated a petition to ask Jackson for the release of the Union men, though Chase doubted their sincerity. Lee reported that two of her friends, Dr. Robert Baldwin and Leonard Swartzwelder, had "been arrested" on orders of General Banks "for refusing to sign the petition" but were released when her friend and lawyer Philip Williams "interceded." On April 10, Banks sent the completed petition to Jackson along with a warning that "if this act be evidence of a determination on your part to carry on the controversy . . . in a manner so utterly repugnant to the usages of war, . . . the responsibility for the initiation of such a policy will rest upon you." Although Chase recorded on April 24 the "glorious news" that her father had been released, these events were just the beginning of military abrasion of local irritations.[41]

Arrests of civilians continued throughout the war. After the first battle of Winchester in late May 1862, when Jackson's army again briefly held the town, more Union men were arrested. One was Joe Meredith, taken on evidence presented by two young women, according to Chase, that he "was a Union man, strong abolitionist & black Republican." Charges of being a "Union man" seemed to be enough to send people to prison, suggesting that loyalty to one side was dangerous for the other, whether or not there was proof that a person's actions were detrimental to the opposition forces. Arrests on flimsy evidence indicate that the occupying commanders were either caught up in the civilian resentments or attempting to eliminate the annoyance.[42]

40. HHG, Mar. 1862; JC, Mar. 10, 1862.

41. JC, Mar. 17, 1862; MGL, 46 (Apr. 1, 1862); Banks to Jackson, Apr. 10, 1862, OR, ser. 2, 3:438–39.

42. JC, May 27, 1862.

"The Dooley affair" removed some of the most prominent secessionists from town. On January 14, 1864, while attending evening services at Market Street Methodist Church, William Dooley was arrested by four Confederate soldiers on charges of spying. The peaceful sanctuary erupted, with women screaming and men shouting, as Dooley reached for his pistol. The soldiers, aided by one male worshipper, subdued him and took him away.[43]

Julia Chase suspected that "some of the Secesh women" had caused the arrest, which could have been true. Mary Greenhow Lee believed Dooley to be "one of the most malignant Union men of Winchester," a "detective, spy & informer." Robert Y. Conrad, according to Lee, deemed him an "infamous scoundrel & low creature." Ultimately, it was proven that Dooley had been working as a "detective . . . on secret service" for the Federals. In the meantime, however, Chase reported that "our cavalry" arrived in Winchester from Martinsburg to hold Mayor J. B. T. Reed and "50 secessionists . . . as hostages" until Dooley was released by the Confederates. Two days later they arrested Conrad, but Chase reported sourly that he was immediately released "through the interference of some of the Union men" who were "so fearful of being carried off . . . that they seem obliged to do all in their power to prevent the arrests of secessionists." Fear of retaliation rather than community spirit seemed to motivate such intervention.[44]

That April, however, Philip Williams, Conrad, and Rev. Andrew H. H. Boyd were arrested and sent to Martinsburg, then on to prison at Wheeling. Lee recorded that these prominent "elderly men" were being held captive "in an immense room with 180 prisoners of every variety from felons to military prisoners, many of them dragging a ball & chain." The Winchester men kept themselves separate from the other inmates by a "chalk line . . . drawn across the floor" and the threat of "death for those who dare[d] to cross the line." Mary Williams wrote to her son, a Confederate soldier, asking if he could use his influence "to have this matter of civil arrests investigated." She went on to argue, "our men do little good" arresting "Union people of no standing" when it causes "the men on the Border who are battling slowly . . . for the sake of the South" to be taken as hostages. Gen. Robert E. Lee agreed. He sent "general instructions" to his officers "not to molest private citizens who do not take an active part against us" because it would "lead to retaliation on the part of the enemy."[45]

43. MGL, 557 (Feb. 16, 1864), 576–78 (Apr. 1864); Delauter, *Winchester in the Civil War*, 63–64.

44. JC, Jan. 15, 16, 18, 22, 1864; MGL, 541, 543, 548 (Jan. 1864).

45. JC, Apr. 22, 1864; MGL, 576–77, 584–85 (Apr. 1864); Mary Williams to Clayton or John J. Williams, Apr. 18, 1864, Philip Williams Family Papers (172 WFCHS), HL; Lee to Jefferson Davis, Apr. 22, 1864, printed in Delauter, *Winchester in the Civil War*, 67–68.

Such incidents of arrests do not illustrate clear lines of sentiment in Winchester. Philip Williams was moderately pro-Confederate by March 1862 and became more convinced of his stand as the war went on. Although he effected the release of Swartzwelder and Baldwin, two vehement Secessionists, his wife, Mary, attempted to secure the release of a Unionist.[46]

Yet another arrest gives evidence of Mary Greenhow Lee's internal conflict. A young Union orderly by the name of Dutton was arrested for desertion. Lee had become acquainted with the man through one of her boarders, a Dr. Love, and through her visits to the patients at "the York," a hotel-turned-hospital. Federals found the man wandering "five miles beyond their picketts" and brought him in. Without waiting for a court-martial, the soldiers were ready to hang Dutton when Dr. Love made a quick appeal to General Sheridan to postpone the execution until he could try the man. Lee did not believe Dutton had intended to desert. As she saw it, "the poor creature" was "almost childish" and "had not the moral courage to form such a plan." Not willing to leave Dutton's fate in the hands of the court, she pleaded with Philip Williams to draft a petition on Dutton's behalf. When she read Williams's petition, however, she found it "so flat & puerile" that she "ignored it altogether & wrote another, much more urgent & politic"; walked through snow and slush to get it signed by her friends and neighbors; and then sent it to Sheridan on the first day of January 1865.[47]

Whether or not her petition influenced the court, Dutton did not hang, but he was sentenced to "imprisonment during the war." Lee's efforts to save a Union orderly from capital punishment adds one more layer to the complex tensions she and the other citizens of Winchester suffered during the war. Suspicion and resentment among citizens points to the complications that arose in the divided town, sitting on the border lands between nations, home to both Secesh and Unionist as well as to those who continued to feel the pull from both sides.[48]

Winchester's children also had to adjust to the war's confusion. When Jackson evacuated the town in March 1862, Cornelia McDonald's children felt disgraced. They had heard others interpreting Jackson's move as a flight or retreat, neither of which seemed heroic to youngsters who had witnessed almost a full year of Confederate drills, parades, and prancing horses with banners flying. According to McDonald, her son Kenneth "looked very

46. Mary Williams to Gen. Thomas J. Jackson, Mar. 11, 1862, Stonewall Jackson Collection, ESB.

47. MGL, 749–52 (Dec. 28–31, 1864).

48. Ibid., 752 (Dec. 31, 1864), 761 (Jan. 11, 1865).

wretched," and young "Nelly's face was bent in deepest humiliation." Mc-Donald described son "Roy's black eyes" as "blazing, as if he scented a fight but did not . . . know where to find it," and two-year-old Donald, unable to comprehend the reasons but sensitive to his family's distress, "turned his back to weep silently." The scene reminded the mother that protecting her children from war was suddenly added to her list of responsibilities.[49]

Indeed, McDonald learned during the battle of Kernstown on March 23, 1862, that "the old life was over" for her children. When the fighting first began, her sons Harry and Allan asked if they could "go to the top of the hill . . . to see what was going on." She let them go but "repented" her decision later as the sounds of battle grew louder and the boys had not returned. She "sat all that fearful afternoon in terror," waiting. Civil War battles were confusing and frightening to the grown men engaged in them; it must have been much worse for young Harry and Allan as they watched. In the words of David Bard, an Ohio volunteer, he hoped to never "behold such a scene" as Kernstown again. Even though he was not hit, a "ball struck the ground" beside him and threw up dirt in his face; dead and wounded men lay beside him. This was part of the scene Harry and Allan watched from the top of a fence for a time until "a man's head rolled close to where they were, and they prudently retreated to a more secure position." They arrived home about nine o'clock that night, seeming to be different boys, "so sad and unnatural was their expression." Winchester children would become accustomed to such violence before the war ended.[50]

Some children in the area recorded their wartime experiences. John Magill Steele was eight years old when the war began; his sister, Sarah Eliza Steele, was ten. Living along the Valley Turnpike at Stephens City, a village on the edge of Winchester, they watched the war pass as the players migrated from one area to another or lingered near. Wounded Federals sometimes boarded with the Steeles. The children did not label them "our men" but "Yanks," and they reported that "about twenty Yanks" knocked at their door, asking for water and "Rebs." They also noted personal losses at the hands of "Yanks," echoing the opinion of their parents. "About daylight . . . some infantry passed through and stole our onions," they wrote, then added, "'Ugly Yanks'!" The evidence suggests, however, that children became acclimated to the violence, danger, and confusion of war just as adults did. Diary entries

49. Ibid., 1–3 (Mar. 11, 1862); McDonald, *Reminiscences of the War,* 41.

50. McDonald, *Reminiscences of the War,* 52; David Bard to Alice Underwood, Mar. 23, 1862, David Bard Papers (361 WFCHS), HL.

made by the Steele children reveal a growing complacency over the vicissi-
tudes of life in a war zone. For example, one contained three sentences of
nine words reporting two events over which the boy and girl had no control
bracketing one over which they did: "Cold. Set three hens to-day. Some Yankees came to-day."[51]

Children endured the same inner conflict that Mary Greenhow Lee experienced, resenting Yankees as a group but learning to like them as individuals.
Three-year-old Donald McDonald boldly warned the first Union soldier to
approach him and tap his head to "take your hand off my head, you are a
Yankee," causing the man to scowl and walk away. But he later had time to
grow fond of a "Capt. Pratt" who stayed with the McDonalds while recovering from a wound. As Pratt rested on the sofa one evening, Cornelia, with
Donald leaning against her lap, examined and admired the captain's pistol,
"very finely mounted with gold." Donald tapped her hand, however, and said,
"take care, Mama, you will shoot Captain Pratt." When she asked him "ought
I not to shoot him" since "he is a Yankee," the young boy thought a moment,
then looked sadly at the man and said with a sigh, "well, shoot him then."
This signifies the extent to which war in Winchester had taught even the
very young the seriousness of national loyalty. The extended crisis also made
children almost immune to the violence. In amazement, McDonald watched
her children "playing in the yard in the bright summer sunshine" while "ma-
neuvering troops scud[ded] over the hills" and artillery, infantry, and ambulances passed the house. "Poor little things," she wrote, "they have long been
used to scenes of strife and confusion, and I suppose it now seems to them
the natural course of things."[52]

War did not seem natural to Mary Greenhow Lee, but since war had been
forced on her, she wanted to be fully informed on its progress. Her identity
as a strong southerner heightened when she could impart military news to
her neighbors. She labeled her house "Head Quarters" when friends came
by to learn the latest news. She sorted through all that she heard, qualified
unsupported data, then advanced with assurance the news she believed.
Neighbors who received their information late and tried gifting Lee with the
tidbit forced her to "go into second hand ecstacies" to be polite. Peyton
Clark, under house arrest for "overlooking the fortifications, with a spy-

51. "Diary of John Magill Steele and Sarah Eliza Steele," in Quarles et al., *Diaries, Letters,
and Recollections*, 65, 69, 72, 73, 76, 79, 93 (Feb. 26, May 22, 14, June 15, July 8, 1863, Jan. 6,
1864, Apr. 14, Apr. 3, 1863).
52. McDonald, *Reminiscences of the War*, 41, 63, 174.

glass, & giving information to" the army, relied on "Mrs. Lee and Miss Laura Lee" for information. Unable to go out of his home to "understand the meaning" of the "bustle in the street," he felt frustrated until the Lee women came to him after dark to let him know of the enemy's evacuation of Winchester.[53]

If Lee could not obtain southern newspapers, she read northern ones. She also sifted through the "flying rumours" constantly coming her way to ascertain the true military positions of both armies. She counted a day lost if there was "no army news." When she could not read the papers, Lee analyzed the events surrounding her, using her intuition and recent experiences to inform her. If northern journals were available, she only half believed their stories. When they were suppressed, she found hope. Keeping track of how long it had been since she had read a northern paper, Lee suspected "there was something in them they did not wish us, or their army, to know."[54]

Lee also studied the faces of incoming Union soldiers for any signs of "exultation." If they "looked puzzled & harassed," she counted it good news for her own army. If she noticed her street "thronged with wagons, with the horse's heads to the Depot, & those wagons . . . heavily laden," she correctly predicted "a retreat." Just before the Federals' first stay in Winchester ended, Lee noted, "the Hospitals were cleared to-day, of all who could be moved. They are preparing for a battle, or an evacuation. I believe the latter." She was right.[55]

Stonewall Jackson's Valley campaign in the spring of 1862 tested everyone's ability to keep track of the army. The general forced his men to march over six hundred miles as he provoked Union commanders into chasing him up and down the Shenandoah Valley. In the words of one of his soldiers, Jackson would begin a march in one direction, then turn around and march the other way, just to keep the "yankeys rather by the horns." Newspapers, Union dispatches, and private journals expressed concern and puzzlement over his whereabouts. Speculation on where Jackson was and when he might strike became dinner conversation for citizens, the subject of numerous Union communications, and fodder for the presses. Peyton Clark reported, "the question 'Where is Jackson?' was upon the mouth of . . . every man." Even Unionists acknowledged the Rebel commander's effectiveness in puzzling his opponents. Julia Chase admitted, "tho' there are so many [Union]

53. MGL, 81 (Apr. 27, 1862), 754 (Jan. 2, 1865), 212 (Aug. 24, 1862); JPC, Sept. 8, 1862.
54. MGL, 146 (June 15, 1862), 534 (Dec. 26, 1863), 19 (Mar. 18, 1862), 71 (Apr. 19, 1862).
55. Ibid., 32 (Mar. 25, 1862), 57 (Apr. 8, 1862), 109 (May 23, 1862).

Genls. in the valley, . . . we have our fears in regard to Gen. Jackson, and think he may again give them the slip." Jackson's ability to confuse the enemy also perplexed his admirers in the Valley, but Lee appreciated this facet of his style. She reported: "We cannot find out about Jackson, who is ubiquitous; here, there, and everywhere." Later, after learning how his subterfuge worked against the enemy, she happily stated that the general was "in his hole again, & they cannot find him."[56]

But Unionist Julia Chase interpreted the news from the opposite perspective. For instance, after learning that Confederate cavalry general Turner Ashby was only six miles from Winchester, Lee reported, "our deliverance is drawing near," yet Chase moaned, "God have mercy on us." When the Secessionists exhibited "great glee," it meant bad news for Chase's army. If she learned good news about the Federal army from the Secessionists, then she could believe it. Hearing that the Federals had gained a "victory in Maryland" was "almost too good to be true" for Chase, but since the news came from Secesh, she could not "doubt it." This last bit of news was a relief for Chase; she and the other Unionists in town had "been very much cast down for months" since it had "seemed as if the Federal army had fallen asleep, or were extinct." By the following summer, however, she was again in bad humor. Almost as if she were shouting at the Union army, Chase wrote, "God forbid that the nation has become a nation of cowards . . . ; every man . . . nerve himself for the struggle & not allow our country to be trodden down & destroyed by these southern people." Her phrase "southern people" implies that she wanted deliverance not from Confederate armies, but rather from her neighbors.[57]

Both Unionists and Secessionists, depending on the army holding the town, looked for signs of liberation. Lee could become frustrated with faulty or flimsy information. "The Secesh of Winchester are punished," she pouted,

56. John Selby, *The Stonewall Brigade* (New York: Hippocrene, 1974) 37; *New York Times,* Apr. 1, 1862, 4; *OR*, 12(1):336, 347–48, 540, 626; 12(3):51, 52, 77, 78, 94, 95, 134–37, 140–44, 150, 152, 154, 162–63, 315, 323–25, 330, 332, 337, 841; 11(1):36; 12(3):173–74; Charles Royster, "The Aggressive War: Jackson," chap. 2 of *The Destructive War: William Tecumseh Sherman, Stonewall Jackson, and the Americans* (New York: Alfred A. Knopf, 1991); Bevin Alexander, *Lost Victories: The Military Genius of Stonewall Jackson* (New York: Henry Holt, 1992); Jedediah Hotchkiss, *Make Me a Map of the Valley: The Civil War Journal of Stonewall Jackson's Topographer,* ed. Archie P. McDonald (Dallas: Southern Methodist University Press, 1989), 58; William Groves Morris to Louisa Costner Morris, Sept. 8, 1862, William Groves Morris Papers (No. 3626), SHC, photocopy; JPC, 24 (May 26, 1862); *OR*, 12(3):330; *Charleston Mercury*, May 24, 1862; JC, June 4, 1862; MGL, 147 (June 17, 1862), 150 (June 20, 1862), 152 (June 22, 1862).

57. MGL, 107 (May 21, 1862); JC, May 23, Apr. 14, Sept. 16, 1862, July 1, 1863.

"by having the accounts withheld." At one point she grumbled that she had "heard for the 700oth time that A[mbrose] P. Hill was in the Valley" and that, if he did not appear soon, she would "be in the Valley of Despair." In addition, she had to endure "the croakers," those who believed all of the bad news they heard and "only half" of the good.[58]

Neither Lee nor Chase required newspapers to learn about the third battle of Winchester on September 19, 1864, when Confederate Jubal A. Early lost to Phil Sheridan's forces on the northeastern edge of town near Opequon Creek; they could hear the battle as it transpired. In fact, Lee found herself in the middle of it when Confederate cavalrymen ran from the fight, their line of retreat leading past her front door. She stood on the porch and "shamed" the men for leaving the battle and "by dint of reproaches and encouragements succeeded in turning some back." Chase was jubilant, recording in her journal two days later, "our troops are driving the rebels at a rapid rate and do not give Early scarcely a chance to take a stand." Assessing the history of the war to date, she acknowledged, "for the first time I have seen a glorious victory in the Valley of the Shenandoah on the part of our troops."[59]

It is important to note that the war years in Winchester were not all grim. Sadness and joy mixed together as they would during normal times; but each was felt more acutely—the highs and lows of life emphasized by uncertainty. Winchester Secesh erupted into celebration when the Confederate army returned, sometimes even while battles spilled over into the streets. During the first battle of Winchester, as Confederates chased Union soldiers out of town, Ranny McKim remembered that citizens rushed into the streets and greeted the Rebels troops "with the most enthusiastic demonstrations of joy . . . regardless of the death-shots flying around them."[60]

Cornelia McDonald recalled "the beaming countenances and the congratulations passed between citizens, . . . some weeping or wringing their hands over the bodies of those who had fallen before their eyes . . . and others shouting for joy at the entrance of the victorious Stonewall Brigade." Upon their release "from bondage," residents began "embracing the precious privilege of saying what they chose, singing or shouting what they chose," and "people in different spheres of life . . . were shaking hands and weeping together." Col. James K. Edmondson wrote to his wife on May 26, 1862, that they had "routed the Yankees completely" and that when Confederate forces

58. MGL, 303 (Jan. 31, 1863), 628 (June 30, 1864), 671 (Aug. 25, 1864).
59. Ibid., 685 (Sept. 19, 1864); JC, Sept. 21, 1864.
60. McKim, *Soldier's Recollections*, 101–3.

"entered Winchester," they were treated to "a demonstration . . . by the citizens, the ladies especially, . . . waving handkerchiefs and flags." McKim reported that the celebrations continued inside the homes as residents took soldiers in to feed them. He enjoyed "a joyous breakfast table that Sunday morning at Mrs. Lee's" until someone came in to report that his cousin Robert had been killed in the battle. Joy and sadness collided continually during the war, the height of one deepening the other, emotional vacillations that most keenly took their toll on Mary Greenhow Lee's household.[61]

61. McDonald, *Reminiscences of the War*, 64–68; Edmondson, *My Dear Emma*, 95; McKim, *Soldier's Recollections*, 103.

6

"We Share & Bear"

Wartime Domestic Politics in the Lee Household

The roomy house at 132 North Market normally could accommodate a large family comfortably. Shortages in firewood during the war, however, made it necessary to limit the number of fires burning in the house, often forcing Mary Greenhow Lee's family to spend most of their days together in the same room. Life in flux, anxieties over friends and family members in harm's way, worry about finances, boredom, and sometimes "intolerable" weather all served to prevent "five women . . . shut up in the house" from remaining "cheerful all the time." A "dismal day" for the Lee household usually found Mary at least attempting to lighten their spirits, but occasionally she "was utterly unable to keep up a show of interest" and figured the other family members considered her to be "out of sorts." Lee knew they did not understand how "old grief" could overcome her will to be cheerful all of the time, but she reasoned that, although they did not quarrel, each of them had "their own private grievances."[1]

In fact, she knew that the suspense of wartime and worry over nephews Lewis and Robert, "too deep for words," could lead one family member to

1. MGL, 499 (Oct. 23, 1863), 316–17 (Feb. 17–20, 1862), 744 (Dec. 22, 1864).

"resent the anxiety of the others" because, as a family, they were expected to "share & bear" each other's trials. For that reason, although she did occasionally fall into depression, she maintained the physical needs of her large—at times very large—household, while also trying to protect their emotions.[2]

Evenings could be the worst part of the day. War news and town concerns filled some of the time until they had talked themselves out. Then nothing could be heard except for "the rattling of leaves" as each turned the pages of their books. To prevent "the gloom of total silence," they often read aloud.[3]

Of course, visitors broke the monotony. Impromptu evenings could go either way, and Lee was always surprised and pleased when "agreeably entertained" by them. Planned events sometimes caused her momentary relief from the dread that seemed to hang over the household, but even then Mary felt the need for diplomacy with other family members. For instance, when the new minister and his wife arrived in town, Lee and her sisters-in-law planned a welcome party for the couple. "The Maury affair" was scheduled for New Year's Eve, 1864. Mary's guest list and menu met with criticism, however, until all of her plans became "disarranged." Antoinette objected to the number, Laura "to the refreshments," convincing Mary that the evening would turn into a "stiff, meagre affair," but she refused to force the issue. In the end, the party "went off well," even though only three of the fifteen guests were men, an odd composition in Mary's view. Significance of the incident lies in her accommodation to family, at least as she related it in a journal destined to be read by family friends. Lee once wrote that she was "tired of everybody" else in the town, the demands of polite society outside of her family requiring more effort than she could marshal at times. But she called upon reserves of energy to "keep up uniform cheerfulness" for those under her roof.[4]

Unfortunately, the identities of Lee's family members remain obscure. Her journal is almost the only source available to uncover descriptions of the household, and since she wrote the journal for Jeannie Mason, an intimate family friend, Lee had no need to expand on individual characteristics and personalities. Nonetheless, tight reading of the journal does provide some insight. Mary's sisters-in-law, Antoinette and Laura Lee, ages forty and thirty-eight respectively when the war began, were examples of a growing

2. Ibid., 595 (May 9, 1864), 499 (Oct. 23, 1863), 761 (Jan. 11, 1865).
3. Ibid., 730 (Dec. 3, 1864), 733 (Dec. 7, 1864).
4. Ibid., 458 (Aug. 14, 1863), 535–36 (Dec. 31, 1863–Jan. 2, 1864), 316–17 (Feb. 17–20, 1863), 761 (Jan. 11, 1865).

trend by the mid–nineteenth century. Whether called "spinsters" or "maiden aunts," women were increasingly remaining single throughout their lives. Some did so to maintain more financial power, for married women had few economic and civic rights under most antebellum state laws, being considered "covered" by their husbands' civil identity. The rising number of widows who chose not to remarry points to this legal cloaking as a reason for that trend. It is uncertain why Antoinette and Laura never married, but since they had been left an inheritance and had each other for emotional support, perhaps they fell into the category of women who, rather than being unclaimed, chose not to marry. Given their apparent personalities, evidence also suggests that they may have been afraid to marry.[5]

Laura Lee is revealed more clearly because she too kept a Civil War journal, though less detailed than Mary's. At times, the parallel journals almost repeat each other in wording, as though the women discussed the news of the day over dinner, then retired to their rooms to echo their conversation in writing. The documents do not reveal discrepancies in events but do reflect differences in temperament. Mary's journal continues doggedly through bad times and good, through excited exertion and dragging inactivity. Laura's leaves major gaps in time, and although she kept at it until word of Robert E. Lee's surrender at Appomattox, she often threatened to "stop writing" because the news was too depressing.[6]

In their reports of the Union provost's order against showing "exultation" over Confederate victories, Laura stated that "any woman" who did so "would be shot." Mary did not note a distinction between sexes in the command, suggesting that, as head of her household, gender lines had grown less noticeable for her. In any event, although Mary often complained about the males with whom she had to deal, her journal reflects a more balanced attitude about the turmoil of their lives than does Laura's, as if she were more cognizant of other points of view. She also seems to have been less excitable than her sister-in-law. After the dust had settled from the first battle of Winchester in May 1862, Mary wrote: "Joy, joy, dearest Jeannie; the battle has been fought; the victory won; we are free," while Laura recorded, "Thanks

5. Lee Virginia Chambers-Schiller, *"Liberty, a Better Husband": Single Women in America, the Generations of 1789–1840* (New Haven: Yale University Press, 1984), 3; Lebsock, *Free Women of Petersburg*, 116; Michael O'Brien, *An Evening When Alone: Four Journals of Single Women in the South, 1827–67* (Charlottesville: University Press of Virginia, 1993), 1–2; Victoria E. Bynum, *"Unruly Women": The Politics of Social and Sexual Control in the Old South* (Chapel Hill: University of North Carolina Press, 1992), 61.

6. MGL, 40 (Mar. 28, 1862), 114 (May 27, 1862); LL, Mar. 28, 27, Apr. 21, 1862.

be to the Lord we are free!!!!!!!!!!!!!!!!!!!" Further, while Laura admitted that the Union occupiers had them "in their power," Mary refused to admit that the Federals had any power over her, but she "remained firm" in her stand, intimidated them with "a bold front," and maintained "a defiant course" within the restraints of genteel behavior.[7]

Mary's characterization of Laura included descriptive phrases such as "so gentle & so unwilling to give trouble," "the good, the perfect," and "the shrinking Laura Lee." Laura appears quite different on the pages of her own journal, making bold statements against "Yankees," Abraham Lincoln, and the "dreadful Germans." She appears very brave when, upon learning that the Seever family had invited Secretary of State William H. Seward to stay with them, she proclaimed that she "would not submit to such degradation" even if she were "to be beggared by refusing." A few days later, however, found Laura complaining that they had *"no ice."* Although Laura Lee exhibited less patience with inconvenience than she boasted, she provided more help to Mary during the war than did her sister.[8]

Antoinette Lee left even fewer traces of her identity. Referred to alternately as "Nettie," "Nett," "Netsy," and "Nette," Antoinette evidently had a delicate constitution. She suffered from various illnesses, depression, nervousness, and "spells" throughout the war, causing the family grave concern and forcing them to divide their time between sitting by her bed and caring for wounded soldiers. Clearly, the war must have exacerbated her health problems, but Mary indicates that Antoinette's health had been a well known, lifelong concern when she wrote that, although the rest of the family survived on meager fare, Antoinette was not "condemned to this fate" because Mary had reserved "cold chicken for her." By announcing this in her journal, Mary ensured that anyone personally acquainted with the Lees who might read the journal would be reassured that one so delicate as Antoinette would not have to suffer privations.[9]

When Antoinette's health permitted, and because her own frailty provided

7. LL, May 24, 27, 1862; MGL, 111 (May 24, 1862), 112 (May 27, 1862); LL, Apr. 3, 1862; MGL, 206 (Aug. 19, 1862), 623 (June 20, 1864).

8. MGL, 354 (Apr. 12, 1863), 51 (Apr. 4, 1862) 55 (Apr. 6, 1862); LL, Mar. 29, May 1, 6, Mar. 28, Apr. 3, 1862 (emphasis hers).

9. MGL, 96 (Jan. 21, 1863); Colt, *Defend the Valley,* 125; MGL, 598 (May 12, 1864), 734 (Dec. 8, 1864), 277 (Dec. 19, 1862), 297 (Jan. 14, 1863), 328 (Mar. 13, 1863), 333 (Mar. 19, 1863), 344 (Apr. 3, 1863), 545 (Jan. 25, 1864), 703 (Oct. 10, 1864), 705 (Oct. 12, 1864), 708 (Oct. 19, 1864), 712 (Oct. 25, 1864), 739 (Dec. 15, 1864); LL, Oct. 9, Sept. 11, 1864; MGL, 734 (Dec. 8, 1864).

empathy, she cared for other family members and friends who were ill. She also enjoyed a good reputation for her singing talents and, when able, soothed wounded patients and grieving mothers with song. Despite both Mary's and Laura's depictions of Antoinette, a neighbor remembered her quite differently. Randolph "Ranny" Barton's memoirs of the war include a scene after the battle of Kernstown, when both he and the Lees' nephew Robert Burwell were marched past their house as prisoners of war. Antoinette Lee, then forty-two years old, seems almost unrecognizable. She brought a "cullender full of beaten biscuits" out to the men, which, when emptied, she waved in the air as she "cheered most lustily."[10]

In neither Mary's nor Laura's journals would one find anything about Antoinette Lee to even remotely link her to the word "lusty." It could be that Barton's memory confused the event, but since he was especially fond of Antoinette, it is difficult to believe that he would have depicted her so far out of character. It is more probable that using sources limited mostly to those most responsible for her care renders the evolving picture of her identity incomplete. In any event, as the war drew to a close, and as food and fuel grew more scarce, Mary found a way to transport Antoinette to her brother George Lee's home in Clarksburg, by then in West Virginia, where she could enjoy "all the comforts and luxuries so necessary for her delicate health."[11]

The other members of the household, the Burwell children, had been living with Mary off and on since their mother's death in 1848. They are listed in the 1850 census under Hugh Holmes Lee, and under both Mary's name and their father's name in 1860. By then, Burwell had remarried to Ann Rea Reily, a widow with a young son, Brisco Reily, born in 1849.[12]

The children's father, Philip Lewis Carter Burwell ("P.L.C."), was a descendant of Robert "King" Carter of Corotoman, one of the most economically and politically powerful men of Virginia's colonial period. When his own father, Carter Burwell III, died in 1819, Philip was only a small boy, but he inherited Carter's Grove, the Burwell plantation in James City County, and a tangled web of legal fights managed by administrators of the estate. He lived at Carter's Grove for a few years after his marriage in 1836, finally selling the plantation after Susan's death in 1848, after which he moved to Frederick County. There he bought and sold various properties, including land

10. MGL, 436 (July 16, 1863), 665 (Aug. 16, 1864), 582 (Apr. 18, 1864), 657 (Aug. 2, 1864); McDonald, *Reminiscences of the War*, 87; Colt, *Defend the Valley*, 125, 340.

11. MGL, 764 (Jan. 16, 1865).

12. U.S. Bureau of the Census, Seventh and Eighth Census, LOV, microfilm.

owned by his mother-in-law, Elizabeth Lee. In 1853 he purchased 471 acres in Clark, an adjacent county, but continued to live in Winchester. Selling that large parcel two years later, he then purchased an acre near Berryville in 1856. This small piece of land very probably had an inn on it, for it was situated near a turnpike. At the same time, he also owned the Taylor Hotel in Winchester, making a fairly successful business out of it until Gen. Nathaniel Banks took it over as a hospital in 1862. While his famous ancestor, the aristocratic "King" Carter, had held almost every position of governance in the colony and owned 300,000 acres and approximately one thousand slaves when he died, Burwell had moved west and made his living in the service industry, lodging travelers. Whether or not the children lived with Mary because their father thought that her home would make a better environment for them remains uncertain. In any case, they became members of her household.[13]

Absent from the home throughout most of the war, nephews Lewis and Robert "Bob" Burwell, twenty-three and nineteen respectively in 1861, were often mentioned by both Laura and Mary in their journals, mostly through the prism of concern for their welfare. The young men served in the Confederate army, thereby earning their aunts' highest respect along with their love. Images emerge from the journals of the two "affectionate" young men, colored by the passion of worry. Mary counted it a special day when letters arrived from them, more often from Bob than Lewis. Bob also came home more often than Lewis, but every visit, though brief, caused joy to the female household. Most arrivals were a surprise, sometimes announcing themselves at the door, sometimes accidentally coming upon family members as they rode into town. Similar to her reaction to a visit from brother James Washington Greenhow when she was young, Mary Lee would drop what she was doing, or hurry to dress, and run to greet them. One visit from Lewis came about from Mary's long-distance needling of Gen. Jubal Early. Encountering Hunter McGuire, by then a member of Early's staff (on which Lewis Burwell also served), on the street one day, she asked him why the general gave a

13. Florence Tyler Carlton, *A Genealogy of the Known Descendants of Robert Carter of Corotoman* (Richmond, Va.: Whittet and Shepperson, 1982), 113, 128–35; Burwell, "Sketch of Carter Burwell," 70–72; Mary A. Stephenson, *Carter's Grove Plantation: A History* (Williamsburg, Va.: Research Department, Colonial Williamsburg Foundation, 1964), 85–88; Stuart E. Brown Jr., *Burwell: Kith and Kin of the Immigrant Lewis Burwell (1621–1653) and Burwell Virginia Tidewater Plantation Mansions* ([Berryville, Va.]: Virginia Book, [1994]), 29; Cartmell, *Shenandoah Valley Pioneers*, 162; Dabney, *Virginia*, 82–83; Eighth Census; Frederick County Deed Book 76:92–94; Clark County Land Tax Registers, 1845, 1855, 1856, 1860, LOV.

furlough to everyone but Lewis and requested that McGuire tell Early, with her compliments, that "he was the greatest tyrant" she ever saw. General Early allowed Lewis a one-night leave.[14]

Although older and already trained in the medical profession, Lewis seemed to cause Mary the most concern. In the first place, it took three years for him to visit home the first time. In the second, he evidently had a "reckless bravery" that she feared "might lead him into unnecessary danger." In the end, Bob's "reckless bravery" sent him home wounded from a bullet hitting his hip, spiraling down his leg, and coming out near his knee. Enjoying a night's furlough with friend and neighbor Ranny Barton, spending the night in the countryside, and planning to hunt partridges the next day, he awoke to the sound of musket fire and decided it was coming from Union cavalry. The two ventured off to rob the enemy of saddles and bridles and then return for breakfast when they found a column of infantry forming for battle. Bob lit out to warn Confederate general Fitzhugh Lee and received the wound for his efforts. He started immediately for home.[15]

Ranny soon followed and found Bob "comfortably helpless" at Mary Lee's. It amused him to see Bob so debilitated when just two hours before he had been boasting of his plan to refurbish his tack at the expense of the Yankees. Through laughter, Ranny asked, "How about that saddle?" Bob absently brushed at a fly and remarked, "Never mind, you'll be in here yourself after awhile." Sure enough, Ranny headed out of town and encountered Jubal Early "returning at top speed, with his little army of eight thousand infantry, to meet Sheridan's formidable advance of twenty-five thousand." Before the third battle of Winchester ended, Ranny was also wounded in the leg. He slowly made his way back to "Mrs. Lee's," where he was "laid alongside of Bob Burwell," who, after assuring himself that Ranny's wound was not life threatening, greeted him with "repeated grunts" that were "aggravatingly expressive" and could be translated to mean "what-did-I-tell-you-this-morning?"[16]

Nieces Louisa "Lute" and Laura "Lal" Burwell, ages twenty-four and twenty-one respectively at the start of the war, shared their Aunt Nettie's

14. MGL, 682 (Sept. 15, 1864), 371 (Apr. 30, 1863), 394 (June 2, 1863), 507 (Nov. 5, 1863), 529 (Dec. 15, 1863), 567 (Mar. 11, 1864), 617 (June 10, 1864), 705 (Oct. 12, 1864), 714 (Nov. 1, 1864), 748 (Dec. 25, 1864); LL, June 9, 1964; MGL, 230 (Sept. 13, 1862), 420 (June 21, 1863), 629 (July 1, 1864), 630 (July 1, 1864), 657 (Aug. 2, 1864), 674 (Aug. 31, 1864), 684 (Sept. 18, 1864), 685 (Sept. 19, 1864), 674 (Aug. 30, 1864).

15. MGL, 630 (July 1, 1864), 601 (May 16, 1864); Colt, *Defend the Valley*, 332–35.

16. Colt, *Defend the Valley*, 332–35.

musical skills, with Lute often called upon to sing and Lal offering music lessons. They not only provided Mary with extra hands for work in the household but also gave her more responsibility. She never begrudged them her protection; their father probably provided for some of their expenses. Indeed, she dreaded the future without them, knowing that they would eventually marry and make their own homes, "remov[ing] one of the few sources of happiness" she had left. Although, or maybe because, Mary never had children, she seems to have adopted her husband's nieces and nephews and treated them as she would have her own. Thoughts of their marrying could lead her into depression, and she wished they could stay with her the rest of her life, "if they were content."[17]

Nevertheless, she participated in their courtships. Mary's characteristic censoring of affairs of the heart from her record continued regarding her nieces. Early in the war Lal became engaged to Capt. Alexander "Sandy" Pendleton, a member of Stonewall Jackson's staff from Lexington, Virginia. For some reason, Pendleton's mother was not pleased with the match. In a letter to her husband, she wrote, "do you want to know who is to be your daughter? . . . the same Miss Laura Burwell I warned him against last winter." The reason Pendleton had to be warned against Lal can only be guessed. In defense of his intended, he had assured his mother that Lal was connected to a George Burwell, seeming to sidestep her father, P. L. C. Burwell, as if her father's reputation would not suffice. P.L.C.'s economic status would not have ruined Lal's standing with the Pendletons. It could be, however, that his presence at the hotel led him into questionable activities. An obscure reference by a soldier stationed in Winchester could apply to Burwell. Answering his sister's letter, Ted Barclay responded: "You wish me to go see the prettiest girl in town. The prettiest one and the belle is the daughter of the gambler; would you advise me to see her?" Although Barclay does not mention Burwell's name, his reference to "the belle," as distinct from being pretty, implies that she enjoyed a status equal to that of the Burwell sisters. It also seems reasonable to assume that a hotel owner would be well situated to put together a gaming table on a regular basis. In any event, the problems with Lal's reputation remain unclear.[18]

Mary Greenhow Lee's notations about the couple are brief and mysteri-

17. MGL, 657 (Aug. 1, 1864), 717 (Nov. 8, 1864), 876 (Oct. 5, 1865).
18. Alexander Pendleton to mother, Oct. 8, 1862, William Nelson Pendleton Papers (No. 1466), SHC; Ted Barclay, *Liberty Hall Volunteers: Letters from the Stonewall Brigade (1861–1864)*, ed. by Charles W. Turner (Berryville, Va.: Rockbridge, 1992), 50.

ous. She wrote merely, "Capt. Pendleton here to-night; affairs getting into a twist," and "Sandy came before church & there was a denouement." Captain Pendleton's version of the "denouement" was more revealing. For him it was more "an explosion." He evidently had no trouble writing about affairs of the heart. In a letter to his mother, he revealed that he had finally realized that he was infatuated, but not in love, with Lal. He arrived at the Lee home on a Sunday morning in October 1862 and was "most cordially received" by "the worthy Aunt in the parlour." When Lal appeared, he complimented her on how well she looked, which "was rather coolly received." Then, before he had a chance to deliver his well-rehearsed speech to end their engagement, to his "extreme astonishment," she dealt her own rejection of him, "final, immediate, unequivocal." Although surprised and without the "faintest conception" of her reasons, he also felt "most intensely delighted" to be "unexpectedly free again." Yet seeing her independence and fire, and realizing that she had not been trying to "cozen" him into marriage, piqued his interest in her once again. Whether or not Lal had gotten wind of his family's opinion of the match is unknown. In any event, when he approached her on the street a short time later, she "cut him dead" and walked away. By December, she had softened somewhat toward him, but soon after, he began seriously courting a Kate Corbin, whom he married and then left widowed with a small child before the war was over.[19]

The first young man Mary Greenhow Lee picked out for Lute was David Gregg McIntosh, a Confederate artillery officer who boarded at Lee's and whom she liked "exceedingly." She corresponded with him after he left and knitted slippers for him for Christmas. When the army came within reach of Winchester, McIntosh managed to stop by and even convalesced there once, recovering from typhoid after the battle of Sharpsburg. Mary's interest in McIntosh evidently was not shared by Lute. Although Mary reported that Captain McIntosh and Lute had gone riding together, making "a very fine looking couple," McIntosh complained later that, as he left to rejoin the army, "Miss Lieut. Burrill" gave him "a very chilling good bye with the tips of her fingers, which I shan't forget." The captain had evidently never seen Louisa's name written; "Lieut.," is an understandable spelling from a military man. ("Burrill" is the correct pronunciation of Burwell, at least for this historic family.)[20]

19. Alexander Pendleton to mother, Oct. 8, Dec. 5, 1862, Pendleton Papers; W. G. Bean, *Stonewall's Man: Sandie Pendleton* (Wilmington, N.C.: Broadfoot, 1987) 75; MGL, 692 (Sept. 24, 1864).

20. MGL, 481 (Sept. 20, 1863), 487 (Oct. 1, 1863), 423 (June 24, 1863), 485 (Sept. 25, 1863), 526 (Dec. 9, 1863), 541 (Jan. 14, 1864), 552 (Nov. 27, 1863), 248 (Oct. 25, 1862); David

Mary had more success with her second try at matchmaking for Lute. On June 12, 1864, Benjamin Mellichamp Cromwell, a young surgeon, wrote to the Confederate surgeon general, requesting transfer from field duty to hospital duty since there was "an adequate supply of medical officers in the field," and he "desire[d] to perfect the knowledge" he had gained by "more extended observations that can only be obtained in the Hospital." His request was denied, but because he was soon taken prisoner, he ironically got his wish when the Union command put him to work in the Winchester hospitals.[21]

Cromwell became "all the rage" among young Winchester women and soon met with Lee's approval as well when he began boarding with her. She found him "high toned and congenial," a "very nice gentleman," and then began noting significant exchanges between him and Lute. He had a "passion for music & was perfectly delighted . . . by Lute's voice," she wrote; she also recorded that Lute gave Cromwell private French lessons. Lee's record of Lute's courtship with Cromwell, the man she eventually married, is cryptic. The only sign in her journal that the young couple was becoming more serious is a mention that Mary and Cromwell had "a very private & confidential chat" and that she then "had a quiet talk with Lute." Besides mentioning the various activities the couple engaged in together, she also wrote, "a balcony scene has been going on, which portends a development." That development, of course, was marriage for the two after the war.[22]

Gregg McIntosh, "A Ride on Horseback in the Summer of 1910," 1910 (No. 1889), SHC, 21, photocopy; David Gregg McIntosh to Mary Greenhow Lee, Nov. 10, 1862, McIntosh Family Papers (Mss1M1895a), VHS; MGL, 244 (Oct. 17, 1862). In his memoir of the war, David McIntosh states that, while suffering the fever after the battle of Sharpsburg (Antietam), he stayed in "the hospitable care of Mrs. Fitzhugh Lee, afterwards spoken of as the Mother of the Confederacy." Since Mary Greenhow Lee's journal has him at her house recovering from typhoid after the battle, McIntosh has obviously confused in his memory Gen. Fitzhugh Lee's wife with Mrs. Hugh Holmes Lee. The southern army tended to name battles after nearby towns, while the northern army named battles for nearby landmarks (e.g., the First Battle of Manassas [southern] v. First Battle of Bull Run [northern]). Since this biography is of a southern woman, I have used the southern name for the battle.

21. Cromwell's obituary, *Confederate Veteran* 25, no. 8 (Aug. 1917): 374; order of J. P. Benjamin, acting secretary of war, Oct. 28, 1861; Appointment Certificate, May 26, 1862; and Cromwell to Moore, June 12, 1864, with responses on back by G. W. Briggs, Senior Surgeon, June 12, L. Guild, June 13, and S. Moore, June 20, 1864, Medical and Hospital Collection, ESB; George H. Weaver, M.D., "Surgeons as Prisoners of War: Agreement Providing for Their Unconditional Release during the American Civil War," *Bulletin of the Society of Medical History of Chicago* 4, no. 3 (Jan 1933): 249–61; MGL, 689 (Sept. 22, 1864).

22. MGL, 689 (Sept. 22, 1864), 693 (Sept. 22, 1864), 698 (Oct. 1, 1864), 700 (Oct. 4, 1864), 701 (Oct. 6, 1864), 702 (Oct. 7–9, 1864), 710 (Oct. 23, 1864), 717 (Nov. 6–7, 1864), 236 (Oct.

Courtships under Lee's roof during the war began as a result of the family mixing with boarders, despite the pledge Mary made the girls sign against such "designs." In part for this reason, Lee fought with every ounce of ingenuity she could muster when faced with the threat of boarding Union officers. For her own army, though, Lee was more obliging. Most of her boarders were officers, some sick or wounded. She also had "applications for board" from military surgeons and foreign correspondents. Her house attracted so many applications—as many as six in one day—until she had to turn some away or search out other arrangements for them. Having surgeons in the house provided both protection for the family "if the Yankees should come" and help with sick and wounded boarders. Further aid came when some of the men offered to assist with heavy work, mending locks and doorbells, moving furniture, tacking down carpets, and cutting and carrying firewood.[23]

Dislocation occurred then, even within her own home, as Mary Lee struggled to make room for everyone. The office, back parlor, and dining room became bedrooms, and a room in the attic became a "chamber" as well. A "Capt. Gibson from Georgia" applied for boarding and found himself "duly installed in the back room up stairs, with typhoid fever for his companion."[24]

For some reason, Mary adamantly resisted boarding women, no matter their regional origins or national sympathies. She mentioned this in her journal as though anyone reading it would understand, rendering explanation unnecessary. It could be that she did not want the additional responsibility of protecting an unrelated female under her roof, or perhaps she believed women to be more exacting in their expectations, especially difficult under the circumstances. Other possibilities include the fact that she felt competition from other women. It is true that she expressed less patience with unrelated women than with her female kin. In any event, she "never intended under any circumstances, taking ladies." When pressed, however, she "could

1, 1863), 238 (Oct. 4, 1862), 718 (Nov. 9, 1864), 722 (Nov. 18, 1864), 725 (Nov. 23, 1864); Bean, *Stonewall's Man*, 73–76.

23. MGL, 704 (Oct. 11, 1864), 233 (Sept. 20, 1862), 235 (Sept. 26, 1862), 236–37 (Oct. 1862), 241 (Oct. 11, 1862), 413 (June 16, 1863), 442 (July 23, 1863), 230 (Sept. 13, 1863), 232 (Sept. 16, 1862), 234 (Sept. 23–25, 1862), 237 (Oct. 1, 1863), 241 (Oct. 11, 1862), 246–47 (Oct. 21–24, 1862), 251 (Oct. 31, 1862), 256 (Nov. 8, 1862), 257 (Nov. 11, 1862), 413 (June 16, 1863), 420 (June 21, 1863), 431 (July 7, 1863), 433 (July 10, 1863), 436 (July 16, 1863), 437 (July 17, 1863), 442 (July 23, 1863), 444 (July 26, 1863), 499 (Oct. 23, 1863), 716 (Nov. 5, 1864), 722 (Nov. 16, 1864).

24. Ibid., 252 (Nov. 1, 1862), 431 (July 7, 1863), 433 (July 10, 1863), 261 (Nov. 21, 1862).

not refuse" Maj. Gen. John B. Gordon's wife, Frances "Fanny" Rebecca Har-relson Gordon, who arrived by stage one morning in July 1864.[25]

Fanny Gordon became known by Gordon's men as the "Bride of the Bat-tlefield" for her determination to follow her husband throughout the war. She left her children with her mother-in-law in Georgia when the war broke out and her husband offered his services to the 6th Alabama Infantry. By the time she arrived on Mary Greenhow Lee's doorstep, she had survived a train wreck, nursed her husband through the effects of five bullet wounds suffered in the battle of Sharpsburg, watched other engagements from hillsides, and seemed to have no trouble finding any conveyance available to be near her husband. General Early's initial frustration over Gordon's wife following the army caused him to grumble that he wished "the Yankees would capture Mrs. Gordon and hold her till the war is over!" He later offered grudging appreci-ation for how well she could keep up with the army when he often had to issue orders to his own men "against straggling." In the end, he bestowed high praise on Fanny Gordon when he told her, "General Gordon is a better soldier when you are close to him than when you are away; so hereafter, when I issue orders that officers' wives must go to the rear, you may know you're excepted."[26]

Whether or not Fanny's reputation for pluck and strength made the differ-ence, Mary Greenhow Lee ultimately became very fond of the "lovely" and "remarkable" woman who had "annoyed" her for intruding upon her family. In fact, when Fanny left again to follow her husband, Mary felt "as if parting with an old friend." With their relationship thus founded, Fanny took refuge at Mary's house various other times when the army was near Winchester, so much so that Mary noted Fanny's presence with the words "returned home."[27]

Taking in boarders during the war became a necessity for Lee and for the officers who stayed with her since there were few options open to the men, and she needed the extra income. The disruption in her life was rendered more tolerable when the guests were southern officers, and the experience proved useful later when she opened her first boarding house in Baltimore to make a living after the war.

Lee drew distinctions between "visitor" and "family," whether that family

25. Ibid., 638 (July 13, 1864); LL, July 12, 1864.

26. "The Bride of the Gray Chevalier," *Hollands' The Magazine of the South*, Feb. 1938, Gor-don Family Papers, Hargrett Library, University of Georgia, Athens, 19, 63.

27. MGL, 638–41 (July 13–18, 1864), 645 (July 20, 1864), 658 (Aug. 3, 1864), 659 (Aug. 5–6, 1864), 661 (Aug. 10, 1864), 662 (Aug. 11, 1864), 673 (Aug. 28, 1864), 684 (Sept. 17, 1864).

was related to her by kinship, friendship, or ownership. The former could expect to drop by for tea, talk with her on the street, or ask a favor. The latter could at any time be a member of her household. One hot summer evening in 1863, Mary fretted over the sad state of her supplies. "I have nothing in the house for dinner tomorrow," she wrote, "for the nine men, eight women & one child, constituting my *family*." One of those men, three of the women, and the child were slaves.[28]

One dynamic of the turmoil in Winchester came from the changing relations between whites and blacks. When General Banks first occupied the town, he and his soldiers spread the word among the slaves that Federal forces would defend their departure if they attempted to flee. A few at a time initially, then in larger numbers, slaves left the homes of their masters and were carried off in railroad cars or remained in town and congregated in hotels set up as temporary housing by the occupying officials.[29]

Early in the war, Union general Benjamin Butler issued an order that if slaves were property as southerners argued, then they would be considered "contraband" when within his lines and would be confiscated. Congress backed up his proclamation by law in August 1861, passing the First Confiscation Act. A growing resentment among Union soldiers was that they had left their farms to fight the war in the South, leaving their livelihood in the hands of their wives, families, and maybe a hired hand, while southern troops, at least in northern minds, had left slaves to keep their farms and plantations running as usual. This resentment, along with those soldiers and officers who were abolitionist in conviction, led to an easy assumption that they had the duty to liberate slaves in Union-occupied areas for both humanitarian and military reasons.[30]

28. Cynthia Kierner, "Hospitality, Sociability, and Gender in the Southern Colonies," *Journal of Southern History* 62, no. 3 (Aug. 1996): 449; MGL, 434 (July 13, 1863, emphasis added); Censer, *North Carolina Planters*, 7; Hareven, "Family Time," 60–61. For a discussion of how, under the patriarchal system and given the South's sense of honor and responsibility, white slaveholders explained all of the people under their care as members of their household—their family—see Eugene Genovese, "'Our Family, White and Black': Family and Household in the Southern Slaveholders' World View," in *In Joy and in Sorrow: Women, Family, and Marriage in the Victorian South, 1830–1900*, ed. Carol Blesser (New York: Oxford University Press, 1991), 69–87.

29. MGL, 7 (Mar. 13, 1862), 20, 22, 23, 25 (Mar. 1826), 75 (Apr. 22, 1862), 89 (May 4, 1962), 111 (May 25, 1862); JC, May 25, 1862; LL, May 24, 1862; McDonald, *Reminiscences of the War*, 79; JPC, Mar. 15, 20, 1862; Mrs. Philip Williams to Mrs. Averitt, Mar. 24, 1862, Philip Williams Family Papers (172 WFCHS), HL; Robert Y. Conrad to Union general Williams, Mar. 20, 1862, Holmes Conrad Papers (Mss1C7637b), VHS.

30. Paludan, *"A People's Contest,"* 65, 79.

Women left in control of slaves faced more management difficulties than their men encountered, for war opened up southern society to northern influence on the slaves to rebel. Less docile and obedient, slaves began to increasingly entertain notions of freedom. Although many had few options but to remain where they were, they still pushed at their restraint and made their management a more difficult task for the women left with the responsibility. Mary Greenhow Lee's example reinforces this argument since she had been the head of her household for several years when the war began. Her experiences with her slaves did not arise from a sudden change in command from master to mistress, but from wartime alterations of the institution.[31]

Lee is a female representative of the middle-class slaveholders in urban areas who, James Oakes has argued relative to small farmers, held more political sway in the antebellum South, from mere numerical strength, than the comparatively smaller group of planter elites studied elsewhere. The slaves in her household also experienced a distinctive type of small-town slavery in which, for the most part, there was no defined spatial separation between whites and blacks, at least in the form of slave quarters as on plantations. Also, as opposed to urban slavery, small-town blacks, whether free or slave, had less opportunity to blend into large populations to form black communities. But slaves in rural towns did have an opportunity to form bonds with slaves belonging to their owners' friends, especially since they were often sent on errands between households.[32]

Relations between the Lee women and their household slaves deteriorated as a result of war's interference. The women also contended with their slaves' fears from the violence surrounding them. News of the Union army returning could send the servants into a panic. Lee recorded that Emily, "who was terrified" and wanted to run to the countryside, "had to be reasoned with & to be assured that they were in far more danger out of town than in it." Betty also decided to go "into the country for safety" and packed her clothes to leave, but Laura "relieved her" of the clothes "and locked them up, . . . determined not to lose" both the clothes and the slave.[33]

Laura Lee complained that "the sauciness of the servants" was becoming "hard to bear" and that "even Betty" had become "infected with uppishness." Although Mary Greenhow Lee stated that she "despise[d] altercations with

31. See Faust, *Mothers of Invention*, 54–58.
32. James Oakes, *The Ruling Race: A History of American Slaveholders* (New York: Knopf, 1982); Tolbert, *Constructing Townscapes*, 193, 196, 204–5, 210.
33. MGL, 406–7 (June 1863); LL, June 13, 1863.

servants," she found it necessary on one occasion to "reprove" Emily for dis-
obeying her, "but not harshly." Even so, with the disruption of war and the
recent examples of slaves liberating themselves, Emily "became infuriated,
seized her bonnet . . . , & went off saying she was going to ask the Yankees
to take her away" but later returned. Fully aware that Emily had "the power
to go" if she chose, Lee wrote that she "would not raise [a] finger to prevent
it."[34]

It is evident that Lee would have preferred not having the additional responsibility of providing for slaves at this point, but she did not know how to
get along without them. Her journal reflects her uncertainty. "I feel like a
reprieved criminal each morning when I see ours come in my room." Stating
that she felt like a "reprieved criminal" could mean many things, but it is
doubtful that she thought she deserved punishment for owning slaves. More
likely, the simile reflects her feeling of doom at the prospect of doing all of
the housework without her "servants" rather than any feelings of guilt over
keeping them in bondage. What the slaves themselves felt can only be
guessed. Although it is clear that they had asserted their wishes in the past,
as evidenced by a reference Mary made about the family being reduced to a
diet during the war that her slaves would have complained about earlier, the
war certainly gave them more leverage than they could have employed in the
past.[35]

Sarah reported to Mary one day that, when a Union soldier on the street
tried to convince her that she was free, she maintained that she was not. This
exchange points to the complexity of black and white relations. Sarah must
have had a reason for relating the conversation to her owner. It could be that
she wanted to earn credit for her loyalty. It could be true also that on some
level she wanted to allay Mary's fears. The point is that, even though Sarah,
Emily, and Betty must have comprehended that their opportunities for escape had greatly improved, they never left Mary. In fact, in the end, she abandoned them. It is possible that the unpleasant scenes in town of suddenly
freed blacks trying to find shelter convinced them to stay put and wait for the
chaos to fade. It is also possible that they were comfortable where they were,
having known no other life but as slaves. Besides, at least one of them had a
growing family.[36]

34. MGL, 439 (July 22, 1863), 459–60 (Aug. 1863); LL, Apr. 14, Aug. 27, 1862, Aug. 13,
1863.

35. MGL, 300 (Jan. 20, 1863), 734 (Dec. 8, 1864).

36. Ibid., 662 (Aug. 12, 1864); JPC, July 28, 31, Aug. 18, 25, 1862; Jacqueline Jones, *Labor of
Love, Labor of Sorrow: Black Women, Work, and the Family, from Slavery to the Present* (New York:
Vintage, 1995), 46.

Emily delivered two babies within two and a half years, one of them, according to Laura, "in the most unexpected and unnecessary manner." The Lee women took the new additions to the household in stride, however, sewing baby outfits for them and giving Emily time to recover before asking her to return to her duties. In addition, Emily "married" a George Washington, a free black man who moved in with the Lees some time in 1864. Clearly, no minister in wartime Winchester would have performed a legal ceremony, but Mary considered George to be Emily's husband. So Mary's slaves did not leave and, in fact, added to her household staff, and so did, unwittingly, the enemy.[37]

The Lees' household slaves became such an attraction for the free-black male servants employed by Union officers in town that their kitchen became crowded with extra people, rendering it less productive. Mary complained that "Sheridan's staff, messing next door," was "a serious annoyance on that account," but she handled the problem by assigning tasks to her slaves' visitors. As Lee noted the visiting servants pitching in to aid her own slaves, cutting wood, taking messages, and "even scour[ing] for Emily," it is possible that she began to change her attitude toward them. She admitted to giving them an "occasional 'Thank you,'" which implies a sense of obligation toward them, though she probably rarely, if ever, bestowed the civility upon her own slaves.[38]

Therefore, the Lee household grew through the war, including family, "servants" both free and slave, and boarders. Having a houseful of people other than family strained Mary's nerves at times, but it provided diversions from war. They spent "cozy evening[s]" playing chess, backgammon, "consequences," reading to each other, "telling ghost stories," or making "a frolic of shelling . . . corn." They also planned, hosted, and attended parties when possible. When the house was vacated, not only by soldiers but also by the rest of the family on various excursions, Lee enjoyed "a good quiet time on the porch" with her thoughts. One of her favorite pastimes was an "interesting ramble" in the countryside. During good weather, walks were a frequent occurrence, with several women in the neighborhood joining the family in

37. MGL, 23 (Mar. 21, 1862), 354 (Apr. 12, 1863), 716 (Nov. 3, 1863), 718 (Nov. 9, 1863), 758 (Jan. 7, 1865); LL, Mar. 22, 1862, Nov. 5, 1864; MGL, 549 (Feb. 1, 1864), 675 (Sept. 1, 1864), 784 (Feb. 15, 1865); Brenda Stevenson, "Distress and Discord in Virginia Slave Families, 1830–1860," in *In Joy and In Sorrow: Women, Family, and Marriage in the Victorian South, 1830–1900*, ed. Carol Blesser (New York: Oxford University Press, 1991), 103.

38. MGL, 23 (Mar. 21, 1862), 354 (Apr. 12, 1863), 716 (Nov. 3, 1863), 718 (Nov. 9, 1863), 758 (Jan. 7, 1865); LL, Mar. 22, 1862, Nov. 5, 1864; MGL, 769 (Jan. 22, 1865).

their "brigade," as they called their "walking party." On occasion, their "brigade stormed the fortifications," as Lee termed their jaunts to former military strongholds outside of town.[39]

The women made their way to the Kernstown battlefield one evening and, while there, created a monument of stones in honor of the Louisiana Tigers, led by Brig. Gen. Richard Taylor, who had, according to Laura Lee, "charged down the hill upon the Yankees." In the week following, the younger women "added to the pile until it ha[d] become quite a respectable monument." When they ventured to the area again, they realized that "several groups of" Union soldiers were watching them, so the women made a show of "running about collecting the stones with great apparent eagerness and then waving . . . sun bonnets and parasols when [they] added to the pile." They then "found an old fruit can" and placed it "on the top pointing towards the Yankees." Before leaving, "Mary wrote on a leaf of her pocket book, 'Attention Yankees! This is a masked battery and highly dangerous, we charge you not to take it. Rebels,'" then left the can and its message for the soldiers to find. Thus the Lee women amused themselves, when they could, at the expense of the occupation army.[40]

When possible, and when there were no other amusements, they made sport of the soldiers from within their home. Lee enjoyed "listening to the repeated 'talkings' of the sentinels . . . on the pavement & sometimes" sitting on her porch. Or, when the streets were particularly treacherous with snow and ice, the whole family watched as Sheridan's staff passed her porch to go to dinner. Lee recorded that "they knew we were laughing at them & the more they tried to walk steadily, the more they slipped." She appreciated the diversion because she "had not had a good laugh" that day and "could find no other amusement." The effect of this ridicule on the officers can only be imagined.[41]

One characteristic deeply ingrained in Lee was her ability to find humor in bad circumstances. While she mocked Union officers, she was also quick to ridicule herself. When she wrote in her journal that she had "slipped on the ice," she added, "(I heard I did it very gracefully)." A severe cold settled in her jaw one rainy season, swelling her face until it appeared as if she "had an immense plug of tobacco in it," and she admitted, "I am an absurd looking person." Within a short period of time, Lee fell down the stairs twice, once while rushing to help chase Yankees from her door; she termed the incident "comic." Always one to look for a positive side to every situation, she also stated that, even though she was bruised, at least the noise of her fall "drove the men off."[42]

Most studies of women living through the Civil War dwell mainly on the dangers, responsibilities, and depression affecting their lives. It is true that war depressed, frustrated, and drained Mary Greenhow Lee, but an intensive study of her experiences contributes a three-dimensional illustration. Lee's intelligence helped her find solutions to the challenges of war. Her faith gave her added strength to stand up under the pressure. But her sense of humor kept her sane.[43]

Lee's goal was "to try to be light hearted"; she was "grateful to everyone who made [her] laugh." Consistently throughout her life, certain things drained her more than others: "middle aged evenings," "inaction," and pretending to be someone she was not. She much preferred "young company" and stimulants such as coffee or a good cause to work for. The war deprived her of good coffee most of the time but gave her something for which to fight. "All the old enthusiasm of my nature has revived in full force since the war," she wrote, and "it is an effort to keep within proper bounds, suitable to my age & grey hairs." There were times when the mature widow seemed very similar to the young Mary Greenhow playing pranks on her friends in Washington. For instance, one evening while visiting a neighbor, the Lee women were treated to "delicious pure Java coffee" with "white sugar" and "rich cream." It "exhilarated" them to such a degree that on the way home they "came down the street in a great gale." On an "expedition to Swartz Mill," the women encountered Swartz himself driving his wagon back to the mill. Lee, now in her forties and with hair turning gray, "sans ceremonie, . . . jumped into the wagon" with the other women, "made him drive" them to the mill, and "had a merry time." When friends played an April Fool's joke on her by "sending in empty plates & dishes, nicely covered up," she appreciated the foolery because it proved "there was life in the old land yet."[44]

To further lighten the otherwise dreary details of destruction and human suffering, Lee sprinkled humor throughout her journal. Wit helped her cling

42. Ibid., 774 (Jan. 31, 1865), 511 (Nov. 10, 1863), 104, 106–7 (May 1862).

43. Faust, *Mothers of Invention*, 18.

44. MGL, 732 (Dec. 5, 1864), 773 (Jan. 29, 1865), 487 (Sept. 30, 1863), 526 (Dec. 6, 1863), 582 (Apr. 18, 1864), 530 (Dec. 17, 1863), 760 (Jan. 9, 1865), 509 (Nov. 7, 1863), 343 (Apr. 1, 1863).

to the center of her identity and remain balanced, displaying a slightly irreverent opinion of the political and military leaders who had propelled the country into the insanity of war and then could not seem to either win it or end it. Reporting on a couple of Yankee skirmishes, she related that "some of their cavalry came dashing into town, thinking" that Confederates "were after them," when, in fact, it proved to be a cow that, Lee presumed, must "have had secession proclivities." She reported another "brilliant charge" the Yankees performed "through Main" Street, resulting in the "wounding [of] one woman & two dogs." Enjoying the "squabblings about the [1864] Presidential election" in the northern papers, she listed the six possible candidates and suggested that "Grant is their best man; I hope he gets the nomination," which would, of course, keep him busy elsewhere than the battlefield. Upon hearing a rumor that two Confederate generals, Fitzhugh Lee and Richard Ewell, were "in the Valley" and another "that Lincoln is dead," she decided that both were "too good to be true."[45]

During one Union occupation, Lee became so frustrated waiting for deliverance by her own army that she saved herself from going "crazy" by imagining it first on the pages of her journal. If not freed soon, she wrote, "I intend to turn Yankee—wear my nice clothes—eat the remains of a fruit cake I have been keeping for our men, &, in short, be utterly desperate." This is not to say that Lee never gave in to sadness. One of the most depressing problems she faced was an inability to alleviate the suffering she encountered at the hospitals each day. Sights of destruction tormented her as well. "This poor old town," she wrote, "is sorely afflicted." The strain of responsibility she felt for her household made her feel "utterly lonely" at times, and she would be overcome with a "finished feeling," having "nothing to live on or for." During one of her periods of depression, "weary & worn out," she informed her journal that her low energy level came from having the opposition gone. "When the Yankees were here," she wrote, "their outrages roused such a feeling of resistance that I was nerved for anything." In between occupations, however, uncertainty drained her.[46]

The "old enthusiasm" of Lee's nature revived when the presence of Union troops reminded her daily that she was being controlled by forces with whom she had not contracted a relationship. Lee was more than a Secessionist. True

45. Ibid., 509 (Nov. 9, 1863), 343 (Apr. 1, 1863), 107 (May 20, 1862), 177 (July 17, 1862), 468 (Sept. 1, 1863), 562 (Apr. 28, 1864), 757 (Jan. 6, 1865).
46. Ibid., 153 (June 23, 1862), 476 (Sept. 13, 1863), 691 (Sept. 24, 1864), 476 (Sept. 13, 1863), 529 (Dec. 16, 1863), 533 (Dec. 24, 1863), 472–73 (Sept. 8, 1863), 444 (July 26, 1863), 454 (Aug. 8, 1863), 206 (Aug. 19, 1862).

to her character, she was also a rebel, straining against the rules imposed upon her. When "several Yankees" stepped onto her porch one night and "shouted 'Lights out,'" even though the rest of the family blew out their candles, she "re-lit" hers almost immediately. When Lee heard that orders had been issued by the provost marshal "that no citizen was to be seen on the streets," she "immediately determined to go out, though" she had "had no such intention before." A member of the provost guard stopped her on the street, then escorted her home. When she asked him what he would have done if she had told him she "was going to, instead of from, home," he answered that he would have followed her "to ascertain the truth & when he found out he was deceived," he would have forced her to "follow him up and down the streets for two hours." It would have been uncharacteristic of her to yield to such a sentence.[47]

During a particularly bad spell in the weather, Sheridan "issued his royal release that all pavements were to be cleaned off in a given time." When the guard came around to ask her why she had not cleaned hers, Lee said that the "Yankees had stolen" her "negro men," and she could not do the job herself. As time went on, she gratefully reported that "the walking was very good" since everyone had been cleaning their pavements. She, however, had not done so, for she "did not choose to obey" Sheridan's orders. Instructions from occupation generals meant little to Lee, who had been raised to discern between those responsibilities she was obliged to meet and those she was not.[48]

War for Mary Greenhow Lee was abominable. She felt grief for the destruction of her "poor old town," anxiety for her friends and family in harm's way, and mournful for the men who died in battle. Yet the turmoil the war visited upon Winchester also enlivened her to fight back in ways suited to her character. Toward the men in her life for whom she had respect and with whom she accepted a subordinate position, Lee gladly behaved in a socially accepted manner. For those men who demanded her allegiance, however, or with whom she had not freely entered into a social relationship, she turned those same standards into weapons to use against them.

47. Ibid., 131 (June 5, 1862), 592 (May 5, 1864).
48. Ibid., 752 (Dec. 31, 1864), 754 (Jan. 2, 1865), 775 (Feb. 1, 1865), 776 (Feb. 3, 1865), 777 (Feb. 5, 1865).

7

"Nothing to Interfere with My Soldier Work"

Mary Greenhow Lee's Warfare Disguised as Housekeeping

*O*n a summer day in 1863, Mary Greenhow Lee and her family worked in the garden behind her home on North Market Street. As they "dug the manure & wheeled it down to the [garden] bed," Union soldiers watched from a distance, and Lee felt certain that it "very much amused" the soldiers "to see the Secesh, the F.F.V.s, working like day labourers." A reduced household staff, the scarcity of free labor for hire, and the irksome, constant reminder for Lee that she was under the oppressive scrutiny of an unfriendly army set this scene. War or no war, management of the household still required her attention. More important to Lee, housework camouflaged her support of the southern army, offering a legitimate means to exercise her patriotism.[1]

It is evidence of Lee's strong character that she continued her housekeep-

---

1. MGL, 399 (June 8, 1863). "F.F.V." stands for "First Families of Virginia," implying descent from colonial founders and its attendant status. Portions of this chapter reprinted from Sheila Phipps, "'Their Desire to Visit the Southerners': Mary Greenhow Lee's Visiting Connexion," in *Negotiating Boundaries of Southern Womanhood: Dealing with the Powers That Be*, ed. Janet Coryell, Thomas Appleton Jr., Anastatia Sims, and Sandra Gioia Treadway (Columbia: University of Missouri Press, 2000), by permission of the University of Missouri Press.

ing tasks at the same time she added the responsibilities of taking care of southern soldiers to her schedule. The work she did for her family and for the Confederacy gave her a sense of fulfillment. Socially defined roles for women kept Lee out of uniform and safe from battle, but she found ways to be useful that also made a vital difference for the Confederate soldiers within her reach. She aided the war effort by working in hospitals, building up a contraband store for her army, and running an underground mail service. Lee applied the phrase "soldier work" to her additional responsibilities during the conflict, implying that the extension of her normal homemaking duties to caring for soldiers was work she did *for* soldiers and, on another level, work she did *as* a soldier, a vent for her patriotism that also accommodated her gender restrictions.[2]

Lee's experiences during the war fell well within the "Cult of True Womanhood," the ideal for white, middle-class women in nineteenth-century American society. Leading a pious life, working primarily for others, and giving of herself, the nineteenth-century woman was charged mainly with maintenance of the domestic realm. Creating a safe and cheerful atmosphere at home, she was expected to focus on the emotional well being of family members, temper her anger, and comfort the sick.[3]

Lee's war work had a nurturing character not unlike the extension of women's work observed in antebellum associations. Although historians have believed that the plantation economy of the South hindered the growth of benevolent organizations, more recent research has refuted this assumption. In Virginia around the beginning of the nineteenth century, women began forming organizations not so much to correct the corruption brought on by capitalism, but to take up where communities and churches had left off. Where local governments drew back from helping the community's poor, Virginia's women formed associations to fill that need. Although almost excluded from the public sphere, women created a space for themselves in service to the public, writing constitutions for their benevolent organizations, electing officers, and raising money. By 1850, women were taking their nurturing and selfless concern for others and applying it to fill civic obligations. It is not certain that Mary Greenhow Lee was involved in reform organizations before the war, but she was active in several at the beginning of the

2. Ibid., 814 (Apr. 16, 1865), 573 (Mar. 24, 1863).

3. Rosemarie Tong, *Feminist Thought: A Comprehensive Introduction* (Boulder, Colo.: Westview, 1989), 137; Cott, *Bonds of Womanhood*, chap. 2; Welter, "Cult of True Womanhood," 135, 141, 143, 145; Ryan, *Cradle of the Middle Class.* For the southern view of the ideal woman, see Anne Firor Scott, *Southern Lady*, chaps. 2–3.

conflict. She named two in her journal—the County Society and the Harmon Society—formed by Winchester women to provide uniforms for the soldiers.[4]

Lee found war to be a "barbarous mode of settling national disputes," but southern editorials had persuaded her that she had a role to fill in the struggle. Warfare gains legitimacy through national rhetoric, compelling citizens to take part. Young men grow up hearing war stories and understanding that there is a certain virtue in being willing to die for a cause. Women are told war stories as well and have been summoned to help on the home front and to applaud the heroism of their men. Men fought. Women did not. Men risked their lives. Women merely risked their men. Mary wrote, "if I were only a man," but "being only a woman & of no account, I have to fold my hands & try to keep quiet & calm." At another point she considered disguising herself so she could enter "the ranks & get shot," forcing "the Yankee government . . . to waste the lead that might be used to kill a better person." Nonetheless, she created a way to become an asset to the Confederate cause that helped her compensate for being "only a woman" in a war zone.[5]

The rhetoric of the South that fueled Lee's patriotism compelled her to offer up the men in her life to the dangers of battle in direct contrast to the nurturing role she had grown up to fill. She wrote that it was "sad to see these men . . . preparing to go out to hunt the enemy" but felt it her duty to "cheer & encourage them & repress" her "own feelings." To sustain that sacrifice, Lee needed to cling to her patriotic impulse. In so doing, she searched for ways, compatible with her role in society, to fight the men of the opposition while at the same time continuing to nurture and comfort the men with whom she sided.[6]

---

4. Faust, "Peculiar South Revisited," 92; Suzanne Lebsock, *Virginia Women, 1600–1945: "A Share of Honour"* (Richmond: Virginia State Library, 1987), 61, 70; Lebsock, *Free Women of Petersburg*, 211; MGL, 47 (Apr. 1, 1862); C. A. Porter Hopkins, ed., "An Extract from the Journal of Mrs. Hugh H. Lee of Winchester, Va., May 23–31, 1862," *Maryland Historical Magazine* 53 (1958): 380. For northern women's perspectives during the war, see Jeanie Attie, "Warwork and the Crisis of Domesticity in the North," in *Divided Houses: Gender and the Civil War*, ed. Catherine Clinton and Nina Silber (New York: Oxford University Press, 1992); and Elizabeth D. Leonard, "'Men Did Not Take to the Musket More Commonly Than Women to the Needle': Annie Wittenmyer and Soldiers' Aid," chap. 2 of *Yankee Women: Gender Battles in the Civil War* (New York: W. W. Norton, 1995).

5. MGL, 185 (July 1862); Drew Gilpin Faust, introduction to *Macaria; or, Altars of Sacrifice*, by Augusta Jane Evans (Baton Rouge: Louisiana State University Press, 1992), xiii; MGL, 565 (Mar. 1863), 449 (Aug. 1, 1863). See also Faust, "Altars of Sacrifice."

6. MGL, 646 (July 21, 1864).

Gender construction is a bundle of expectations and limitations based upon sex. Women during the American Civil War are usually studied in light of their society's expectations that they be protected from warfare, nurture their families and soldiers, and be spared the rigors of violent conflict. Such a perspective characterizes women as witnesses or victims of the grand drama, rarely as participants. Mary Greenhow Lee's life, however, exemplifies a more complex view of women's warfare roles. Her strong character, patriotism, gender awareness, and class-based sense of responsibility combined to help her do battle within the confines of her socially acceptable role.

When Confederate general Thomas J. "Stonewall" Jackson evacuated Winchester on March 11, 1862, and Federal general Nathaniel P. Banks led his troops in the next day for the town's first Union occupation, Lee recorded in her journal, "all is over and we are prisoners in our own houses." She did not remain confined to her home but went out frequently "on the street to attend to . . . business." Instead of merely running a household, Lee's daily life became dramatically complicated with the intrusion of wartime activities. Housekeeping continued as before but became much more difficult, especially since two of her male slaves ran away, leaving fewer hands to do the work. She added to her schedule, supplying the hospitals and tending to wounded and sick soldiers, operating an underground mail service, and obtaining, storing, and distributing contraband goods for the army.[7]

Lee's "soldier work" did not lessen her duties as the head of her household. She still had housework to oversee, food to supply, wood to procure for heat, and clothing to find for her two sisters-in-law, two nieces, and the men, women, and children she held as slaves. War simply made the process more difficult. In addition, she sacrificed all of the money and labor she could spare to build up a store of supplies for the soldiers and other patients in the hospitals. When soldiers were close by or when she could send supplies through the lines, she worked to have the items they needed available.[8]

7. Ibid., 4–5 (Mar. 12, 1862), 60 (Apr. 11, 1862). See Linda Kerber, "Separate Spheres, Female Worlds: The Rhetoric of Women's History," *Journal of American History* 75, no. 1 (June 1988): 9.

8. Lee claimed only two slaves in the 1860 personal property assessment, although during the war she lost two male slaves—Hugh and Evans—while three females—Betty, Emily, and Sarah—remained with her. On occasion she used the possessive "our" or "my" when speaking of slaves belonging to other family members who lived in her home. A slave named William belonged to James Murray Mason, who left him in the Lees' care when the Masons fled Winchester. Adding to the household during the war, Emily delivered two babies within two and a half years. She later married George Washington, a free black in Winchester, who also became a member of Mary Greenhow Lee's "family." See Winchester Personal Property Tax Lists,

At the opening of the conflict, women who owned slaves were not immediately faced with an increased demand on their own labor, though they did take on the burden of handling household finances and securing their property. Later, however, women in households throughout the South took on chores they had not attempted before; historian Drew Gilpin Faust estimates that many of them resented or feared the changes to which they had to adapt because they had not been reared to feel competent in the new skills required of them. Mary Greenhow Lee did complain at times about the new labor she had to perform, but she rarely mentioned feeling unequal to, or fearful of, the tasks, only weary from the demands on her time. As a widow, Lee had clearly become used to assuming the financial responsibilities for her household. In addition, her strong character served her well when circumstances demanded extra duties of her during the war.[9]

The work that tired Lee the most, however, was that which had been hers to oversee all along, housekeeping. It depressed her; she could not "tolerate" it. Besides the accumulation of the normal dust and disarrangement that comes from everyday living, the addition of military men as boarders in her home created even more work to keep her house in top order. "Whitewashing," cleaning windows, "putting down matting," "dismantl[ing] the parlours," "taking up carpets," and putting up curtains all required the same amount of labor and organization during war that they had in peacetime. Now, however, "all of these extra jobs had to be done regardless of the cannon pointing" at the town. Spring cleaning took on new meaning as well, for they were not only shaking out the "dust of ages" but also preparing for another season of battles. Most of the armies went into winter quarters during the colder months, so the hottest campaigns and the highest casualty lists occurred from spring through fall. Spring cleaning for Lee meant making her home ready to receive patients and boarders and ensuring free time later for her attendance at the hospitals.[10]

1860, LOV; MGL, 61 (Apr. 12, 1862), 23 (Mar. 21, 1862), 354 (Apr. 12, 1863), 716 (Nov. 3, 1863), 718 (Nov. 9, 1863), 419 (June 6, 1863), 452 (Aug. 4, 1863), 641 (July 18, 1864), 344 (June 4, 1863), 522 (Nov. 27, 1863), 537 (Jan. 3, 1864), 654 (July 28, 1863), 339 (Mar. 27, 1863), 346 (Apr. 6, 1863), 365 (Apr. 24, 1863).

9. Faust, *Mothers of Invention*, 22, 49, 52; LeeAnn Whites, *The Civil War as a Crisis in Gender: Augusta, Georgia, 1860–1890* (Athens: University of Georgia Press, 1995).

10. MGL, 297 (Jan. 15, 1863), 555 (Apr. 10, 1864), 109 (May 22, 1862), 172 (July 13, 1862), 176 (July 1862), 340 (Mar. 28, 1862), 396 (June 5, 1863), 399 (June 9, 1863), 458 (Aug. 14, 1863), 485–86 (Sept. 1863), 584 (Mar. 1, 1864), 597–98 (May 1864), 604 (May 1864), 682 (Sept. 15, 1864).

Gardening and sewing were additional tasks on her list of responsibilities that continued as before, only now with more frustration. The garden itself was a source of food for the family and, therefore, a necessity, except that when she thought about "horses wallow[ing] over the beds" and the fact that the family might "be turned out & sent South in a day," she believed it to be a "hopeless task." So that no one would "reproach" her "for having neglected it," Lee kept up the gardening even while admitting that it was her "pet aversion." Another job women were expected to perform graciously was sewing, a task Lee hated. During the war, most of her sewing involved "fixing up old clothes" and making dresses for her female slaves. Scarcity of material forced Lee to remodel outdated dresses into new ones. In fact, she "cut out a new linen garibaldi" from a garment twenty-one years old. The only sewing occupation Lee seemed to enjoy was a patriotic one. "When I am not jobbing about, & decency compels me to employ my fingers," she wrote, "I knit for the soldiers." She procured yarn from wherever she could to provide socks for her army, even resorting to unraveled tenting material at one point.[11]

Lee's soldier work required her to take on household tasks she had not previously performed. Slaveowning women often described work done in the household as their own when, in fact, the labor came from their slaves, the mistresses merely overseeing or directing the tasks. In other words, white women seemed to view their slaves as extensions of their own hands. Mary Greenhow Lee also used the pronouns "I" or "we" when describing work actually performed by her slaves. There were instances in her journal, however, when she stopped herself from taking full credit for the work. For example, after writing "I have been gardening . . . energetically," she added, "that is to say *having it done*," which suggests that she refrained from taking credit

11. Ibid., 74 (Apr. 21, 1862), 109 (May 22, 1862), 359, 368 (Apr. 1863), 569–70 (Mar. 17, 1864), 581, 584, 586 (Apr. 1864), 596–98, 606, 608 (May 1864), 687 (Sept. 20, 1864), 310 (Feb. 9, 1863), 321 (Feb. 26, 1863), 487 (Sept. 1863), 613, 615 (June 1864). A garibaldi, named for the Italian military hero Guiseppe Garibaldi and the garments he and his troops wore, was a shirt and waist outfit, usually with full sleeves sometimes pleated or gathered where they met at the bodice. What made the ensemble a garibaldi was the shirt, so it is uncertain if Lee made a full shirtwaist or merely the shirt in this reference. Since a garibaldi requires a good deal of material, it is probable that she could only produce the shirt from old cloth. See Joan L. Severa, *Dressed for the Photographer: Ordinary Americans and Fashion, 1840–1900* (Kent, Ohio: Kent State University Press, 1995), 197, 227, 403, 496; MGL, 522 (Nov. 27, 1863), 548 (Jan. 30, 1864), 577 (June 1864). The socks Lee knitted from this tent material are located at the Museum of the Confederacy in Richmond, Va.

for actual work that others performed. She also hired help when available for housework and "attended to having the garden ploughed."[12]

Free labor was scarce during the war, further limiting Lee's soldier work, and she learned on more than one occasion that, even though a person might promise to work for her, there was no guarantee that he would show up for duty. In writing about such matters, Lee often made the description almost poetic in its presentation, giving the reader an idea that she took the problem in stride: for example, "I went in various directions this evening to see about a gardener; the man who was to plough the potato ground, said he had no horse; I got him a horse & then he discovered he had no plough." This incident could have made her angry, but her depiction of it suggests that she was simply amused over her own bad luck. In each of these instances, the labor she used was free labor, not that of her slaves, all of which points to the complications war brought to her responsibilities for her family.[13]

Conscious of the social demands on nineteenth-century women of Lee's class, prescriptive literature advised them to make the most efficient use of time for housework to free them for more enriching activities, making them both interested and interesting in regard to others. Whether using slaves or hired help, middle-class women were expected to "do" housework by organizing it and overseeing it, not by performing most of the labor. War, however, necessitated the need to summon all possible hands to work, thus Lee performed some household chores herself. She mentioned "helping Emily" on a number of occasions, and she ironed her own family's clothing, "45 pieces" in one day. Trimming the raspberry bushes left her "hands and arms . . . so scratched & full of splinters" that she had trouble holding the pen to write in her journal. In another instance she had planned to bake sugar cakes, only giving the task to Sarah to do after realizing that she was too ill to bake them herself.[14]

Although she "dread[ed] having to do . . . servant's work" because she "despise[d] it more & more each day," she did not complain about it as though it was beneath her but for the same reasons that most people hate it: house-

---

12. Fox-Genovese, *Plantation Household*, 109–30; MGL, 570 (Mar. 18, 1864, emphasis added), 384 (May 21, 1863).

13. MGL, 356 (Apr. 14, 1863).

14. Alan Grubb, "House and Home in the Victorian South: The Cookbook as Guide," in *In Joy and in Sorrow: Women, Family, and Marriage in the Victorian South, 1830–1900*, ed. Carol Blesser (New York: Oxford University Press, 1991), 174; MGL, 381 (May 17, 1863), 383 (May 19, 1863), 386 (May 23, 1863), 394 (June 2, 1863), 396 (June 5, 1863), 725 (Nov. 24, 1864), 728 (Nov. 30, 1864), 513 (Nov. 14, 1863), 745–46 (Dec. 23, 1864).

work is messy, boring, and tiring. Describing a day of "thoroughly cleaning" several upstairs rooms, she admitted, "I took off my hoops, tied up my head & was a figure of fun." For the most part, however, she did not like housekeeping because it hindered her "soldier work."[15]

The soldier work that required most of Lee's energy involved taking care of the sick and wounded. As early as January 1862, Union sympathizer Julia Chase reported, "our town has become a complete hospital," and Winchester retained that image through most of the war. All the buildings that could be commandeered into service took on the task of housing the sick and wounded: hotels, churches, and private homes. The Union Hotel became a hospital under General Banks and remained so until December 1864, when "the poor old" structure "fell down & seven Yankees were crushed in the ruins." At one point there were twenty buildings in town designated as "hospitals," needed most after some of the worst battles. It is doubtful that the casualties actually coming to Winchester ever reached the rumored numbers, but word through town after major engagements gave women pause to wonder how they would be able to handle the casualties. Nearly three thousand wounded were expected in Winchester after the battle of Sharpsburg, and residents believed that five thousand casualties were headed their way after Gettysburg. Occasionally, generals sent word to town that their wounded were on the way, such as the "dispatch . . . from Jackson, to the ladies to prepare for his sick & wounded." Lee watched sadly as ambulances arrived, then got to work, along with other women in town, to meet the needs of the ailing.[16]

When Lee's "soldier work" extended to "hospital work," one of her most important tasks was to provide food. Scarcity affected her own family until they "adopt[ed] the prevailing style of two meals a day instead of three" and began accepting "good things" from their friends. But she tried to ensure that the patients in the hospitals had appropriate things to eat, depending upon their needs. Besides the "tea, coffee, bread, flaxseed tea & lemonade," "hot biscuits & (rusks)," "cimblins" (or "sago"), and "blanc mange and marmalade" she took to the hospitals, she also begged others for "some lemons for [her] wounded men" and treats "of apples and onions" to fend off scurvy. Keeping track of which patients had the capability of taking solid foods, she "sent

15. MGL, 176 (July 16, 1862), 396 (May 1863), 573 (Mar. 25, 1864).

16. JC, Jan. 12, 1862; MGL, 741 (Dec. 16, 1864), 690 (Sept. 23, 1864), 125 (June 1, 1862), 228 (Sept. 10, 1862), 430 (July 6, 1863); JC, Sept. 20, 1862; MGL, 228 (Sept. 10, 1862), 631 (July 4, 1864), 672 (Aug. 27, 1864).

chicken soup and rice to one room . . . , blanc mange to one—baked apples to another set," and "currant jelly to one poor Lt., . . . wounded in the mouth," who could "only take liquids." A patient named Ivey asked her for "egg-pie" and listed what he imagined to be the recipe. When she presented it to him, "he pronounced [it] excellent." Upon finding that men in the "Louisiana ward" at the Union "had not been well fed," Lee took the "ward master home" with her and had him carry "soup and milk" back to the hospital.[17]

Nursing during the Civil War did not become the gateway to equality that has been supposed. Scholars find that the work performed by most southern women during the war is better designated "hospital work" rather than the conventional perception of "nursing," for their activities had more to do with seeing to men's needs than to their infirmities. For the most part, this argument agrees with Mary Greenhow Lee's activities in the hospitals, yet she approached her hospital duties with the determination of a combatant. Her hospital visits and errands through town, making sure that supplies were available to keep the hospitals running, at times wore her down, saddened and depressed her, and took her away from her family responsibilities. Yet the activity gave her one of the most immediate ways to aid in the war effort and express her patriotism. Other women of leading families in Winchester made the same commitment, providing constant care for wounded and sick soldiers in their town.[18]

Although the nursing care women gave their families was supposed to have come naturally, modesty dictated that they not be intensively involved in nursing men in the hospitals. For the most part, male nurses filled that function. Lee did not comment specifically on actual nursing restrictions, but she did note how "murderous" the "horrible minie balls" were to the men, checked for a "bright hectic flush" on patients' cheeks, and commented on the "shocking wounds" of one group of men coming in who had "so many" wounds "in the face, . . . shot through the jaws & tongue." She also helped dress wounds.[19]

17. MGL, 717 (Nov. 1864), 761 (Jan. 11, 1865), 33 (Mar. 25, 1862), 36 (Mar. 26, 1862), 138 (June 9, 1862), 416 (June 17, 1863), 502 (Oct. 26, 1863), 435 (July 15, 1863), 699 (Oct. 2, 1864), 742 (Dec. 17, 1864), 746 (Dec. 23, 1864), 674 (Aug. 30, 1864), 486 (Sept. 28, 1863), 693 (Sept. 26, 1864).

18. Faust, *Mothers of Invention*, 102, 109, 110, 111, 112. For references to Lee's work in the hospitals, see MGL, 33–36, 137–40,147–48, 177–78, 183–84, 228–37, 277–81, 430–40, 455–61, 485–91, 633–42, 698–703, 716–22. See also Leonard, " 'No Place for a Woman'? Sophronia Bucklin and Civil War Nursing," chap. 1 of *Yankee Women*.

19. Faust, *Mothers of Invention*, 102, 109, 110, 111, 112; MGL, 48 (Apr. 2, 1862), 278 (Dec. 23, 1862), 233 (Sept. 1862).

Lee often approached her soldier work as if she were an officer. Because of her position in Winchester society and as the head of her household, she commandeered others into her service. She set Lute and Lal Burwell to rolling bandages and received donations of furniture and sheets for the hospitals. "I staid some hours distributing supplies & running about to collect more. . . . By to-morrow," she wrote, "I hope things will be more in order & some stores collected." Lee also saw to patients' personal needs, locating crutches, pipes, tobacco, "some gospels," fans, shirts, tin cups, and "tracts" to give them as requested. There were days when she not only fed patients but also spent time "preaching to some, scolding some, cheering others, writing letters, reconciling differences," and "getting whatever clothing" they might need. For patients in which she had taken a keen interest, Lee even made arrangements for their burial. When a man named Pringle died, she acquired "a lot in the cemetery for him, . . . placed flowers over him, . . . then followed him to his very grave." For another, she "found enough white flowers" in November 1864 "for a wreath" and placed it on his breast before they closed the coffin.[20]

Visits from women in town must have given the patients a lift. Owen J. Edwards of the 114th New York Volunteers woke up on September 20, 1864, after the third battle of Winchester, to find that his arm had been amputated. The surgeons moved him "to Winchester to the old church hospital" a couple of days later. Mary Greenhow Lee did not serve at any of the church hospitals, restricting her time to the Union and the York Hotels, but Edwards's experiences must have been similar to the patients she attended. Besides his "old stub of arm paining [him] some," his main complaint was boredom. "I have nothing to do here," he wrote, "but lay in bed," a grievance probably similar to many of the patients once they began to heal. Any visit from the town's women, therefore, would have been a welcome diversion.[21]

Lee's soldier work had the nurturing and spiritual character expected of nineteenth-century women. "The men always have so much to tell me," Lee wrote, "or ask me to do for them," but she asserted that it was her "chief pleasure to contribute to the comfort of" her soldiers. During one visit, Lee noticed a man she called "the poor red headed Catholic" in a "dying condition," and when he expressed interest "in the plan of salvation" she had "told him of," she wrote "down a simple prayer for him that he might read it all

20. MGL, 63 (July 4, 1864), 724 (Nov. 21, 1864), 634 (July 8, 1864), 635 (July 9, 1864), 700 (Oct. 4, 1864), 712 (Oct. 26, 1864), 708 (Oct. 19, 1864), 234 (Sept. 23, 1862), 715 (Nov. 2, 1864).

21. Owen J. Edwards Diary, HL, typescript. Edwards was a member of Co. D, 114th New York Volunteer Infantry.

day"; he was dead by the time she returned to visit him again. Writing was a large part of her hospital work. Since many of the men could not write, or they were too injured to do so, she wrote "notes and letters . . . to their friends" and families. When soldiers died, she notified their families when she had complete names and addresses.[22]

An excerpt from one of South Carolinian David Gregg McIntosh's letters shows that he understood Mary Greenhow Lee and the basis of her war effort. After expressing a wish that she could get more rest, McIntosh added, "though I sometimes think that without some wounded and sick Confederates to look after, or Yankees to circumvent, you [would] be at a loss as to how to exercise your patriotic energies." This is key to understanding the force Lee put into her work for the Confederates; she needed a vent for her feelings. When battles raged near enough for men to stop in town afterward, taking advantage of the hospitality of Winchester's female patriots, Lee's "soldier work" included "the feeding process," which she continued as long as she "had a mouthful of food" left to offer. Her dining-room table would be surrounded by exhausted, hungry soldiers, then she would clear the table and fix it again "for stragglers." Even after she thought she was done with the "feeding," she would hear "the bell ring and two or three more" weary Rebels would sit down to her table. She also fed captured Confederates before they were marched out of town, sending them "bread, soup, coffee," and "bacon and greens." Energy for the ordeal came from her patriotism. Food for the table, however, provided another dilemma.[23]

Her work included efforts to provide for both her family and her army, often stymied by both finances and availability of supplies. Although she had various financial resources, interruptions in mail delivery kept some of that money from coming in until at times she was past hoping for it. After assessing her situation one evening, she figured she would "have but twenty-seven cents" for two months' expenses. Money dribbled in from members of her network of family and friends who owed her money, such as her brother-in-law, William Powell in Loudoun County, and she occasionally rented out her stable to people who followed the army into town and sold wheat to Swartz Mill, presumably grown on land left from Elizabeth Lee's estate. Taking in boarders added to her income, but she also had to supply food for them as

22. MGL, 466 (Aug. 28, 1863), 468 (Aug. 30, 1863), 695 (Sept. 28, 1864), 699 (Oct. 1864), 688 (Sept. 21, 1864).

23. David Gregg McIntosh to Mary Greenhow Lee, Oct. 21, 1863, McIntosh Family Papers (Mss1M1895a), VHS; MGL, 116–17 (May 29, 1862), 412 (June 15, 1863), 678 (Sept. 6, 1864), 688 (Sept. 21, 1864).

part of the agreement. Lee never mentioned what she charged for a night's room and board, but other soldiers in the Valley recorded costs ranging from $1.50 to $4.00 at other boarding houses, with the higher cost the most often required. Some of her income came from her investments, from which she became forced to draw principal since it was not earning interest enough to live on. Giving up her investments was her positive option to "starvation," but she realized she had little choice and finally admitted, "I shall have to work hard the rest of my life."[24]

For her army, however, Lee was not too proud to take donations. At times, men who boarded with her and saw the work she was doing left money behind for her "sick family at the hospitals." She also "sent off . . . begging letters for Northern money for the soldiers, to Baltimore & New York," and once received ten dollars "mysteriously placed in [her] hands." Her sister-in-law Rose Greenhow sent "$20.00 in Greenbacks" that arrived by going first to "a Mrs. Boyd" and then to Ned Brent in Baltimore, who sent it on to Lee in the care of a resident on his way back to Winchester. Throughout the war, Baltimore members of Lee's circle continually funneled money or supplies her way by whatever clandestine means they could find. One of these benefactors was Henrietta Henly Smith, a childhood friend of Lee and wife of Bayard Smith. Another was Dr. Philip C. Williams, son of Lee's lawyer. Her network extended even to Philadelphia and New York, from where she gained additional economic support. The dispersion of these members to other urban areas, especially those outside of the Confederacy, proved to be a boon to Lee in her soldier work. She kept track of the considerable funds accumulated to supply the soldiers in an "account book of money received for Confederates & disbursements."[25]

Although cash eventually dribbled in, Lee's soldier work taxed her further in actually spending it. "It is tantalizing," she wrote, "to have plenty of money & nothing to buy with it." War interrupts commerce in no small way.

24. MGL, 519 (Nov. 23, 1863), 520 (Nov. 24, 1863), 523 (Nov. 28, 1863), 614 (June 4, 1864), 620 (June 15, 1864), 735 (Dec. 10, 1864), 500 (Oct. 24, 1863), 520 (Nov. 24, 1863), 523 (Nov. 28, 1863), 725 (Nov. 25, 1864), 525 (Dec. 5, 1863); James M. Cadwallader Diary, J. Paul Cadwallader Collection (683 THL), HL, Feb. 5–8, 1864; MGL, 180 (July 20, 1862), 182 (July 21, 1862), 479 (Oct. 20, 1863), 531 (Dec. 19, 1863), 567 (Mar. 11, 1864), 614 (June 4, 1864), 620 (June 15, 1864), 650 (July 23, 1864), 735 (Dec. 10, 1864), 744 (Dec. 22, 1864), 766 (Jan. 19, 1865), 744 (Dec. 22, 1864).

25. MGL, 246 (Oct. 22, 1862), 304 (Feb. 2, 1863), 470 (Sept. 4, 1863), 467 (Aug. 30, 1863), 314 (Feb. 15, 1863), 467 (Aug. 30, 1863), 507 (Nov. 4, 1863), 527 (Dec. 10, 1864), 346–47 (Apr. 6, 1863).

In Winchester the occupying government did have supplies on hand, but citizens had to apply to the provost marshal for a permit to purchase goods from the sutlers by first taking the oath of allegiance to the United States, a demand that Mary Greenhow Lee never fulfilled. There were several reasons why the Union commanders insisted upon these criteria: to assure that enough supplies were first available to their army, to deter hoarding, and to guard against hostile citizens supplying the enemy. To an extraordinary degree, whether because of her status or her attitude, Lee was able to get around the prerequisites to purchasing goods. After a year in the military environment, she wrote, "it is strange how those people [sutlers] all sell to me; I have bought six or seven hundred dollars worth from them, without permits." She had other means of supply as well. If friends obtained a pass or planned to run a blockade, they asked her for a shopping list they might fill. At one point she had "eight different lists out, some, months old."[26]

Lee's role of "shopper" during the war entailed much more than a list, a basket, and a walk to the Market House. Trying to fill her shopping needs herself demanded more soldier work. Her word choice in describing this effort suggests that she indeed saw herself taking on the role of a combatant. Most of her purchases came "by dint of looking out for & embracing every opportunity" or by making "purchases on the sly" or "sub rosa," receiving goods "smuggled through" the lines by those willing to "run the blockade," by "fortunate inspiration," or by "a lucky hit." Instead of going shopping, Lee "went out on a chase," ventured "on a foraging expedition," "laid the train," and "tramp[ed] through the mud." In one instance she decided that if Union general Joseph "Hooker ha[d] the same difficulty in crossing the sacred soil at the Rappahannock" that she encountered seeking out some organdy, then Gen. Robert E. Lee would "not be gobbled up for some time." En route, "mud pulled the shoes" off of her feet, and she "was very much afraid the Yankees would laugh at the F.F.V. stuck in the mud." When Mary finally arrived at the house in question, she noticed that it stood immediately in front of a Union cavalry camp, forcing her to whisper her request to the resident, a futile endeavor since the woman selling the cloth was deaf. Ultimately, she decided she was "between Scylla & Charybdis" and left with only the promise that she could come back and try again later.[27]

26. Ibid., 263 (Nov. 26, 1862), 302 (Jan. 1863), 304 (Feb. 4, 1863), 320 (Feb. 25, 1863), 325 (Mar. 8, 1863), 344 (Apr. 4, 1863), 370 (Apr. 29, 1863), 207 (Aug. 20, 1862), 218 (Aug. 30, 1862), 292 (Jan. 7, 1863), 370 (Apr. 29, 1863), 320 (Feb. 25, 1863), 560 (Feb. 1864), 625 (June 23, 1864), 766 (Jan. 18, 1865).

27. Ibid., 207 (Aug. 20, 1862), 318 (Feb. 21, 1863), 343 (Apr. 1, 1863), 404 (June 11, 1863), 464 (Aug. 25, 1863), 623 (June 20, 1864), 338 (Mar. 26, 1863), 437 (July 1863), 500 (Oct. 24, 1863), 527 (Dec. 1863), 591 (May 5, 1864), 635 (July 9, 1864), 724 (Nov. 1864), 338 (Mar. 26,

At least some of her supplies came to Lee courtesy of the U.S. government. In May 1862, when President Abraham Lincoln received word that General Banks intended to move his command from Winchester to Strasburg, he insisted that Banks report Stonewall Jackson's position before making the move. Lincoln's fear was that Banks would be exposing his "stores and trains at Winchester" if he moved out too quickly. The next day Jackson attacked Banks, and the safety of Union "stores and trains" was a moot point. As James W. Beeler of Cutshaw's Battery described it, besides prisoners, the road from Winchester "was full of captured wagons." Unionist sympathizer Julia Chase reported sourly, "what a glorious capture Jackson has had." He had "taken some 1100 prisoners" and "captured [a] great many valuable stores." Some days later Chase complained, "the citizens in town have been stealing at a great rate, sugar, cheese, crackers & many other things the sutlers & Commissary Master left behind." She noted that the "stealing" was being carried out by the women more than the men in town.[28]

When Federals evacuated Winchester the following September, they also left behind their stores, and Confederate commissary Col. M. G. Harman wrote to the inspector general to learn what he should "do in regard to the stock of goods" left behind. Harman need not have bothered the inspector general. Chase again reported, "the people here are perfectly happy with joy, and have been going in crowds to the fort" and returning "with carts and wagons loaded." One woman in particular earned special notice from Chase. "Mrs. Robt. Conrad, it is said, had her wagon filled with different things. So much for our F.F.V.'s." Elizabeth Conrad was not the only woman in the wagon, however. Mary Greenhow Lee reported: "Mrs. Conrad & I went out in a common cart, much to the amusement of the passers by." Lee did not mention any guilt associated with this event, suggesting that she found nothing ethically wrong with supplying her household at the expense of the Yankees. With women in charge of supplying the needs of their families, scavenging for goods from abandoned Federal installations was both convenient and patriotic.[29]

1863). In Greek mythology Scylla was a nymph who could change into a monster and terrorize sailors in the Strait of Messina; Charybdis was the name of a whirlpool off the coast of Sicily that symbolized a female monster. To be between the two means choosing between two equally hazardous alternatives.

28. Edwin M. Stanton to Nathaniel P. Banks, May 24, 1862, OR, 15:527; James W. Beeler Diary, May 25, 1862, Rubye Hall Collection (73 THL), HL, typescript; JC, May 25, June 4, 1862.

29. Harman to Cooper, Sept. 5, 1862, OR, 19(2):594; JC, Sept. 3, 1862; MGL, 222 (Sept. 3, 1862).

The second battle of Winchester in June 1863 afforded the same opportunity. As Cornelia McDonald recounted, "Milroy evacuated the fort during the night," and the Confederates "captured all their baggage." Lee reveled in their good fortune, stating that the Rebels had "captured more from the Yankees now than ever" and went on to claim, "if Banks was our Quarter Master, Milroy is our Commissary." In fact, a page and a half of her journal is written in red ink that, Lee explained, was from their "Yankee stores." This opportunism evidently had taken place earlier in the war since Mary's sister-in-law Laura Lee used for her journal a ledger stamped "U.S. Ordnance" on the cover.[30]

Whatever the source, Lee succeeded in amassing a great store of supplies for her own household and for her *"large family,"* meaning her soldiers. Laura Lee reported, "Mary goes on buying everything," from sugar to coffee to molasses, "oil, [and] dried fruit." Mary reported both her successes and her failures in accumulating goods. She "succeeded in getting two immense hogs," yarn, honey, "hdkfs," mackerel, mustard, hair brushes, and "the best sirop [*sic*]" she "ever tasted." Yet when she ventured "to look at an old house . . . to buy for fire wood," she found "nothing left but the brick chimneys." Keeping her large family warm and fed seemed to be two of Lee's greatest trials. But what seemed most important for her to accumulate was sugar and shoes. She hoarded sugar, amassing as much as 170 pounds at one point, yet leaving the family to drink their "tea & coffee without sugar, & without murmur" so there would be plenty on hand "for the army when it comes." Demanding patriotic behavior from her charges was another facet of Lee's soldier work.[31]

Shoes and boots for the troops also ranked high in importance on Lee's shopping lists. Besides sewing "soldier's shirts" made from calico and handing out underwear and uniforms, she gathered as many forms of footwear for the servicemen as possible. Keeping shoes on soldiers' feet was a vexing problem for Confederate officers. Robert E. Lee reported to President Jefferson Davis in September 1862 that, although they had obtained "a thousand pairs of shoes" in "Fredericktown, 250 pairs in Williamsport," and "about 400 pairs in" Hagerstown during his Maryland campaign, the amount would "not be sufficient to cover the bare feet of the army." By November, with winter clos-

30. McDonald, *Reminiscences of the War*, 175; MGL, 414 (June 16, 1863), 408 (June 14, 1863); LL, front cover.

31. MGL, 346–47 (Apr. 6, 1863, emphasis hers); LL, Mar. 16,1863; MGL, 416 (June 17, 1863), 469 (Sept. 1863), 522 (Nov. 27, 1863), 527 (Dec. 1863), 622 (June 19, 1864), 641 (July 1864); LL, Mar. 16, 1863; MGL, 461 (Aug. 1863), 469 (Sept. 1863), 496 (Oct. 19, 1863), 484 (Aug. 23, 1863), 641 (July 17, 1864).

ing in, Lt. Gen. James Longstreet estimated that "the number of men in his corps without shoes . . . [was] 6,648." When Mary Greenhow Lee realized the extent of this problem, she did her part to correct it, giving away at one time "10 prs. shoes & 20 prs socks, to the infinite delight of our poor barefooted soldiers."[32]

Even when Mary Greenhow Lee had the finances and could find the necessary items, her soldier work was challenging. For one thing, the values of the various currencies available fluctuated to such an extent that there were some merchants who eventually accepted only gold. At first it seemed disloyal to use U.S. currency, but then it became apparent that "greenbacks" were the least likely bills to lose their value. But the money she used depended upon Lee's supplier and what she bought. "Went out this evening," she informed her journal, and "amused myself playing the broker; I bought Va. money with Yankee, & Confederate money with Va." and finally "invested $25.00 Va. money in candles." She then had to find ways to transport her larger purchases. Begging, borrowing, and demanding netted her everything from an ambulance to a spring wagon to a rail truck in order to move her supplies. At one point the genteel widow found herself in "the bar room at Stottlemeyer," where she finally secured a buggy, suggesting that her soldier work overruled her sense of propriety.[33]

Lee was fairly forthcoming in her journal about where she kept all of the contraband she gathered. Some of it was in a "black hole" in the house next door without the residents' knowledge. Some of her friends stored supplies for her; others were under planks in her floors, under her beds, and at times "worn under our hoops." But she also kept them in plain sight, "mixed together in most natural disorder" among her own household supplies. To camouflage her stores of "U.S. blankets" and sheets, she made them into a mattress or had them "bundled up" and "carried to a place of safety." They hid some of the food and "treasonable supplies" in slaves' bedrooms or "in concealment in the garret." Large amounts of male footwear created another

32. MGL, 441 (July 23, 1863), 538 (Jan. 7, 1864), 216 (Aug. 28, 1862), 171 (July 12, 1862), 412–14 (June 1863); LL, Mar. 16, 1863; R. E. Lee to Jefferson Davis, Sept. 12, 1862, OR, 19(2):604–5; Robert E. Lee to Secretary of War George W. Randolph, Nov. 14, 1862, ibid., 718; R. E. Lee to Secretary of War George W. Randolph, Dec. 12, 1862, ibid., 21:1041; MGL, 431–32 (July 1863).

33. MGL, 452 (Aug. 4, 1863), 614 (June 4, 1864), 620 (June 15, 1864), 476 (Aug. 30, 1863), 519 (Nov. 23, 1863), 559 (Feb. 19, 1864); McDonald, Reminiscences of the War, 63; Douglas B. Ball, Financial Failure and Confederate Defeat (Urbana: University of Illinois Press, 1991), 5–17; MGL, 654 (July 28, 1864), 262 (Nov. 25, 1862), 522 (Nov. 27, 1863), 537 (Jan. 3, 1864).

problem. Since there was only one man in her household at the time—a slave named William, who belonged to James Murray Mason—having several pairs of men's shoes on hand would have drawn enough suspicion to have her "sent to Fort Delaware." In the first place, in order to purchase shoes from the sutlers, she had to prove a need for them and usually explained that they were for her slaves. Lee admitted to her journal, however, that "if William were to wear all the shoes I have bought for him, he would be shod for life." In the second place, she had to store them all. For that, her scheme required the aid of several men in town. She gave John Peyton Clark "a present of some boots & shoes," then "sent him down the street to please himself," knowing that he would return them when her army returned. She also "made . . . a present" of shoes and boots to brother-in-law P. C. L. Burwell, to a "Mr. Taylor," and to "Mr. Brown, Mr. Dosh, & Mr. Baker," and she had additional pairs "carried . . . over to Mrs. Tuley's" next door for safekeeping.[34]

Lee's soldier work attracted the attention of Union officials, who searched her house on a number of occasions, but she strained to keep her cache safe, taking advantage of gender assumptions to lower her risks. She merely played her role as female to the fullest extent and assumed that Federal military commanders would follow the same rules of genteel society she followed. Lee had evidence that this was true. Relying upon the social graces, she once willingly invited the provost, who stood on her front porch, to search her house. Her attitude disarmed him, leading him to search carelessly and then provide her with a certificate against further searches, proclaiming her house free of contraband and signing the certificate on the same desk that held her journal, with "only a blotting sheet between the paper, on which he was writing" and her "account book." Another ploy to protect her contraband stores used during that same search also depended upon the gender code and social protection of women's modesty. Both of her sisters-in-law, Antoinette and Laura Lee, were wearing men's shirts under their dresses, and her nieces, Louisa and Laura Burwell, "were walking about under the weight of grey cloth." Lee felt certain that the illegal items were safely hidden on these women's bodies because she believed in the gender code and expected the inspecting officer to abide by it as well. Ironically, these genteel women who could not fight the men's battles were "in uniform" participating in Lee's soldier work.[35]

34. MGL, 339 (Mar. 27, 1863), 365 (Apr. 24, 1863), 554 (Feb. 8, 1864), 592 (May 5, 1864), 346 (Apr. 6, 1863); LL, Feb. 28, 1863; MGL, 509 (Nov. 1863), 539 (Jan. 8, 1864), 551 (Feb. 5, 1864), 184 (July 24, 1862), 320 (Feb. 25, 1863), 365 (Apr. 25, 1863), 319–21 (Feb. 1863), 365 (Apr. 24, 1863), 744 (Dec. 22, 1864).

35. MGL, 320 (Feb. 25, 1863), 338 (Mar. 25, 1863), 346 (Apr. 6, 1863).

Another gender expectation demanded that nineteenth-century women uphold and maintain family connections. Confederate prescriptive literature enjoined southern women to write cheerful letters to their men in the army, thus putting them in charge of morale. But how were they to mail letters through enemy lines? The first words in Lee's journal state her difficulty: "I know not how a letter can be sent, or to whom to address it, as our Post Office is removed to Harrisonburgh." Initially, she relied on friends or acquaintances heading south, but this became a problem too. One such acquaintance, an Englishman named Buxton, offered to take letters for her and ultimately caused Lee a great deal of apprehension when she heard a rumor that he was a spy. The rumors flew back and forth for several days, intimating first that he was a Yankee spy, then a double agent, then a reporter for the *Herald Tribune*, and then a correspondent of the *London Chronicle*. But she grew weary of sorting out rumors and finally decided, "whether he is a Spy or not, if he carries my letters, I will make use of him." Ultimately, although she termed him a "will-o-the-wisp," she decided Buxton could be trusted.[36]

Lee needed to trust her carriers because she put herself at risk. "I have written to Turner Ashby," she wrote, "telling him of traitors in his camp, & I have sent my letters & lists of killed & wounded to Genl. Jackson." She also informed Ashby that "one of his men, had deserted" and was scheming "with the Yankees . . . to lead a Cavalry force to his camp, for the avowed purpose of capturing him." Lee, in effect, took on the role of spy herself. Word soon spread that the Lee house could be counted on as a "Confederate Post Office," possessing a "secret means of communication with Dixie." Mary became creative in sending out her packets of mail, secreting some of them away in pin cushions and the hems of skirts, with the help of local seamstress Julia Kurtz. Within one month of Winchester's first Union occupation, Lee had sent over fifty letters from her house via one route or another. "Outwitting the Yankees is my only amusement," she stated in January 1863. But it became a pattern in her life, and by the end of the war, she had become adept at the subterfuge. She considered it "a pleasure to outwit" men like General Sheridan, the last Union commander in Winchester, but she became more

36. Faust, "Altars of Sacrifice," 1211; MGL, 1 (Mar. 11, 1862), 39–40 (Mar. 28, 1862), 52 (Apr. 4, 1862), 60 (Apr. 11, 1862), 61 (Apr. 12, 1862), 87 (May 2, 1862), 57 (Apr. 8, 1862). For an understanding of the importance of letters between families, see Wylma Wates, "Precursor to the Victorian Age: The Concept of Marriage and Family as Revealed in the Correspondence of the Izard Family of South Carolina," in *In Joy and in Sorrow: Women, Family, and Marriage in the Victorian South, 1830–1900*, ed. Carol Blesser (New York: Oxford University Press, 1991), 3.

prudent in her movements and more protective of her cohorts, eventually ceasing to name her carriers in her journal for their own safety.[37]

Clearly, Mary Greenhow Lee's nurturing character had plenty of opportunities to manifest itself during the war. She aided the southern war effort by building up a contraband store for her army, running an underground mail service, and working in the hospitals, "willing to endure any privation to become a beggar" for the cause.[38]

Some months after the war, as she struggled to organize details for the next phase of her life in Baltimore, Lee met with, and was entertained by, several people who had heard of her strenuous activities during the conflict. One such hostess greeted her warmly and offered her services whenever Lee might need them. The woman's warm reception made Mary feel as if she "were a Confederate soldier," and she admitted that she "appreciated the feeling" of being included in that group. Lee contributed to the war effort to the extent that her gender, abilities, and resources allowed. She used the phrase "soldier work" in reference especially to the "feeding process" when her army camped nearby, an acceptable activity for women during wartime. Her efforts included preparations for the army over an extended time and also involved accumulating contraband and circumventing postal inspectors, both of which carried personal risk. In Lee's own estimation, she had won the right to claim the identity of not only a Confederate but also a soldier. For purposes of studying women during the Civil War, she also provides a more complex perspective, suggesting that women were much less passive in their war efforts than even their own words may, on the surface, express.[39]

37. MGL, 52 (Apr. 4, 1862), 65 (Apr. 14, 1862), 86 (May 2, 1862), 66 (June 14, 1862), 192 (Aug. 2, 1862), 66 (June 15, 1862), 219 (Aug. 30, 1862), 341 (Mar. 29, 1863), 88 (May 3, 1862), 40 (Mar. 28, 1862), 304 (Feb. 2, 1863), 210 (Aug. 22, 1862), 68 (June 16, 1862), 300 (Jan. 20, 1863), 772 (Jan. 26, 1865), 729 (Dec. 1, 1864), 785 (Feb. 18, 1865), 778 (Feb. 7, 1865), 783 (Feb. 14, 1865).

38. Ibid., 814 (Apr. 16, 1865).

39. Ibid., 888–89 (Nov. 8, 1865).

8

"This Is Surely the Day of Woman's Power"

Mary Greenhow Lee's Gender Warfare

*M*ary Greenhow Lee recorded that, upon returning to Washington after a tour of the Kernstown battlefield, Secretary of State William H. Seward was asked how he found Union feeling in Winchester. His reply: "The men are all in the army, & the women are the devils." Lee was one of those women. She played no part in the decision to go to war or in its prosecution, but she found herself and her family squarely in the middle of the conflict for almost four years. How does a woman wage war when she is expected to be passively patriotic, to sacrifice male family members and friends, to sew flags and uniforms, and to remind God constantly whose side he should be on? She does so by taking advantage of her status in society and by pressing contemporary gender ideology to its limits. Lee recognized that, as a woman, she faced some limitations, but being a woman also afforded her a way to wage war against northern male invaders that her male Confederates did not have.[1]

Lee knew well the rules of the patriarchal society into which she was born. Those rules not only restricted her rights but also afforded her protection

---

1. MGL, 58 (Apr. 8, 1862); LL, Apr. 7, 1862.

and a certain deference from gentlemen. She waged her warfare based on those assumptions. At the same time, Lee's social standing relied upon how well she adhered to her prescribed gender role. Her class identification was integrated with her gender. Therefore, Lee used a dynamic mix of class and gender against the enemy. War forced her, however, to alter the guidelines she adhered to for each. Lee's personal sense of social place remained unchanged, but the sustained crisis of war forced her to reexamine qualities she judged essential in those around her, eventually raising patriotism above all other criteria for being included within her social circle.

War, in fact, drove both men and women to make use of a complex combination of gender and class when dealing with members of the opposite sex. Union general Benjamin Butler's solution for dealing with women's disrespect and scorn in New Orleans was his General Order No. 28. Not knowing how long his "flesh and blood" soldiers could withstand the epithets and "insulting gesture[s]" directed at them "by these bejeweled, becrinolined and laced creatures calling themselves ladies," he ordered his men to treat those who behaved in this fashion as "common women plying their vocation." According to Butler, it worked. "These she-adders of New Orleans," he reported, "were at once shamed into propriety of conduct by the order." In this case, with few options available, he used class as a weapon against women.[2]

Butler explained later that he had feared his soldiers would relax the gender rules requiring them to be gentlemen in the presence of a lady, and granted his men the assumption that unladylike behavior voided the title of "lady." Seemingly, this theory meant that as "common women" a female's insults would have no effect because her opinions were not valued as a "lady's" would be. Drew Gilpin Faust has noted that Butler fought women's insults toward his soldiers by making women accountable for their actions in the public sphere, the location where "ladies" had been presumably immune from responsibility.[3]

Butler is the best-known and most publicized commander for taking such a stand. Others, however, followed the same strategy, including commanders in Winchester. Colonel William D. Lewis Jr. posted a proclamation there on April 17, 1862, giving both men and women equal warning against "circulating flying rumours and creating false excitements." The next month the provost marshal ordered that Winchester "ladies shall not . . . insult the soldiers." And, in a similar move to Butler's General Order No. 76, which stated that

2. *Charleston Mercury*, July 21, 1862 (order given May 15, 1862).
3. Faust, *Mothers of Invention*, 207–14.

women as well as men must take an oath of allegiance to the United States, Winchester women were being ordered to take an oath as early as August 1862. Eventually, Maj. Gen. Philip H. Sheridan arrested all Winchester men of conscription age. He explained his actions by stating that, although he had "no especial charges against" the men, "he chose to show this community that he had the power to compel respect to his soldiers." Sheridan knew that men were not the only ones disrespecting his troops; the women were perpetrators too. As long as he remained within the acknowledged social parameters, the general had few weapons to use against the women, and as Mary Greenhow Lee reported, "he could not resist the women because that would be called brutal." Since Sheridan could not arrest the women, he simply deprived them of their husbands.[4]

Butler and other commanders were forced to use imaginative ways to defend against patriotic southern women because they were constrained by gender construction from treating them as they would men. The same frustration also affected the women. Winchester "ladies" could not defend against the invasion of northern forces by taking up arms. They could, however, use their social status and gender as weapons, Mary Lee's tactic. She incorporated into her circle members of a lower social class while denying that right to Union officers of her own social standing. In addition, she adopted a mode of warfare against the occupiers that consisted of a refusal to play the role of helpless female, thus denying them the role of protective male, the designation she reserved for patriotic southern men. Lee worked out this system of warfare within the confines established by society.[5]

That Lee felt herself to be waging warfare is obvious from her choice of metaphors and imagery. She "armed" herself with a basket of food when she knew her presence at the hospital would be challenged. During another conflict at the hospital, she "took the position of the Cavalry & brought up the rear, protecting the retreat" of her allies. At still another time, when denied the right to take pudding to wounded Confederates, she argued until she finally "came off conqueror & was left in undisputed possession of the field." At times, even nature seemed to be her enemy. When she got stuck in a snow drift, she described her reaction to the contretemps in military terms: "I al-

4. Lewis's proclamation reprinted in JPC, Apr. 18, 1862; Faust, *Mothers of Invention*, 207–11; MGL, 66 (Apr. 15, 1862), 102 (May 15, 1862), 200 (Aug. 12, 1862), 728 (Nov. 29, 1864).

5. For comparison, see Jane E. Schultz, "Mute Fury: Southern Women's Diaries of Sherman's March to the Sea, 1864–1865," in *Arms and the Woman: War, Gender, and Literary Representation*, ed. Helen M. Cooper, Adrienne Suslander Munich, and Susan Merrill Squier (Chapel Hill: University of North Carolina Press, 1989), 59–62.

most cried from fatigue, cold & the dread of either advancing or retreating," and she finally "had to fall back very much demoralized."[6]

Lee conducted her campaigns not only against invaders from the North but also against northern men who, in her estimation, had neither an understanding of southern women nor a right to demand that she respect them as men. Gender ideology in the South developed differently than it did in the North. Southern historian Bertram Wyatt-Brown has identified the "Code of Southern Honor" as both a solution to woman's physical weakness and a reason to keep her restricted politically and economically. This code rested in part upon the institution of slavery. White male power drew upon their obligation to provide for both blacks and whites within their households while protecting their women from any dangers inherent in the slave system. Although southern justification for slavery included the paternal care of slaves, paradoxically, those same slaves could not be trusted to be loyal and respectful to those who provided for them. This was the male side of gender ideology in the nineteenth-century South.[7]

If women had a distinctive set of societal roles, this assumes that it was the complementary opposite of that for men. Gender difference must be understood in terms of a relationship, an "other" against which one gender operates. Women's assumed vulnerability thus necessitated a protective capacity in men. Historians debate whether or not southern women were unhappy and frustrated with the institution of slavery because it was either immoral or annoying, but several agree that slavery had become a burden to many southern women. Although some might have been dissatisfied with slavery, the abolitionist movement in the North drove southern women to defend the decisions of their men. The best way to do that was to uphold the identity of the "Southern Lady," which, in turn, emphasized the chivalrous identity of their men.[8]

The resistance waged by the women of Winchester, according to Mary Lee, escalated correspondingly with the length of the war. Having the enemy in their midst merely made home-front women more determined to annoy them. "The feeling against the women is increasing every day," Lee wrote, and "they say 'the revolution can never be quelled, till the Secession women

6. MGL, 448 (July 31, 1863), 38 (Mar. 27, 1862), 167 (July 8, 1862), 779 (Feb. 9, 1865).

7. Wyatt-Brown, *Southern Honor*, 227; Faust, "Altars of Sacrifice," 1213.

8. Chodorow, *Feminism and Psychoanalytic Theory*, 99–113; Claudia Bepko and Jo-Ann Krestan, *Too Good for Her Own Good* (New York: HarperCollins, 1991), 166–67; Suzy Clarkson Holstein, "'Offering Up Her Life': Confederate Women on the Altars of Sacrifice," *Southern Studies* 2, no. 2 (1991): 121.

are subdued.'" Warfare for Lee and her neighbors consisted not of weapons, but of words and an attitude of disrespect. They fought as women fight, not as soldiers do. They took up the habit of wearing thick veils and sunbonnets and carrying parasols to keep their faces from revealing any signs of acknowledgment. Lee took note of those she saw "passing unveiled" as if they were out of uniform. If forced into contact with the enemy, women's facial expressions registered lack of interest or disrespect. In effect, patriotic southern women in Winchester withheld their countenances from Union soldiers to show that they did not consent to the presence of northern forces in their town.[9]

Julia Chase commented critically that the Secessionist women had "all adopted sun bonnets, . . . some with long curtains, called Jeff Davis bonnets. They put on many airs and frowns and sneers, and . . . are certainly bold and impudent." She looked forward to the arrival of Union forces and could not understand why Secessionist women thought of the Yankees as "monsters in human form." Chase did not seem to adopt the same tactics for use against her enemies when Confederates held Winchester, nor did she understand the reasons for these efforts on the part of secession women. Although Unionists were outnumbered in town, the best interpretation of this discrepancy might be that Chase did not feel invaded by either Union or Confederate forces since she welcomed the former, and the latter, though Rebels, were southerners at home on their own ground. In any event, Chase seemed to resent secession women more than Confederate military men, making hers less a gender conflict than a growing feud with members of her own sex.[10]

Lee and her friends, however, were trying to combat the presence of men who assumed the right to dominate them without earning the women's consent to do so. Writing about the effect of the Secesh women of Winchester on the Union soldiers, she wrote, "I am delighted to hear that they . . . say they were never treated with such scorn as by the Winchester ladies" and that soldiers were boasting that they would "make the Secession women hold their tongues." Later, when reporting that fifteen thousand northern troops were massed at Harpers Ferry and forty thousand at Middletown, Lee wryly suggested that these combined forces might be enough to "subdue the women of Winchester." Although her position in society demanded that she

9. MGL, 8 (Mar. 13, 1862), 15 (Mar. 16, 1862), 37 (Mar. 27, 1862), 95 (May 11, 1862), 102 (May 16, 1862).

10. Julia Chase, diary, May 16, 1862, quoted in Quarles, *Occupied Winchester*, 40; JC, Mar. 9, 1862.

remain a "lady," Lee wanted northern soldiers to fear her as "a great Virago." The Secesh women of Winchester gained a reputation among the Union soldiers for their defiant Rebel spirit. This reputation grew, at least in the minds of the women. Mary Magill recalled later that Union soldiers "almost invariably . . . held exaggerated ideas of the power, influence, and knowledge possessed by the Southern women."[11]

Although none of the Winchester diarists reported that women fired weapons at Union soldiers, Col. George H. Gordon of the 2d Massachusetts Regiment believed they did. In his report on the first battle of Winchester, Gordon claimed, "males and females vied with each other in increasing the number of their victims, by firing from the houses," and declared, "this record of infamy is preserved for the females of Winchester." Whether or not this actually happened, the perception of the colonel that it did might explain some of the enmity Union soldiers felt for the town's women.[12]

If antebellum women thought of themselves as restrained within gendered boundaries, war—at least in Winchester—broke those borders. As Lee noted early in the war, it surprised her to find "timid, retiring women . . . who have kept off the Yankees, defended their property, & when depredations were committed have gone alone (for there are no men to go about with the women now) to" the Union commanders in town "for redress. They get none," she continued, "but still it is not because they do not boldly maintain & claim their rights."[13]

During the war, Lee grew to appreciate women outside of her social circle who showed that they were able to handle the stress of military rule under an occupation army and not buckle under the strain. Lizzie Doods, for instance, earned Lee's respect by being "the embodiment of wit & sarcasm, in her talks with Yankees." She learned that Doods had been arrested for expressing "strong Southern sentiment," but she had "indignantly refused to take the oath" before being released and had "ordered the guard to fall back and not to dare walk by her side." Lee was "amused at her pluck," convinced that "this spirit of patriotism" was a gift from God "in His elevating & refining influences," a gift that "enlarges & expands minds, that before, had been of the lowest calibre." Her reference to Doods as being among "the lowest calibre" suggests that the two women had not moved in the same circles before

11. MGL, 12 (Mar. 14, 1862), 94 (May 10, 1862), 162 (July 2, 1862), 281 (Dec. 25, 1862); Magill, *Women*, 202.

12. *OR*, 12(1): 616–18.

13. MGL, 54 (Apr. 6, 1862).

the war, but it must have been an assessment made on other than economic grounds. Doods headed her own household and paid taxes on two pieces of property and one slave, placing her on an approximately equal financial footing with Lee.[14]

The households on both sides of Lee "changed hands" from one class to another during the war. In October 1863 her longtime neighbor and friend Dr. Robert T. Baldwin died. She not only grieved over Baldwin's death but also dreaded the prospect of the requisite social civility toward the local family who had purchased the house, whom she described only as "people of that class." Lee's new neighbors, Charles F. Eichelberger and his family, had moved from a house worth five hundred dollars into the one next door to Lee, valued at over ten times that amount. Improvement in Eichelberger's economic status did not, in Lee's opinion, move him into her social circle merely because it enabled him to move into her neighborhood. He and his family lacked other qualities she believed essential in making them "visitable," the contemporary rubric she applied to values such as education, good manners, family heritage, and civic responsibility. By the end of the war, however, Lee had relaxed the standards by which she measured the "people of that class" next door.[15]

As the war ground on, Lee began to see the Eichelbergers in a new light. Whatever their class, she appreciated the family as patriotic Secessionists who were willing to help her as she struggled against an invading army. A brief visit by her nephew Bob Burwell could have had severe consequences, for example, if not for her new neighbors. Upon hearing of a Union scouting party nearby, niece Louisa "piloted Bob over to Eichelberger's & concealed him in a vault" until the scouting party left. By the end of the war, Lee was "pay[ing] . . . semi-annual visit[s]" on the "people of that class" next door, for they had proven by their patriotism to be *visitable*.[16]

Lawyer David Barton, owner of the house next to Lee opposite the Baldwins, died in July 1863. His widow eventually moved her family to their rural property outside of town and leased the Winchester house to the Tuley family. Mrs. Tuley, a widow, was a woman of "that class," so designated by Lee for various reasons, not the least of which was Tuley's limited education. Although Lee ultimately became fond of her and appreciated especially her pa-

14. Ibid., 66 (Apr. 15, 1862), 200 (Aug. 12, 1862); Winchester Personal Property Tax Lists, 1860, LOV; Winchester Land Tax Registers, 1860, LOV.

15. MGL, 498 (Oct. 22, 1863), 619 (June 13, 1864); MJCG/MHS, 11 (Sept. 23, 1837); *Etiquette at Washington*, 45–50; Winchester Land Tax Registers, 1859, 1860, 1865.

16. MGL, 630 (July 2, 1864), 761 (Jan. 11, 1865), 866 (Sept. 7, 1865).

triotic thoughts, she often cringed at how Tuley presented them, stating that she was as "promiscuous as usual in her grammar & pronunciation." Tuley's patriotism made her *visitable* during the war, but her speech pattern signified to Lee that her education had not prepared her for a genteel life.[17]

Tuley received an unexpected visit from her neighbor one Sunday. The call seemed to surprise Lee as well. "I did not think, a week ago," Lee wrote, "I would ever pay Mrs. T. a Sunday visit, but we all feel equally helpless." Enemy occupation of Winchester denied the *connexion* the power and influence they had relied upon, thus bringing the classes closer together, at times, in their common vulnerability. As the war continued, money had even less to do with social position for Lee than it had before. She even admitted to having stolen "some delicious little ginger cakes" while visiting Tuley to take home as a treat for her nieces, hardly an action of an F.F.V. lady. The old measurements of class fell away, and a new one took over. Now, national sentiment and patriotism drove her away from old friends and propelled her toward new ones. During those years, she began spending her time with some of the people she would have jealously guarded herself against before the war.[18]

Lee found one woman in particular, a Mrs. Sperry, to be "very smart . . . & very entertaining." She identified Sperry as plain and uneducated, a woman who had "always associated with common persons." When Lee heard, however, that this "plain person" had written a "poetic sketch of the war," she invited her over to read it to the family and "was perfectly astonished" at her talent, commenting that, despite her background, Sperry had a "decided genius." Wartime gave Lee an opportunity to see past social barriers to the assets in new acquaintances. Eventually, she concluded that she "prefer[red] people of that class next door" to those she had felt "obliged to be more sociable" with before the conflict. Because war had forced Lee to reevaluate the values necessary for inclusion in her company, placing patriotism above all others, she began associating with "common persons" herself.[19]

Julia Kurtz was another woman whose relationship to Lee changed because of the war. A woman in her fifties, single, and making her living as a seamstress in Winchester, Kurtz owned real property valued at just five hundred dollars less than Lee's, yet she owned no slaves. With little difference in

17. Ibid., 431 (July 7, 1863), 325 (Dec. 5, 1863).
18. Ibid., 16 (Mar. 17, 1862), 814 (Apr. 16, 1865), 559 (Feb. 19, 1864), 100 (May 15, 1862), 783 (Feb. 14, 1865), 16 (Mar. 17, 1862).
19. Ibid., 594 (May 8, 1864), 614 (June 4, 1864).

the economic status of these two women, their social valuation stemmed from the other attributes associated with position, placing Kurtz outside of Lee's circle. By the end of the war, however, they had become co-conspirators against the Union. The most important activity that the seamstress and the genteel widow took part in together was the underground post office Lee ran, with Kurtz helping her get the mail through by various means (such as sewing up the letters in the hems of dresses). The two women came from greatly different backgrounds, but the war provided them with enough common interests in the present to overcome the disparity. Kurtz became *visitable* for Lee, at least for the purposes of patriotism.[20]

As war modified class lines, it strengthened the barrier between the Secesh women and male occupiers, and Lee worried about the consequences to manners, suspecting that she could lose her gentility while maintaining her patriotism. In dealing with the enemy, women had little recourse but to ignore them or address them severely when forced into an encounter. "Scorn & contempt are such habitual expressions," Lee wrote, "that I fear they will not readily give place to more lady-like ones." Although proud that "the women of Winchester [were] so utterly fearless," she pronounced some of their behavior "perfectly ludicrous," and when she heard them using "strong language," she became concerned that "the Billingsgate style [would] become habitual," referring to the name given to coarse language, often heard in the London fish market of the same name, adopted by some of the Winchester women—language that ran counter to gentility.[21]

Such behavior drew comment from both friend and foe of the Winchester women. John Peyton Clark reported that when one "handsomely dressed 'lady'" caught sight of a Union burial detail ushering a Confederate prisoner of war at gunpoint down the street one day, she asked the officer in charge if "that son of a b——h (pointing to one of the Yankees) [was] going to make one of our men dig a grave for a d——d Yankee?" Clark's explanation that this outburst simply "illustrate[d] the intense indignation felt towards" the Union occupiers "by all classes of society" suggests that he did not condemn the "lady" in question because he understood her frustration. Julia Chase,

20. Winchester Land Tax Registers, 1850, 1854, 1859, 1860, 1865; Winchester Personal Property Tax Lists, 1855, 1859; U.S. Bureau of the Census, Eighth and Ninth Census, LOV, microfilm; MGL, 48 (Apr. 2, 1862), 71 (Apr. 19, 1862), 99 (May 15, 1862), 261 (Nov. 21, 1862), 558 (Feb. 19, 1864), 590 (May 4, 1864), 684 (Sept. 18, 1864), 783 (Feb. 14, 1865), 815 (Apr. 16, 1865).

21. MGL, 76, 78 (Apr. 23–24, 1862), 13 (Mar. 15, 1862), 16–19 (Mar. 17–18, 1862), 724 (Nov. 23, 1864).

however, did not. She noted that the Secession women became "bolder & bolder every day, and talk[ed] as saucy as you please," warning that "all pretensions to ladylike actions" were "forever gone, & the F.F.V.'s will long be remembered for their disgraceful conduct and ridiculous behavior."[22]

The women's attitudes provoked notice from as far away as Baltimore and Philadelphia as well. The *Baltimore American* reported that the behavior of Winchester's women had forced "the commanding officer . . . to issue an order advising the citizens to be more discreet." The *Philadelphia Ledger*, reporting "acts of rudeness and insult . . . perpetrated" against the soldiers by the "inhabitants calling themselves 'ladies,'" suggested that, although "Virginia has always boasted of the high tone of its society and the elegance of its manners, . . . with their patriotism, all this refinement and courtesy seem to have fled." In fact, Maj. Gen. Robert Milroy finally issued a proclamation that "if his men [were] insulted by word or manner, by male or female," the offending party risked imprisonment.[23]

The members of Lee's *connexion* guarded against a "habitual indulgence of passion." In fact, one reason more homes had mirrors by midcentury was the need to practice mild expressions in private where, even though families could be more relaxed, they were expected to treat each other and their servants as they would behave with them in public. Disciplined emotions signaled gentility. Anger, however, indicated a loss of self-control, dignity, and composure, but the degree of risk depended upon gender. Men who lost their temper were in danger of questionable decorum. Women, however, lost their femininity if they exhibited anger.[24]

Lee's neighbor, Fanny Barton, became notorious for venting her spleen on the Union soldiers in town. When angered by enemies camping on her grounds, she would tell them that they were welcome to "six feet of Southern land" but nothing else. In relating an outburst Barton visited on General Milroy, Lee declared, "Dickens himself could not have pictured a richer scene." During the shouting match, Barton asserted that "John Brown was the cause of the war," which Milroy termed a "lie." Barton then "drew up close to him & looked, as only Mrs. B. can look & said in a vicious tone, 'Don't you say I lie,'" to which the general "got into such a rage, that he danced about the room & ordered her out in the most insolent manner." Barton withdrew, but slowly, "keeping her eye on him" as she left.[25]

22. JPC, July 7, 1862; JC, Apr. 23, 1862, Apr. 8, 1864.
23. MGL, 389 (May 26, 1863). Both papers copied into JPC, Apr. 18, 1862.
24. Kasson, *Rudeness and Civility*, 147, 148, 157, 161, 165–68.
25. McDonald, *Reminiscences of the War*, 73; MGL, 312 (Feb. 13, 1863).

Anger frustrated these women, but conversations about their feelings seemed to offer relief, and Lee's record of such incidents reflects that she looked for humor in the ways that women expressed their struggle. Fanny Barton's unbridled rancor lent itself well to the release of tension because she could turn it into comic scenes. For instance, early on she told Lee that to withstand the presence of the enemy, she desired "to be put in a paper box, half filled with pink wadding & then to be covered over with it & kept quiet, till the Yankees" left, "except that some friend" should come in "to turn her over occasionally." This image amused Lee, but it also shows the conflict tearing at the women. Barton believed that she risked losing her true identity—a caring and serene woman—and wanted to preserve it in the folds of pink softness until the war ended.[26]

Having an invading army in her town, even camped in her garden for several weeks at a stretch, severely tested Lee's temper. It became a struggle for her to retain her "composure & self command" at times, and she had to keep a constant check on her anger, placing a strain on the gentility she had been conditioned to observe all of her life, a task not always easy. She could become "so mad" that she would find herself "trembling with passion," surprising family members who "had not imagined" that she "could be in such a rage." Lee openly lost her temper at times, as in the instance when "two Yankee negroes" refused to move horses from her path and called her "a God damn rebel woman." She became "so indignant that" she "flew up the street at rail road speed, scorning the Yankees by" her "looks so completely that they gave way right and left before" her. Although Lee refused to "beg . . . favors from the Yankees," one of them, who parked his wagon in her garden, told her servants that, even if she were to ask a favor of him, he would refuse because she did not speak to him "as a lady ought to speak." Her power and position clearly demanded proper gendered behavior or she risked losing both.[27]

In Lee's opinion, however, war had changed the rules of etiquette. Her parents would have been amazed, for example, to know that she and her family observed their custom of afternoon tea while listening to the staccato rhythm of "Confederate sharpshooters" chasing Union soldiers past her door, but the women continued sipping tea without giving the sounds more than brief notice. Lee claimed that war diminished propriety and made every-

26. MGL, 59 (Apr. 10, 1862).
27. Ibid., 448 (July 31, 1863), 715 (Nov. 2, 1864), 734 (Dec. 12, 1864), 9 (Mar. 14, 1862), 491 (Oct. 10, 1863), 777 (Feb. 5, 1865); Bepko and Krestan, *Too Good*, 19.

one "so French," which she equated with "unreserved." The perception that the French were ill mannered seems to have been a common assumption among Winchester women. Cornelia McDonald made a similar comparison in her diary, reporting that a Union officer by the name of Cluseret had resigned from the army over an injustice done to the citizens of Winchester. His behavior toward her and others in town must have impressed her as civil. "He was, it is said, a French barber," she wrote, but added, "he may have been, but he has very good manners," suggesting that she felt compelled to qualify his origins by reporting that he did not fit the characteristics commonly associated with them. During one of the Confederate occupations, a young soldier approached Lee after church and excitedly told her that a telegram had come, in which "all that could be deciphered was, 'Good news; Vicksburgh; 22,000,'" then had the "impertinence . . . to venture to walk" with her down the street, though he had never been introduced to her formally. As she replayed this scene on the pages of her journal, she wrote in resignation, "etiquette is laid on the shelf now."[28]

Gender ideology for nineteenth-century women also enjoined them to be attractive and to be ladylike. Lee's sense of decorum and propriety seemed almost innate. She knew, for instance, that a woman's half of the gender relationship called for both good manners and a pleasant appearance. Her efforts meant that she respected and appreciated the man or men in her company and expected the same in return. Whenever forced into dealings with the enemy commanders in town, Lee admitted that she grudgingly dressed herself "more carefully, because they are far more respectful to one well dressed, than in dishabille." Cornelia McDonald made use of the same rule when visiting the provost marshal's office to ask a favor. She arrived "stylishly dressed," she wrote, and believed that the officer "was perhaps influenced by the better clothes" she wore and more inclined to treat her with the respect due a lady.[29]

Yet when Lee needed nothing from the enemy and wanted to emphasize her disdain, she sometimes took pains not to look her best. On one occasion she wrote that she "went down to the parlor windows entirely in dishabille to enjoy my favorite sight—the retreat of the enemy." Although she made sure all the women in the household donned pretty skirts and shawls to show their respect when Confederate troops came to parade in front of her door, for the

28. MGL, 434 (July 13, 1863), 456 (Aug. 11, 1863), 459 (Aug. 17, 1864); McDonald, *Reminiscences of the War*, 126.

29. Anne Frior Scott, *Southern Lady*, 70; MGL, 697 (Sept. 30, 1864); McDonald, *Reminiscences of the War*, 49.

enemy she did the opposite. In fact, that distinction drove their custom of wearing sunbonnets and aprons in public; it became their uniform, clothing as the language of disrespect. "The Provost says," Lee reported, "the ladies shall not wear sunbonnets & aprons on the street, because they only do it to insult the soldiers." Lee and her friends used gender ideology in their battles with the enemy, and Union officers admitted their effectiveness.[30]

Lee made her position clear to enemy commanders when she told them that even though she and her family were "rebels," she "expected as citizens to be treated according to the usages of civilized warfare" and, as women, "the courtesy that every lady has the right to expect from every gentleman." When the commanders bowed, seeming to agree with her, she "assumed a very lofty tone" and thought she had "inspired them with some respect for" her as a "determined & openly avowed rebel." She never acknowledged, how- ever, that her success at being a good Confederate hinged a great deal on the opposition being good gentlemen. The fact that soldiers rarely violated Lee's home implies that Union commanders in Winchester attempted to follow the rules of genteel society, even though Lee must have severely tested their faithfulness to the rules. According to Lee, her reputation among the Union officers was awesome. "I know I can cow them" she stated, and "make them afraid of me whenever we come in collision." Paradoxically, although Lee expected Union commanders to be gentlemen, she also wanted them to fear her as a Confederate.[31]

Union commanders began to believe, Lee reported, that "the women of Virginia [were] all insane." Indeed, area women kept them busy, if not from dodging minié balls, at least from answering their demands for protection. Brigadier General James A. Shields complained that "these miscreants [Rebels] fly before us and leave their wives and children in our power," understanding that fighting a war among civilians fettered him with the added responsibility of taking over the duties of protecting the families of Confederate soldiers. Mrs. W. Strother Jones wrote to Maj. Gen. Nathaniel Banks about wagon- loads of corn and hay taken from her farm by his quartermaster, asking for payment and ending her request with the hope that he would be "willing to attend to the rights of all helpless women." To another such reminder, Banks wrote, "you are mistaken in supposing we come into Virginia for your protec- tion." In case the woman expected northern men to behave as her husband would, the general disabused her of the notion, stating, "we make no preten-

30. MGL, 666, 668 (Aug. 1864), 102 (May 1862).
31. Ibid., 484 (Aug. 23, 1863), 290 (Jan. 4, 1863), 188 (July 29, 1862), 312 (Feb. 13, 1863).

sions to that Chivalry which vilifies the major part of the American People
. . . and then abandons its own women and children to seek the protection of
those they . . . despise." When Union general Robert Milroy retorted in a
similar fashion to Cornelia McDonald, she responded, "it is only from the
army you command that we want protection." Mary Greenhow Lee also demanded protection, like Cornelia McDonald, on the grounds that the army's
presence occasioned the need for it. In other words, Union occupiers had
created the situation they complained against.[32]

When Colonel Stanton demanded rooms in her home, Lee drew on her
most practiced role as a woman of high social status to create a perception of
control. "I kept my eye fixed on his face," she wrote, and "with a very bland
manner assured him I had not gone to him to argue the question, nor to ask
a favour, but simply to demand the protection that every woman had a right
to demand from every man." Stanton finally gave in, stating, "I must confess
myself out-Generaled." He agreed to take only the rooms she insisted were
available, those in the wing of the house. When Lee won her point, she
"could scarcely restrain [her] exultation," but instead said "something civil
about its only being by a woman." Lee's deference to Stanton on this point
caught him in a net of responsibility based on her acceptance of their relationship on her terms, not from his demands. Whether or not Stanton knew
it, by calling attention to her subordinate position, Lee was actually reminding him of her right to expect his protection. In a sense, this is the first instance of Mary Greenhow Lee submitting to a relationship with an occupying
commander. Granted, Stanton forced her into it, but once there, Lee claimed
the power of the subordinate. To maintain her strength, she emphasized her
weak position in the relationship, forcing Stanton to assume a place of obligation.[33]

Rarely did Lee willingly enter into even a working alliance with a Union
man. When she did, they were usually with men she believed to be in a less-
advantaged social position and whom she required to aid in her activities,
such as laborers, "Yankee nurses," or orderlies like Dutton, the man whose
aid she came to during his arrest for desertion. Southern men who were patriots found it easier to make Lee's acquaintance, though even a Confederate
uniform did not blind her to possible character flaws.

32. Ibid., 14 (Mar. 16, 1862); Nathaniel Banks from Brig. Gen. James A. Shields, Winchester, Mar. 22, 1862, Nathaniel P. Banks Papers, LC; Mrs. W. Strother Jones to General Banks,
Apr. 2, 1862, ibid.; Banks to [?], Apr. 9, 1862, ibid.; McDonald, *Reminiscences of the War*, 127,
128.

33. MGL, 329–39 (Mar. 16, 1863).

Lee was not uncritical of her own soldiers. In particular, she was not fond of Lt. Gen. Jubal A. Early. On July 2, 1864, she played hostess to several Confederate officers, including Early, whom she reported was "very stupid, as he always is." Perhaps he did not fit her definition of "gentleman" because he was, in the words of historian Clement Eaton, "somewhat of an eccentric, an old bachelor of biting and sarcastic tongue who acquired the reputation of outcursing any man in the Confederate army."[34]

Men who were not southerners but favored the southern cause did not easily gain Lee's trust either. British correspondents and officers came to America to follow the events of the war. One of these men was Col. Garnett Wolseley of the British army, who traveled through the South on a mission to educate himself in American warfare. Traveling with Wolseley were two newspaper men: Frances Charles Lawley, a "special correspondent" for the London *Times*, and an artist who worked for the *Illustrated London News*, Frank Vizetelly, "a big, florid, red-bearded Bohemian" with a flare for the dramatic and, according to his biographer, a tendency to spend his leisure time imbibing.[35]

"About dusk there was a knock at the door," Lee recorded, and "it proved to be Mr. Vizitelley [*sic*], the Honble., Frank Lawley & Col. Wolseley (three grand Englishmen) who had come from the army in Genl. Lee's carriage & implored me to take them in; I demurred but they insisted & I consented." When Laura Lee reported their arrival, she wrote: "They are Mr. Lawley, (who knows Mr. [James M.] Mason very well) Mr. Vizetelly, and Col. Woolseley [*sic*]. The first is a dignified, polished gentleman, the two last are not." Mary Lee agreed, stating that Lawley was "evidently a gentleman & Mr. Mason's endorsement settles that point," but that "Col. Wolseley . . . is flash, neither he nor V. compare with our Virginia gentlemen." The Lee women accepted Lawley immediately with his letter of introduction from Mason, allowing the correspondent to borrow on the trust these women held for Mason to quickly establish a willing relationship with them. Vizetelly and Wolseley, however, had to work their way into the women's acceptance. At first Lee deemed Vizetelly a "mendacious snob" and had no little difficulty with his propensity for drinking. He would come in at one in the morning

34. Ibid., 630 (July 1, 1864); Eaton, *Southern Confederacy*, 285.

35. Lehmann, *Model Major-General*, 118–19; Adrian Preston, ed., *The South African Diaries of Sir Garnet Wolseley, 1875* (Cape Town, S.A.: A. A. Balkema, 1971), 26; William Stanley Hoole, *Lawley Covers the Confederacy* (Tuscaloosa: Confederate Publishing, 1964), 12, 13, 15, 52; William Stanley Hoole, *Vizetelly Covers the Confederacy* (Tuscaloosa, Ala.: Confederate Publishing, 1957), 55.

after a drinking "frolic with Wade Hampton, Col. Alexander," and others, kicking the glass out of her lantern as they staggered in, and then try to work his way back into her good graces the next day. After another spree, he stood before her "very penitent," making "humble apologies" and "protest[ing] that he was going to church three times on Sunday to do penance."[36]

Repentant or not, Vizetelly continued this behavior. In September 1864 both he and Maj. Gen. John B. Gordon stayed with Lee. When the artist again arrived home very drunk, Lee tried shaming him but noted out of the corner of her eye that Gordon and her nieces were having a difficult time restraining their convulsions of laughter at the scene. Finally, the general "went out and finding a courier at the door, sent him in to tell Vizetelly that Anderson's corp [sic] was moving and he staggered off." Unfortunately, "he came back later, bringing two more intoxicated men with him." Even with all of the trouble he gave her and the obvious evidence that he lacked the restraint and temperance demanded of genteel society, when he left to follow the army, she wrote, "I miss him very much." Vizetelly could tell a good tale and proved bright and well traveled, all of which appealed to Lee, but his obvious support of the Confederacy is what probably won her over.[37]

Lee did not mention many of Wolseley's characteristics that drew her into a comfortable relationship with him, except for what she learned about his extensive military service. When he left, she "would not take board, but received him as a guest." Whatever qualities he exhibited, their friendship lasted throughout the rest of Lee's life. Eventually knighted, Sir Garnett Wolseley maintained contact with several of the Confederate commanders he encountered during the Civil War and with Lee. Wolseley wrote a significant article about the Civil War, published in *Blackwood's Edinburgh Magazine* in the first half of 1863, after an extensive rewrite by his sister. In the article, although not mentioning Lee by name, which would have breached gender etiquette by placing her in the public eye, he did write that when he and his companions arrived in Winchester, they "drove up to the inn, where as usual no accommodation was to be had; but a hospitable lady kindly took us in, and entertained us during our stay in that place." The "hospitable lady" was Mary Greenhow Lee. She wrote in December 1863, "I never expected to figure in Blackwoods, but I have found myself in many unexpected places, during this war."[38]

36. MGL, 241 (Oct. 12, 1862); LL, Oct. 14, 1862; MGL, 241 (Oct. 12, 1862), 244–47 (Oct. 17–24, 1862), 251 (Oct. 31, 1862).

37. MGL, 679 (Sept. 8, 1864), 255 (Sept. 7, 1862).

38. Ibid., 242 (Oct. 14, 1862); Colonel Wolseley, "A Month's Visit to the Confederate Headquarters," in *Blackwood's Edinburgh Magazine* 93 (Jan.–June 1863): 1–29, 22; MGL, 524 (Dec. 1, 1863).

Lee's relationships with men who supported the Confederacy were based first on their patriotism, then on personal qualities she judged captivating. She appreciated men who were "attractive," "elegant looking," and "well shaped." "Charming" men won her favor as well as those "with refined & cultivated sensibilities; very handsome & exceedingly graceful." Confederate officers who stayed with her earned her approbation and friendship if they were "bright & spirited," "congenial," "pious," and "clever." Some of the same skills Lee had employed as a flirtatious young woman she used in the relationships she formed during the war: wit, intelligence, and what one of the young officers called her "faculty for managing men." This latter ability sharpened during the war, but she also began questioning her relationship with men, whether they were southern or northern.[39]

Historian Drew Gilpin Faust argues that "women . . . began to regard their difficulties as a test of the moral as well as the bureaucratic and military effectiveness of the new nation." She sees women's loss of patriotism as the result of the contradiction between "sacrifice as a means of overcoming uselessness" in the propaganda offered to them at the beginning of the war and the reality that their efforts were failing. When women demanded that their men come home and when they rioted for food, Faust argues, this suggests that women lost interest in maintaining and sustaining the Confederacy because it was not giving enough of a payoff relative to the effort involved and the cost to their families.[40]

Although this is part of the explanation, the conflict was not experienced collectively and daily war-born crises were felt more deeply than were national issues. These struggles they endured at home were personal and much more immediate than prescriptive literature could reach or overcome. Lee read *Macaria*, a novel by Augusta Evans published in 1864, that points to the ambiguous nature of women's lives while detailing the sacrifices women should make for the war. Faust points out that the novel "acknowledg[ed women's] fears of uselessness," a fear that they might remain single or become widows, suggesting they could be fulfilled as women only if they were partnered with men. Although Lee considered "the last part [of the book], about the war," admirable, she deemed the rest to be a "mass of pedantic nonsense." By the time she read *Macaria*, she had been in a war zone for over two years. If women were fulfilled only when they could define themselves in relationship to men, then Mary Greenhow Lee had a problem.[41]

39. MGL, 140 (June 11, 1862), 229 (Sept. 11, 1862), 230 (Sept. 13, 1862), 235 (Sept. 26, 1862), 248–49 (Oct. 24–25, 1862), 271 (Dec. 9, 1862), 694 (Sept. 27, 1864), 739 (Dec. 15, 1864).
40. Faust, "Altars of Sacrifice," 1223, 1228.
41. Ibid., 1219; Holstein, "'Offering Up Her Life,'" 123; MGL, 616, 620 (June 1864).

For instance, when rain had filled the gutters in the streets and a Union commander ordered one of his men to "get a plank to put across for" Lee's benefit, she "cross[ed] the street to another crossing without appearing to acknowledge or see his intentions," refusing to receive even "the slightest civility" from men of the opposition. When Philip Sheridan met her on the street one day, he "had the assurance to bow," a bow that was "not returned." Warfare for Lee meant expecting, but not always accepting, the rules set by society for gender relations. If Union soldiers or officers approached her on the porch, her custom was to turn her back to them as if they did not exist. She did this while visiting with a neighbor one day when "three Yankees" came "galloping" up to her house, but she learned later that this might not always be the best policy. One of the men shouted to her back, asking "where that cavalry had gone." Curiosity overcame her and she asked, "what cavalry?" In frustration the rider shouted, "Yankee, or rebel, or any god damn cavalry!" To that Lee walked into the house without a reply but learned from her neighbor later that "the Yankee had his carbine pointed" at her back the whole time.[42]

But she would have been happy to accept aid from her Confederate gentlemen, if they had been available to render it. One day, as the war neared an end, visiting gentlemen chased away a Yankee who had come into her yard. She discovered it "a new & singular sensation to have anyone" take her "part or act as protector against the enemy." Lee had learned that the men who were supposed to protect her could not and, as she worked out her "military" successes in her journal, harbored little respect for the enemy as men, felt she could outwit them, and sensed that the roles she played contradicted each other. According to Confederate generals, the women of Winchester were "women worth fighting for." According to the Union commanders, these same women were "devils."[43]

Yet how could a "Lady" sustain her nurturing capacity without sacrificing her Confederate identity when wagons loaded with wounded enemies were brought into town? Winchester men were not torn by this dilemma. Peyton Clark "visited all the hospitals" the morning after the battle of Kernstown, though only "for the purpose of finding any *friends* who may have been wounded to minister to their relief." He also reported that "Dr. Baldwin refuse[d] to attend the federal wounded on the grounds that" he would be "rais-

---

42. MGL, 740 (Dec. 16, 1864), 777 (Feb. 6, 1865), 513 (Nov. 14, 1863).
43. Ibid., 704 (Oct. 11, 1864), 120 (May 29, 1862), 201 (Mar. 12, 1862), 411 (June 15, 1863), 12 (Mar. 14, 1862).

ing up men to fight against the country and his friends." Neither of these men seemed to feel the weight of compassion when it came to the enemy. Women in Winchester, however, did.[44]

Mary Greenhow Lee had vowed never to have anything to do with Yankees, but when wounded Confederate soldiers were hospitalized with the Union wounded, she discovered herself "down on the floor, by the Yankees, feeding them." It became a crisis for Lee, tearing her between her female and Confederate identities. "I am trying to do good even to our enemies," she wrote, "but it is a wearisome life." One might suspect that northern military leaders used gender ideology to manipulate southern women, placing Federal wounded in sight of them intentionally, understanding on some level that the nurturing role would overpower the patriotic one.[45]

In fact, Cornelia McDonald knew that Union commanders manipulated women's emotions. When she complained that one of the soldiers kept milking her cow, the colonel in command "punish[ed] the offender" by having the man seated "on a barrel with his hands tied behind him" where McDonald would be sure to see him. She wrote that he looked "so miserable" and had "such a human look, so dejected and wretched," that her "heart was melted." When she asked the colonel how long the man had to stay on the barrel, his reply was "until justice is satisfied, Madam," and then she saw "his eyes twinkle as if he enjoyed the fun of seeing [her] take it to heart." Even so, she pleaded the culprit's cause, he was released, and she "did not annoy the Col. any more with complaints." In the end, she grumbled: "it was malicious in him to punish the man where I could see it. He knew I would not suffer it."[46]

In any event, Lee and other Secesh women of Winchester took care of enemy patients. The woman who imagined she would have nothing to do with Yankee hospitals and who upheld the standards of propriety not only cared for enemies in pain but even carried one northern man's amputated leg out of the hospital. Additionally, men who were upholding the old gender standards, while she had been forced to modify hers, amused her. One of her patients became embarrassed as she tended to his wounds because he had "to be considerably disrobed," which did not disconcert her. "I have seen so much in the last year," she wrote, "that I am nerved for everything." Lee's gender crisis was evolutionary, not revolutionary, but by the end of the war,

44. JPC, Mar. 24, 25 (emphasis added), 1862.
45. MGL, 34 (Mar. 25, 1862), 37 (Mar. 27, 1862).
46. McDonald, *Reminiscences of the War*, 45.

her journal makes it clear that she had incorporated contradictory roles into her identity that she would never have imagined before the war.[47]

It can be argued that women have always stepped into roles that fulfilled the requirements of a crisis, no matter what the dictates of society at the moment. But when that crisis is sustained, as in war, it can also be argued that women have more time to question society's rules. A good woman, for instance, was expected to pray for the cause. The men who had remained in Winchester were afraid to challenge the Federal order not to hold prayer meetings as requested by Confederate president Jefferson Davis, who proclaimed that "a people . . . faithfully relying on their Father in Heaven may be cast down, but cannot be dismayed." Mary Greenhow Lee challenged not only the enemy but also her male friends and conducted her own prayer services in accordance with Davis's proclamation. She also began to question just which gender had the most strength and the larger capacity for protection in the patriarchal order. Lee believed the "dear old men of this town . . . too cautious" and declared, "this is surely the day of woman's power" because "the men are afraid to do, or say, anything, & leave all to us."[48]

On several occasions during the war, Nathaniel Meade met with her to discuss "affairs of church & state." In fact, when a question arose as to whether they could afford to keep their church heated and open during the winter months, she suggested to Meade that he approach the Lutheran minister to see if that congregation would like to join theirs at Christ Church. The two churches could share the costs of heating, and the ministers could alternate Sundays in the pulpit. The Lutherans had lost their church to serve as a Yankee hospital, after all, so the idea made sense. The male leadership followed her advice, and Lutherans and Episcopalians worshipped together that winter.[49]

Early on, at one of those times when the Confederate army had just left Winchester and before the Union troops reoccupied the town, Lee noted that her army had abandoned twelve wagons of powder in the magazine. She suggested to the townsmen that they blow up the magazine to keep the Federals from getting their hands on it, promising to take responsibility for the action with Stonewall Jackson himself if the need arose. "But no one would

47. Sperry, "Surrender!" HL, 153, 154, typescript; McDonald, *Reminiscences of the War*, 54; MGL, 412 (June 16, 1863), 654 (July 26, 1864), 55 (Apr. 6, 1862), 258 (Nov. 12, 1862), 120 (May 29, 1862).

48. MGL, 102 (May 16, 1862), 314 (Feb. 13, 1863), 7 (Mar. 13, 1862), 47 (Apr. 1, 1862), 6 (Mar. 31, 1862), 206 (Aug. 19, 1862), 571 (Mar. 19, 1864); Davis, *Messages and Papers*, 227–28.

49. MGL, 591 (May 5, 1864), 721 (Nov. 14, 1864).

do anything," she grumbled, and "now, the Yankees are here & have put a guard round it immediately." She estimated that "there is enough powder there to blow up the whole town. I wish I was a man, or that our men had some manliness."[50]

The reality of the situation, of course, was that Union commanders perceived that the townsmen were necessarily more dangerous than were the townswomen. Winchester men understood this implication of the "Code of Southern Honor" as well and were thus more circumspect in their behavior. During the first Union occupation, male residents were "not allowed to go to the hospitals" or given a pass out of town "unless ladies [were] with them." Men in Lee's circle knew that they could not behave as they had in the past toward the invaders. Peyton Clark grumbled that the occupiers "shake their fists in our very faces whilst we are powerless to resent it." As Dr. Robert Baldwin left Cornelia McDonald's house one evening after visiting her sick children, he nodded toward the Union officers who had taken over her home and told her "he was sorry to leave" her with them. McDonald seemed to understand Baldwin's feelings of impotence. She wrote, "he looked very sorrowful, poor old gentleman, and mortified that he could do nothing to save me from their presence." Later, when Sheridan took command of Winchester, Lt. Gen. Ulysses S. Grant directed him to hold "all male citizens under fifty . . . prisoners of war," reasoning that if they were "not already soldiers, they [would] be made so the moment the rebel army [got] hold of them." Lee watched the men being taken away, "Dr. Holliday & other grey haired men amongst them," and believed this to be "the fulfillment of the threat they made when they first came, that they were going to send off all the men that the women might be still more unprotected."[51]

Lee proved capable of protecting herself. Ultimately, her social position became the most powerful weapon she used against her enemies. Although the war had moved her into relationships with patriotic citizens of less-connected circles, she refused to extend her sociable self to those of a similar station in the enemy camp. Many of the Union officers occupying Winchester met Lee's prewar requirements for acceptance into her company. As an invasion force, however, they now lacked one obvious value: southern patriotism. Because of her background and the *visitable* assets she had always prized

50. Ibid., 129 (June 4, 1862).

51. Ibid., 45 (Mar. 31, 1862), 50 (Apr. 4, 1862); JPC, Mar. 18, 1862; McDonald, *Reminiscences of the War*, 46; Sheridan, *Personal Memoirs*, 2:486; MGL, 711 (Oct. 25, 1864), 713 (Oct. 28, 1864).

so highly, Lee understood that she had something the Union army could never take from her. Union officers had threatened to take over her house. At one point a "6" was chalked onto her gate, telling her what position her house held in the schedule to be burned. Federal soldiers had also taken down her fences and outbuildings for firewood. But what the enemy could not forcibly requisition from Lee was an invitation into her parlor, even those officers who "under other circumstances" she would have entertained in all "civility." She tenaciously refused formal recognition of northern officers into "the society of Southern women," something she was convinced they wanted.[52]

According to Lee, northern officers were "men of the highest social position—the very elite of Northern society," but inviting them into her home would have been the same to her as welcoming the "murderers of our friends & the enemies of our liberty." She watched the officers make "desperate efforts to get into society, . . . & desir[ing] to be introduced to the Southerners." While some Winchester Secesh succumbed to the temptation of entertaining them, Lee resisted. Union officials had the power to demand entrance into any home they pleased. In fact, many citizens gave up rooms in their houses to board officers or to serve as "headquarters." Lee did not count such instances as social conquests, however. After all, Winchester was under military rule. Although Union officers had "by force, gained the entrance of so many homes," she reminded herself in her journal, "socially they have not gained an inch." For Lee, none of the values encompassed in the term *visitable* could be ascribed to Union military men who refused to acknowledge the South's right to secede. Cornelia McDonald held the same opinion. When a young Union soldier approached her with a letter of introduction, stating that he had family and acquaintances in the town and wondering if he might feel free to call on them, she answered, "they would not see you, coming with this army, and with that uniform on."[53]

Lee's opinion of Yankees as a class fluctuated depending upon gender. She was more antagonistic toward the wives of northern officers than to the officers themselves. According to her, "the [Union] officer's wives" were the ones who explained "the social status" of those in town who had invited northern officers into their homes, suggesting both that women would be more socially

52. MGL, 16 (Mar. 17, 1862), 35 (Mar. 26, 1862), 99 (May 14, 1862), 107 (May 21, 1862), 152 (June 22, 1862), 164 (July 5, 1862), 170 (July 11, 1862), 259 (Nov. 17, 1862), 329 (Mar. 16, 1863), 714 (Nov. 1, 1864), 745 (Dec. 23, 1864), 811 (Apr. 7, 1865).

53. Ibid., 730 (Dec. 3, 1864), 742 (Dec. 18, 1864), 594 (May 8, 1864), 730 (Dec. 3, 1864), 742 (Dec. 18, 1864), 751 (Dec. 30, 1864), 776 (Feb. 14, 1865); McDonald, *Reminiscences of the War*, 57.

discerning than men and that citizens who would deem the invaders *visitable* must not be members of the "better class." One general's wife could not even overcome her northernness by being an acquaintance of Lee's sister-in-law Rose O'Neal Greenhow. Mary deemed her "a coarse, common woman," with "the original Yankee shining out." General Milroy's wife could also never hope to be included in Lee's circle. Hearing that Mrs. Milroy had exhibited the "primitive custom" of blowing her nose through her fingers in public merely confirmed in Lee's mind that Yankees, and especially "Yankee women," were not *visitable.*[54]

In June 1862 Lee penned in her journal, at a time when both armies were absent from Winchester, "we shall declare ourselves a separate & independent sovereignty, & elect a Queen to reign over us, the women hav[ing] proved themselves more valiant than the men." In less than three months of living in a war zone, she had already begun questioning the system that placed men in charge. At the end of the war, Lee was even more convinced that women had done more than their part for the cause, stating, "I hear the women of Richmond are maintaining the honor of the Confederacy—but not the men."[55]

Earlier, as she emphasized her patriotism on the pages of her journal, Lee decided she would protect her family and her town, normally the responsibility of gentlemen, by being a good woman. But the contradictions that troubled her the most were the ones that forced her to play at one gender's role in order to achieve the goals expected of the other. It might be true that a majority of southern women lost faith in the idea of the Confederacy, unable to withstand the sacrifices they were being asked to make. As one southern woman put it, "the mother and helpless woman triumph[ed] over the patriot." But this sentiment cannot be found in the pages of Mary Greenhow Lee's journal. In fact, she tested and used both her gender and her class to wage war against Union occupiers to the very end.[56]

Lee's success might have been her undoing. She gloated that Union officers were disappointed "at not getting into Southern society," serving as "a bitter mortification to them & a great triumph to" her. Disappointment for Union officers and their wives, however, probably translated into the final grievance against Lee. Just prior to Sheridan's order that she would be es-

54. MGL, 524 (Dec. 23–24, 1863), 768 (Jan. 21, 1865), 729 (Feb. 9, 1865); LL, Apr. 4, 1863; Kasson, *Rudeness and Civility,* 124–25.

55. MGL, 127 (June 3, 1862), 818 (Apr. 28, 1865).

56. Quoted in Faust, "Altars of Sacrifice," 1220.

corted out of town in two days, Lee stated that, as she saw to various errands through town, she heard "nothing but the pique of those Yankees at not being received" in her home. She learned after her banishment from Winchester that Sheridan had been "very unwilling to send" her "out but . . . was persecuted into it by his staff because" the Lee women had held themselves "aloof & treated them with scorn & contempt." In Lee's opinion, her banishment had been a direct result of the social and gendered warfare she waged against the northern enemy.[57]

Mary Greenhow Lee had fought the war using the only weapons available to her. She did not risk her life in the process, but she did risk life as she had known it, sacrificing most of her assets and the comforts of her home. The end of the war left Lee wandering in exile, wondering where and how to start the next phase of her life but never questioning the cause for which she had fought.

57. MGL, 751 (Dec. 30, 1864), 775 (Feb. 2, 1865), 787 (Feb. 23, 1865), 813 (Apr. 14, 1865).

9

"I Feel Quite Independent Now"

Mary Greenhow Lee described the details of her banishment calmly, as though it were happening to someone else. Throughout the war, she had strained to keep Union officers from viewing her in distress, refusing to give them the satisfaction of knowing their effect on her. Her journal entries regarding her expulsion have the same detachment, possibly a way to portray the scenes on paper the way she hoped she had played them in front of the Yankees. Another possibility is that she felt some level of relief, like finally hearing the second shoe drop. She had expected banishment almost from the beginning of the first Union occupation. In any event, Lee remained aloof and disengaged when she wrote of being sent into exile, despite the fact that it meant propelling her into an uncertain future. Perhaps the bravado she expressed in front of the Yankees and on the pages of her journal strengthened her in the decisions she would have to make. In the end, although she gave up her life in Virginia and the home she had shared with Hugh, the new life she made for herself in Baltimore included many from her *connexion*, and even though forced into becoming a businesswoman, she maintained her social status for the rest of her life.

On Thursday, February 23, 1865, Lee received an order from Maj. Gen.

Philip H. Sheridan stating, "Mrs. Lee & her family must be prepared to go through the lines the first fair day." She "took it very coolly & sent [her] card to Sheridan asking him to call" on her, "as the weather was too bad." Ironically, although throughout the war she had refrained from inviting Union officers into her home, the order of banishment, in league with the weather, prompted her to send word to a Federal commander that now, at least to help her learn the charges against her, he was welcome. The general did not come but sent a member of his staff to find out what Lee wanted. She answered that she "had some little curiosity to know what were the accusations against" her.[1]

Later, when Sheridan did not answer her request, she and Mrs. Tuley went to his office to find out. Sheridan "shook hands with Mrs. T. & had the impertinence to offer his hand to" Lee, who merely "extended the tips of two fingers & then asked him what accusations he had to bring." The general replied "very rudely [that] there were plenty of charges," without stating any, and promised her "ample time for preparation." When Lee finally received the written order from Sheridan, she learned that she had until Saturday morning to pack. The only charges recorded on the order were that the Lee women had caused Union military personnel "constant annoyance," an open-ended indictment leaving room for several versions, each of which came to Lee's ears later.[2]

Among the reasons Lee heard given for her banishment was that one of her family members "had spit in a Yankee's face." She also read in the *New York Herald* that they had been sent out on "the charge of disloyalty" for conspiring to have Sheridan abducted by Maj. John S. Mosby's "guerrillas" and taken to Richmond. Another version printed in the *Herald* was that she had attempted "to poison Sheridan & his staff." The reason making the most sense to Lee, however, was the official cause, that she had been unsociable to the officers, which was reaffirmed through Lee's cousin Mary Charlton in Petersburg, who reported that the grounds "assigned by some Yankee officers for" their banishment was that the Lee "house was closed to them." The *Confederate Veteran* in 1895 reported that Lee had been banished for "her services and loyalty to the South," which equals all of the versions melted down. Loyalty to the South was the first basis of anything she might have done against northerners, real or imagined.[3]

1. MGL, 787–88 (Feb. 23, 1865).
2. Ibid.
3. Ibid., 799 (Mar. 12, 1865), 804 (Mar. 21, 1865), 812 (Apr. 11, 1865), 813 (Apr. 13, 1865), 824 (May 15, 1865), 831 (May 31, 1865), 880 (Oct. 14, 1865); James Murray Mason to Eliza Mason, Mar. 1865, printed in Mason, *Public Life*, 569; *Confederate Veteran*, 3, no. 11, Nov. 1895, 331.

Although there were usually a variety of reasons for southerners to be forced from their homes, those commanders who expelled them usually did so to remove disruptive citizens from occupied areas, to make an example of individuals to gain control over the rest of the population, or to use dislocation as a weapon against the Confederacy. Lee was not a refugee, meaning those who moved willingly to avoid enemy forces, thus forcing others to aid them in their resettlement or becoming a burden on the new community. She was, instead, forced into exile, having no choice in the decision. Distinctions between the terms probably evolved as war caused further disruption in the South, for Lee had confused the two earlier, long before exile became a reality for her. Although the female imbalance of refugees and exiles stemmed in part from a large percentage of men being in the army, it is interesting to note that the seven people Sheridan chose to remove from Winchester at this time were single women who did not have husbands to protect them, war or no war.[4]

Whatever the charges, Mary's household, with the exception of Antoinette, who by that time was staying with brother George Lee in Clarksburg, had two days to prepare to leave. They would be traveling with three of Joseph H. Sherrard's daughters, Ann, Lizzie, and Mary. Sherrard, cashier at Farmers Bank of Virginia when the war started, lived with his family above the bank. Lee appreciated the Sherrard family's southern sympathies; but she worried about some of the schemes their daughters had gotten into, writing that Lizzie Sherrard was "daring & dashing to an extreme that is perfectly ludicrous." Whatever the charges against the Sherrard women, it is possible that their "perfectly ludicrous" behavior was equal to Lee's "giving constant annoyance."[5]

Although she did not want to abandon her home and did not know what form of shelter she would find, Lee reasoned, "If God permits it, it is all right," placing her faith above her fear. The Lee household worked hard on Thursday night to "do all the packing" possible, taking some possessions to the Tuley's for safekeeping and depositing the family silver in the bank. The next day, even though from the time Lee dressed in the morning until late that night her hours were "filled with visitors" coming to see if the news was true or offering assistance, she attended to "the thousand things necessary to be done in breaking up a home in a day." Nathaniel Meade came by to give

4. Mary Elizabeth Massey, *Refugee Life in the Confederacy* (Baton Rouge: Louisiana State University Press, 1964), 18; Rable, *Civil Wars*, 180; Faust, *Mothers of Invention*, 40–44; MGL, 351–52 (Apr. 10, 1863), 364 (Apr. 23, 1863).

5. MGL, 225 (Sept. 5, 1862), 729 (Dec. 2, 1864), 435 (July 15, 1863), 472 (Sept. 8, 1863), 60 (Apr. 11, 1862).

her "$500 in Bank money," offering it "without interest for 20 years," and others offered "kindnesses" as well.[6]

On Saturday morning, friends gathered in front of the house to see them off. "Many tears were shed," she wrote, "but not by us." Those who cried were "strong men," friends, and "servants," not only their own but also "old attaches of the family . . . weeping bitterly." The Lee women, however, "laughed & talked all sorts of Rebel talk & the Yankees gazed in astonishment at seeing people turned out of their homes & not depressed by it." The assemblage followed their wagon down to the Sherrards' home, where Lizzie, Ann, and Mary Sherrard loaded their belongings and joined the Lees. As though observing her banishment through the eyes of her enemies, Mary Lee reported that, since their departure scene was played in front of the provost's office, she was certain that he "had a full view of [their] movements." As Lee and her family left Winchester, in "two ambulances & an army wagon piled up with baggage" and with "an escort of over twenty men," she stated that they "felt very independent & said loudly what [they] pleased," feeling that there was nothing more the Yankee occupiers could do to them.[7]

The Union escort traveled with the party as far as Newtown, where the exiles were forced to find their own transportation; the U.S. government did not intend to provide the conveyances they would need for their journey. From Strother Jones in Newtown they "procured a road wagon for the baggage & a spring wagon for the" women. Their next stop was Woodstock, thirty miles south. The horse pulling the spring wagon was "a miserable old one," but Louisa and Mary drove it until the animal "gave out so entirely" that, to ease its load, the women rode on top of the baggage wagon.[8]

Their progress was delayed at Mount Jackson from February 27 until March 12 while they waited for the waters of the north fork of the Shenandoah River to recede enough for them to cross. They could have left a day earlier, but their wagon drivers refused to start due to word that Yankees were only five miles away. Even though Lee had been sent within her lines, to her it seemed as though her enemies were following her. Early the next day, however, they set off, walking the mile to the river since "there was a dreadful gully" in the road, then crossing the river while "the girls sang 'On the Other Side of Jordan'" for courage as the Shenandoah swept around the wagon.

6. Ibid., 788 (Feb. 25, 1865), 762 (Jan. 13, 1865), 764 (Jan. 16, 1865), 787–88 (Feb. 23, 25, 1865), 788–89 (Feb. 25, 1865).

7. Ibid., 788–89 (Feb. 25, 1865).

8. Ibid., 789–90 (Feb. 25–26, 1865), 790 (Feb. 26, 1865).

That night they stayed in Harrisonburg, then left on March 13 for Staunton, all the while fearing they would meet Sheridan somewhere along the way. Lee had planned to go on to Richmond immediately from Staunton, but the "croakers" in that town told her "it would be impossible" to reach the capital for a while. She made plans, then, to settle in for some time, although "the idea of staying at Staunton with the prospect of the immense bill at the hotel was rather startling."⁹

Leaving her comfortable home in Winchester behind had been a major concern for Lee, for she had the responsibility of providing shelter for her family. Unlike the problems in some overcrowded regions such as Richmond and cities in the Lower South, where residents faced a massive influx of refugees, the stops on Lee's journey up the Valley afforded available accommodations. Between Winchester and Richmond, Lee's *connexion* offered help with quarters, which, added to public lodging available, provided fairly comfortable situations for the seven exiles. In Woodstock, for instance, Lee wrote that the party had "scattered," some staying with the Hollingsworth family, while others roomed at the Magruders' home; Lee herself was even "comfortably fixed" enough to have a small tea party. As a bonus, "Mrs. Hollingsworth . . . would not receive any pay," so lodging in Woodstock did not stretch the women's slim resources as much as it could have.¹⁰

Their extended stay in Mount Jackson necessitated a more permanent arrangement; some in the group "took rooms at the hotel" and went into "room-keeping." Whiten and Virginia Farra's hotel enjoyed the assistance of four servants, a horse and carriage, and a piano for entertainment. The Lee party felt snug for a time, although Mary described their "style of living" as "very amusing," with the room she and Laura Lee stayed in the "mess room" where they had a "table set out with plates, cups & saucers," some they had brought along and "some borrowed." It was also expensive, costing "$90 per day for . . . two rooms & fire." Within a day or two, local residents began inviting other members to wait out the river in private homes, until Mary and Laura were the only two remaining at the hotel. The group engaged three rooms at the hotel in Harrisonburg and were allowed use of the parlor to receive visitors, of which there were many for the one night they were in town. More than a quarter million southerners found themselves homeless during the war, but their experiences varied, depending upon resources, destinations, and friends along the way. The accommodations many people set-

9. Ibid., 791–800 (Feb. 28–Mar. 13, 1865), 801–3 (Mar. 14–19, 1865).
10. Ibid., 820 (May 3, 1865), 791 (Feb. 28, 1865).

tled for were much less comfortable than those Lee found. Some were forced to find shelter in churches, stables, tents, caves, and even abandoned railroad cars.[11]

Lee's worries about the expense of an extended stay in Staunton proved groundless. She secured rooms at the American Hotel, then asked Colonel Nadenbousch, the proprietor, his terms. Because of the reputation she had gained for her war efforts, Nadenbousch, a veteran, responded that the party would "be his guests," refusing to "receive a cent from ladies who had acted so nobly . . . in risking so much for [the] cause," waiving his normal charge of twenty dollars a day.[12]

The warmth of this former soldier's regard for Mary speaks to a thread that connected Lee's journey in exile. A sign that she had not taken her "soldier work" lightly was her continuance of it away from Winchester. While packing trunks and deciding what to take and leave, she had the presence of mind to pack not only her journal but also items of interest to soldiers and their families, minor details that would normally be forgotten in the haste of preparing for a major life change on short notice. In Woodstock, for instance, a man approached her and asked if she knew a Lieutenant Snarr, who had been wounded and was believed dead. Snarr had been one of Mary's patients. Looking through her portfolio, she found a letter she had received from him a few weeks earlier and gave it to Snarr's sister, letting her know he was still alive. In Mount Jackson a woman whose husband had been one of Lee's "special favorite[s] as long as he lived" asked Lee about her husband's last days, and Lee relieved the woman by relating "his cheerful & brave spirit" to the end. In Staunton, Lee called on a Mrs. Fall "to tell her of her son who died at the Hospital in Winchester." She also sent a ring and a lock of a dead soldier's hair to his widow in Georgia and gave "$5.00 . . . of the little horde" she had put together for the soldiers to a wounded Confederate in Staunton. All of this points to the minute details she saw to during her hurried packing in Winchester.[13]

Banishment did not curtail Lee's other soldier work either, that of supply-

11. U.S. Bureau of the Census, Eighth Census, LOV, microfilm; Shenandoah County Personal Property Tax List, 1861, LOV; MGL, 791–92 (Feb. 28–Mar. 1, 1865), 793 (Mar. 2, 1865), 800 (Mar. 13, 1865); Massey, *Refugee Life*, 22–23, 75, 76, 103; Rable, *Civil Wars*, 181–201.

12. MGL, 801 (Mar. 14, 1865); Nadenbousch to wife, Aug. 26, Sept. 2, 22, Dec. 30, 1863, Jan. 27, Feb. 13, Mar. 9, 1864, Jan. 24, 1865, Col. J. Q. A. Nadenbousch Letters, Soldier Letters Collections, ESB.

13. MGL, 799 (Mar. 12–13, 1865), 790 (Feb. 26, 1865), 796 (Mar. 6, 1865), 802 (Mar. 15, 1865), 830 (May 28, 1865).

ing information about the enemy. In fact, once in the countryside, she had more freedom to note troop movements along the Valley as she passed, assess numbers, and sight "pontoon bridges, &c.," then telegraph the information to her generals. A woman from Woodstock told Lee that "the Yankees said they were amazed at the correctness of [her] information & they were very anxious to overtake" the exiles to stop her. Jubal Early ignored her warnings, however, with the capture of twelve hundred Confederates near Staunton the result. "I have done fighting Early's battles," wrote Lee. He "received my dispatch sooner than any other & it was his fault that he was not prepared."[14]

Exile also did not stop Lee's "feeding process." In Mount Jackson a Confederate regiment stopped by the hotel and "begged for bread." She gave them "a large basket of hard-tack" and watched it disappear in short order. After inviting a colonel to dine with the women in their room one evening, Lee wrote, "wherever we are, . . . I expect we will be entertaining Confederates." Between leaving Winchester and finally settling in Baltimore, Lee received visits from several of her soldiers. The Bartons and Baldwins stopped in to see the family and ate at their table in Staunton several times. She also entertained "Henry Douglass, . . . as handsome & agreeable as ever." Randolph McKim spent time with her in Staunton before moving back to Baltimore. Hunter McGuire visited with her as did her "special favourite," David Gregg McIntosh, and "Genl. Fitz Lee." When "Col. Holliday" stopped in, Lee sadly noted his empty sleeve and made a similar observation on another occasion, mentioning that "Genl. Lilly with one arm & Mr. Ryan with one leg & Col. Skinner with one eye were all here together."[15]

Despite Nadenbousch's generous invitation, Lee and her party again scattered for lodging. Laura Lee and Louisa Burwell accepted the hospitality of one family, Lizzie and Mary Sherrard another, and Laura Burwell and Ann Sherrard yet another, while Mary moved into the home of Dr. Francis Stribling, superintendent of Western State Hospital for the mentally ill. Mary's room was "a beautiful chamber," but she thought that the "quiet household" was "rather stiff after the life of abandon" she "had been leading lately." The

---

14. Ibid., 791 (Feb. 28, 1865), 792 (Mar. 1, 1865), 799 (Mar. 12, 1865), 792 (Mar. 1, 1865), 796–99 (Mar. 6–11, 1865). A search of Early's papers at the Library of Congress turned up no mention of Lee's warning. Whether he did not receive her letter or ignored it remains unknown. Jubal Anderson Early Papers, LC.

15. MGL, 793 (Mar. 3, 1865), 797 (Mar. 8, 1865), 802, 807, 817, 818 (Mar.–Apr. 1865), 834 (June 9, 1865), 843 (July 5, 1865), 855 (Aug. 15, 1865), 859 (Aug. 22, 1865), 871 (Sept. 21, 1865), 886 (Oct. 29, 1865), 889 (Nov. 10, 1865). "Col. Holliday" was F. W. M. Holliday of Winchester, who became governor of Virginia in 1877. See Dabney, *Virginia*, 381.

length of her stay in Staunton stretched into another month and, not wanting to "trespass on the hospitality" of their various hosts, Lee decided in April 1865 to rent a house suddenly available. Fearful, she stated that it required "strong faith to go to housekeeping at this crisis, in a strange place, with very little money," but she could not be sure when she could get to Richmond. With furnishings the former renters left behind and the donations of friends in the area, the scattered family moved back together, a "great comfort" to her.[16]

At this point, signs that she would be able to survive the new life America's Civil War forced her into became apparent. On the morning of May 11 in the Sherrards' kitchen in Staunton, Mary Greenhow Lee, forty-five years old, learned to make bread. Lee, Louisa Burwell, and Ella Stribling had gone to the Sherrards' for breakfast, after which Jeannie Sherrard gave them their lesson. Filled with enthusiasm at the prospect of making bread on her own, Lee hurried home to her rented house to try her hand at it. Even though this was her first attempt, she invited "the Catletts & Mrs. Johnson" for supper, but "being timid, they were afraid to leave home as another Brigade of Yankees came in" that morning. Still determined to share her first bread with friends, she invited Alexander Hugh Holmes Stuart and his family to join her for supper. Instead of Yankees, rain kept the Stuarts from accepting. She "was disappointed" because her "bread was very successful."[17]

The first visitor to sample Mary's bread was Randolph McKim, now a war veteran and ordained minister, who came on a Saturday to tea, which included slices of Lee's newest endeavor. Clearly, McKim would have appreciated her efforts, no matter the outcome, because he had suffered the trials of bread making himself, "on the march," and without the most necessary ingredient: yeast. Innovative and hungry, the young soldier had put flour and water together, wrapped "the dough round [his] ramrod," and leaned "it up before the fire to bake," producing "a loaf of bread about three feet long and one-eighth of an inch thick." With the war over, however, he was again at liberty to enjoy the warmth of bread made properly, baked in an oven, and served on real dishes, even though most of those dishes and the silver cutlery were on loan from Lee's friends and the wood for the fire and ingredients for the tea donated to the widow out of friendship. Despite her straightened

16. MGL, 801–2 (Mar. 14, 1865); Hugh Milton McIlhany Jr., *Some Virginia Families*, (Baltimore: Genealogical Publishing, 1962), 41–42; MGL, 802 (Mar. 1865), 813–16 (Apr. 12–17, 1865).

17. Ibid., 822, (May 11, 1865).

circumstances and her patchwork furnishings, Lee played her role as hostess, serving McKim bread, which "proved a grand success." As she recorded the event in her journal, she announced, "I feel quite independent now."[18]

It is a sign of her character that Lee did not fear taking on this new chore herself, nor did she lack confidence in exposing her first try to dinner guests. She risked the ridicule of her peers if her bread had not turned out well. Bread making is not an exact science in which merely measuring ingredients, temperature, and time will always produce the same results. It requires the senses of sight and touch to know the dough's readiness to move from one stage to the next. When the practiced eye and hand note that the dough has a dull sheen yet no longer sticks to the palm of the hand, then the kneading is done. When an impression in the dough fills in quickly, signaling that it has risen to its fullest point, it is ready for baking. All of these sensory perceptions require time and experience to develop. Yet Lee's confidence and enthusiasm led her to invite critics to supper even as she waited for the bread to come out of the oven.[19]

Significantly, although she had feared that her slaves might leave her and wondered how she would manage her household without them, in the end she left them and, once she learned how to make bread without them, felt "quite independent," suggesting that relying upon the slaves for this housewifely art had kept Lee dependent upon them in order to meet her obligation as a woman. Simply learning to make bread gave her a feeling of independence even in the middle of her future's uncertainty. Women of Lee's era were measured by their ability to provide nutritious meals. She had always counted on her slaves to perform this duty for her, but war and banishment had deprived her of slaves, and although she hired a young cook in Staunton, that woman was "a novice," and Lee admitted to "not know[ing] how to teach her in the plain branches." War propelled Lee into "the servant problem" and left her to provide the best, most complete meals for her friends and family on her own.[20]

Finally, in August 1865, after the war had ended and life in Richmond had become more stable, Mary Greenhow Lee found her way clear to venture

18. McKim, *Soldier's Recollections*, 43; MGL, 816 (Apr. 16, 20, 1865), 817 (Apr. 21, 23, 25, 1865), 823 (May 13, 1865).

19. I would like to thank my mother, Shirlie Islay Smith Baber, for patiently teaching me the art of bread making, a process that feeds the soul as much as the bread feeds the body. During the lessons, I felt an ancient connection to the long line of women from whom I am descended, learning the tricks they had all passed down through the ages.

20. Grubb, "House and Home," 171; MGL, 818 (Apr. 25, 1865).

there. The rest of the family had gone back to Winchester in July, so Lee traveled alone by train, stopping for a short while in Charlottesville to visit with friends Dr. George G. and Caroline Christian Minor. From there she traveled again by rail to Richmond, this time encountering "several Yankee officers" in the car with her. Still determined to withhold recognition of them, she "stretched" herself "out on the seat with [her] back to the aisle," pulled her "hat & veil over [her] face," and pretended to sleep.[21]

Samuel C. Greenhow, George's son, met Lee at the train station and took her home with him, where he and his wife, Mary, settled her into "a delightful room on the first floor, with [a] window opening on a balcony, overlooking a pretty yard" at his house on the corner of Tenth and Clay Streets. Lee spent her days in Richmond, her "dear old home," with friends and relatives. She also ventured off for two short trips out of town: to Petersburg to visit cousins, and in September she traveled to the countryside to renew her friendship with Mona Warren (formerly known to her as "Eddie" Christian) at Runnymede, the Warrens' plantation sixteen miles southeast of Richmond. During her visit, John Warren took Lee for a drive "over historic ground," showing her the landscape on which the Seven Days Battle had occurred in the summer of 1862, explaining "the position of the two armies" as they rode along. The scarred battlefields troubled Lee. "The horrors of war impress me more now," she wrote, "than when they were actually being enacted."[22]

By the time of her Richmond interlude, Lee had finally come to terms with the South's loss of the war, but her first reactions to the news had not been surprising, given the full energy she had applied to the struggle. At first she had been doubtful. In April, upon hearing that Richmond had been evacuated, she wrote, "can the terrible news I have just heard be true?" That day she decided to rent the house in Staunton and stay for a while. Confirmation by telegram that "the Yankees entered Richmond at 1/2 past nine yesterday morning" convinced her, however. The next blow came when she heard that "Genl. Lee & all his army had surrendered," which she first met with her "usual skepticism," then, when "Genl. Lee's farewell address to the army he

21. MGL, 868 (Aug. 25, 1865), 845 (July 14, 1865), 856 (Aug. 17, 1865), 858 (Aug. 18, 1865), 860 (Aug. 25, 1865).

22. Ibid., 861 (Aug. 25, 1865); Mary Wingfield Scott, *Neighborhoods*, 92; Virginius Cornick Hall Jr., *Portraits*, 166–67; MGL, 873–74 (Sept. 29–30, 1865), 862 (Aug. 27, 1865), 865 (Sept. 3–5, 1865), 877–78 (Oct. 9, 1865), 865–69 (Sept. 5–14, 1865), 545 (Jan. 23, 1864), 559 (Feb. 19, 1864), 564 (May 1864), 863 (Aug. 29, 1865), 866 (Sept. 7, 1865); MJCG/MHS, 9 (Sept. 1837); Tubbs, *Rennie Family*, 1:161; MGL, 866 (Sept. 1865).

surrendered" made its way through town, she wrote, "it would be looked on as foolhardy were I still to express a doubt."[23]

She had been devastated. The phrase "after the war" had kept her going for four years, but now there were "no triumphs," "no rejoicings," and she felt "utterly bewildered." Considering the work she had put into the war effort, she lamented: "all the energy & enthusiasm of my nature, which was buried in the graves of my loved ones . . . , was warmed into full development for my country, my beloved Southern Confederacy. . . . [B]ut now . . . all has been in vain." When she watched Ranny and Bob Barton having breakfast at her table in Staunton, she wrote, "I love to see the boys; still it makes me so sad to think their hands are tied & they cannot do anything to save our tottering cause."[24]

Lee became additionally distressed when she heard "an official report that *our* President has been captured & . . . that it is said he was making his escape in his wife's clothes." Historian LeeAnn Whites draws a powerful parallel between this picture of Davis attempting to flee in his wife's overcoat and shawl and the emasculating result of southerners' failure to protect their political independence. She states that "these men had staked their sense of themselves as free men upon their successful founding of an independent nation; the defeat of the Confederacy now presented them with an overwhelming threat to the very deepest level of their masculine identity." Mary Greenhow Lee placed a similar significance upon the scene, but it did not force her to accept defeat at all levels.[25]

Throughout the war, Lee's conditions for association shifted until patriotism ranked second on her list, just below family. When the South lost the war, it compelled her to reassess her views on the subject yet again. No longer sure of what to do with her feelings of patriotism, she transformed that allegiance into conservation of the Old South's traditions. Her struggles and losses, both human and material, had turned Lee against northerners, and "the treatment" of Jefferson Davis "by the Yankees" merely intensified her "hatred of them as a people."[26]

Upon learning that the North's Reconstruction policies were inhibiting former secessionist politicians' political power and securing the election of old-line Whigs and Unionists to the constitutional convention, she became

23. MGL, 809 (Apr. 4, 1865), 808 (Apr. 3, 1865), 812 (Apr. 11, 1865), 813 (Apr. 13, 1865).
24. Ibid., 814–15 (Apr. 14–16, 1865).
25. Ibid., 826 (May 20, 1865, emphasis hers); Whites, *Crisis in Gender*, 132–35.
26. MGL, 836 (June 12, 1865).

further embittered. In fact, it called up her deep reserves of stubbornness, evidenced by her announcement that, although "political reconstruction might be unavoidable, . . . social re-construction" was something that she "might prevent." When forced into company with northerners, she ignored them and steered the conversation to topics they "could not appreciate." She suspected that they thought her "an insufferable aristocrat" but did not care.[27]

As she renewed acquaintances in Richmond, Lee's identity remained unchanged. Still a staunch Secesh, she visited hospitalized Confederate soldiers, treating them with gifts of oranges, and reported with pleasure that "there is a stronger & more united feeling against the Yankees than existed a year ago." She felt no reticence in agreeing with "old & young men" alike who "fire with wrath at our present condition & are ready to side with any party who will chastise our tyrannical foe."[28]

Secesh to her toes, Lee continued fighting a battle of the sexes, now on the side of the men, urging those in her circle to regain their own power. Instead of a war of weapons, she considered the South engaged in a political battle and, without hesitation, proclaimed her opinions on the way to go about winning. Chafing under Reconstruction policies, she stated her case with men of "different interests; some the monied, some the mercantile, the literary, the agricultural & professional," and she found many who agreed with her "views about the proper course for the South to pursue." Lee believed, in "every election where the semblance of free voting is allowed, *we* should vote for our soldiers even though we know they will not be allowed to hold the Office." Clearly, she thought that males who voted for what she believed in were casting her votes.[29]

Historians are now beginning to question if all of the national tensions before the war were merely between the North and South or if there was also growing discontent among southern women with the patriarchal system they lived under, and whether or not the war halted or escalated women's questioning their place in society. War not only created more work and worry for women but also, argues Anne Firor Scott, allowed them to "do business in their own right, make decisions, . . . and in many other ways assert themselves as individual human beings." The myth of the Lost Cause, arising after the war, is credited for postponing an organized women's movement in the

27. Ibid., 844 (July 12, 1865), 868 (Sept. 13, 1865), 870 (Sept. 19, 1865); Eric Foner, *A Short History of Reconstruction, 1863–1877* (New York: Harper and Row, 1990), 90–92.

28. MGL, 874 (Oct. 4, 1865), 877 (Oct. 8, 1865).

29. Ibid., 873 (Sept. 28, 1865, emphasis added).

South. The question now is whether historians are describing the myth or perpetuating it. As Sandra Gioia Treadway has stated, "it is fair to say that the Virginia women of the Civil War era are as obscured today by the spell of the Lost Cause as they were in the 1860s and 1870s." Part of the South's distinction came from its code of honor, with the "Southern Lady" perched atop its pedestal, the reason for white men to assume and maintain their power. When the men lost the war and then had to fight through Reconstruction to regain power, southern ladies could not simultaneously struggle against their men for their own political rights. As opinionated as Lee was, it did not occur to her to argue for a political voice of her own. For her, the course to follow was to bring power back to the men who had led the South politically before and during the war.[30]

Lee also turned her back on Winchester, where she predicted that Reconstruction and emancipation would produce a "heterogeneous mass" of society, and made plans to start over in Baltimore, saving her the trouble of reinstituting *visitable* requirements on associations she had made during the war. Even as she prepared to leave Virginia for good, she remained proud of her "grand old State," which she was sure would "weather this storm even yet, if her true men can get the ascendancy." Although filled with misgivings about her own future, she did not doubt the future of either Virginia or the South.[31]

Her decision to move to Baltimore did not come easily, even though she had no desire to return to Winchester. When soldiers taunted her by singing "impromptu verses" under her window in Staunton such as "There's one light they can't put out & that's a bitter pill; his last name was Sheridan—his first name was Phil," they were disappointed. Although she tried to be angry, she could not help but laugh at their "happy hit," for the soldiers did not realize how "obliged" she was to Sheridan for giving her a reason to leave Winchester. She had not perceived the pressure she had been under until removed from it and began enjoying an uneventful life within her own lines.[32]

In addition, the house in Winchester was in a sad state of disrepair, with "part of the wall . . . caving in," and in need of a new roof. A Mrs. Cochrane moved in the day the Lee family left, then Union officers occupied the house

30. Anne Firor Scott, "Women's Perspective on the Patriarchy in the 1850s," in *Half Sisters of History: Southern Women and the American Past*, ed. Catherine Clinton (Durham, N.C.: Duke University Press, 1994), 78, 87; Sandra Gioia Treadway, "New Directions in Virginia Women's History," *Virginia Magazine of History and Biography* 100, no. 1 (Jan. 1992): 18.

31. MGL, 845 (July 13, 1865), 878 (Oct. 10, 1865).

32. Ibid., 845 (July 13, 1865), 805 (Mar. 22, 1865).

for a time. Conflicting reports came to her from Winchester, and she was never sure what to believe, but when Phil Williams let her know that the house was finally rented to a man named Hollenbach to use as a restaurant, she said, "so the fact is at last established that for six months I am to be a wanderer." The renter "kept such a disreputable establishment," however, that "Williams had to turn him out," putting Lee in "a maze" again.[33]

After deciding not return to the town, her choice of another location became a struggle. She had alternatives. Several friends and family invited her to live with them, at least for the time being. Hugh Lee's brother, Henry, and his wife, Anna, invited the family to New Orleans to live with them, an option that appealed to Lee since they were favorites and it would give her time to make a more permanent decision. The Maurys, Dunlaps, and Powells all offered a place for Lee in Richmond. And James Murray Mason and his family asked her to stay with them for a while in Canada, where the former senator was living in exile pending the resolution of Reconstruction policies, raising vegetables and chickens. Lee did not take advantage of any of these offers. She agonized over the decision, feared that she would "shrink into the insignificance that is the fate of all middle-aged women," felt "bewildered," and wondered if her "darling would approve." But she finally made plans to start over in Baltimore, running a boardinghouse to make a living. It is probable that Lee did not want to live near relatives because she wanted to test her independence. Consistent with her character, she ventured into a new life.[34]

Mary Greenhow Lee "left Richmond with great regret," again traveling by train, under the "nominal . . . protection" of a "Mr. Davenport . . . , who was taking his own family to the North." A "delay in Washington" caused her to miss her connection, so instead of arriving in Baltimore at five in the evening, she "was put out hurriedly" in Philadelphia "at night, by [her]self, [and] some distance from the baggage office." Trying to locate a driver, she "was nearly run over," then "stood at the office in a crowd of men" to get her baggage, and sat on her "trunk till the driver found some one to help him

33. Ibid., 821 (May 6, 1865), 861 (Aug. 25, 1865), 791–92 (Feb. 28–Mar. 1, 1865), 819 (May 2, 1865), 821 (May 6, 1865), 823 (May 12, 1865), 829 (May 25, 1865), 830 (May 31, 1865), 834 (June 8, 1865), 837 (June 15, 1865), 837 (June 18, 1865), 861 (Aug. 25, 1865), 864 (Sept. 1, 1865); Winchester Deed Book 13:273, 275–77, 283–85, 344–45, Frederick County Courthouse, Winchester, Va.

34. MGL, 837 (June 18, 1865), 831 (June 2, 1865), 832 (June 4, 1865), 845 (July 14, 1865), 852 (Aug. 5, 1865), 864 (Sept. 2, 1865), 872 (Sept. 22, 1865), 879 (Oct. 11, 1865); Mason, *Public Life*, 586–87; MGL, 852 (Aug. 5, 1865), 857 (Aug. 17, 1865), 860 (Aug. 23, 1865), 878 (Oct. 10, 1865).

move it." Finally, "after sundry adventures," she was "very kindly received" at the Dorseys' in Baltimore.[35]

She had to make arrangements for a home and furniture. There were times when her feet ached from traversing the city on errands, often feeling "very alone" and close to tears. At the same time, she felt "perfectly independent" and began to see herself as "a mere adventuress." After a month of searching and wrangling with lawyers, Lee finally signed a lease on a house at 160 Calvert Street. She was not happy with its location but felt pressured to get things settled. She wrote, "so the die is cast for a year," then went out for a "lunch of cake & ice-cream." Whether ice cream was a celebratory food or a comfort food is unclear, but it punctuated the end of her old life and the start of a new one. This is the last entry in Mary Greenhow Lee's Civil War journal, which is close to a promise she had made to herself. On August 18, 1865, while visiting in Charlottesville, she wrote: "I have determined to continue with my journal till I have a home again & the scattered members of my family are reunited." Although the family was not with her, she had at least found a home.[36]

Lee did not operate her boardinghouse alone but staffed it with servants. Her slaves had not left Winchester with her, becoming truly liberated with Lee's banishment. It could be that Sheridan would not allow her to take them, though she did not mention it, or Emily and Sarah may have refused to leave their family and friends in town. It is also possible that Lee made the decision herself, not relishing the added worry of taking care of them in exile, a problem many planter refugees faced. The Masons' slave, William, had located Lee in Staunton and moved in with her, though she did not explain how or why he followed them. Witty and flamboyant, "a wag" as Lee called him, William might have enjoyed living in the Lee household, but he did not follow her to Baltimore, returning instead to Winchester, where he found work for "50 cts a day in silver." Lee tried convincing Sarah to relocate in

35. MGL, 882 (Oct. 19, 1865). Research has not revealed conclusively who the Dorseys were. Lee refers to them as "Mr. Dorsey" and "Kate." Margaretta Barton Colt states that a J. T. B. Dorsey was married to Kate Mason, a daughter of James Murray Mason. The Baltimore directory for 1858–59 lists a J. T. B. Dorsey as an attorney located at 35 St. Paul Street. Considering Mary's attachment to the Masons, this is probably the couple with whom she briefly stayed. See Colt, *Defend the Valley*, 243, 422–47; *Woods' Baltimore Directory, for 1858–'59* (Baltimore: John W. Woods, 1858), 147.

36. MGL, 882–91 (Oct. 19–Nov. 17, 1865), 891 (Nov. 17, 1865); Mary Greenhow Lee to Mary Williams, June 6, 1866, Philip Williams Family Papers (172 WFCHS), HL; MGL, 858 (Aug. 18, 1865).

Baltimore with her, but she refused, and Lee was forced into hiring a staff for her boardinghouse. By 1870, she had five "domestic servants" living with her, one of them a white woman from Ireland, Catherine O'Brien; the other four were black women who were natives of Maryland.[37]

When Lee migrated to Baltimore, she was not a stranger in the city. Several of the Winchester *connexion* had relocated there. St. George Hopkins wanted to "take his meals" at her boardinghouse; Ranny Barton boarded with her while he got his law practice going; and Frank Clark, brother of Peyton, relocated there as well. In addition, Lee could call for help and companionship from several native Baltimore friends. In addition to natives who had aided in her war effort, the city became home to some of the young soldiers she had befriended. When Basil Gildersleeve had visited with Lee during the war, he acted out his departure like a scene in a play, throwing "himself against his horse and wip[ing] away imaginary tears with his cuff." Years later, Gildersleeve became a prominent professor of ancient languages at Johns Hopkins University and settled down in Baltimore with his family.[38]

Basil Lanneau Gildersleeve had originally taught Greek at the University of Virginia in 1856. One of his students was Randolph McKim, and the two began a lifelong friendship that intensified through their shared military experiences. Gildersleeve's knowledge of ancient languages and McKim's study of theology prompted discussions of the classics between the two men. There is also some evidence that the Gildersleeves kept in contact with Dr. Philip C. Williams. A letter from Eliza ("Bettie") to Basil from Germany states that she saw the Williams's son, John, during her travels. These relationships do not mean that Mary Greenhow Lee provided all of the links—she obviously did not—but it does depict a tightly woven network of friends and family connecting various urban areas together, not just for the Old South but also for the new.[39]

Lee's friendship with Randolph McKim in Baltimore is one of the best documented of her relationships, beginning with her attendance at Emman-

37. Massey, *Refugee Life*, 109; MGL, 811, 812 (Apr. 1865), 824 (May 16, 1865), 828 (May 24, 1865), 832 (June 4, 1865), 883 (Oct. 21, 1865), 885 (Oct. 25, 1865); U.S. Bureau of the Census, Ninth Census, LOV, microfilm.

38. MGL, 885 (Oct. 27, 1865), 889 (Nov. 10, 1865); Frank P. Clark to Henry Rowland, Oct. 3, 1879, Henry Augustus Rowland Papers (Ms. 6), JHU; MGL, 678 (Sept. 6, 1864), 680 (Sept. 9, 1864).

39. McKim, *Soldier's Recollections*, 258–59 n; Barringer et al., *University of Virginia*, 362, 517–18; letters between Gildersleeve and McKim, July 8, 1898–Dec. 28, 1905, Basil Lanneau Gildersleeve Papers (Ms. 5), JHU; Eliza Gildersleeve to B. L. Gildersleeve, Mar. 24, 1889, ibid.

uel Protestant Episcopal Church, where McKim served as assistant minister, and continuing throughout Lee's life. In 1904, when McKim delivered a speech to Confederate veterans in Tennessee, Lee suggested that he send a copy of the speech to Lord Wolseley. In a postscript to his letter of appreciation to the minister, Wolseley added, "It was most kind of Mrs. Hugh Lee to ask you to send me the copy of the speech," illustrating the contact the three maintained. At this point, Lee lived in Baltimore, McKim in Washington, D.C., and Wolseley in England, remaining connected long after the war. One of Lee's "special favourites," David Gregg McIntosh and his wife, Jennie Pegram McIntosh of Richmond, also left the South to settle in Baltimore, putting the three within close proximity.[40]

This network also helped Lee in her business. Even if they did not live with her, they sometimes stopped by for dinner at her boardinghouse. When Gildersleeve's wife, Bettie, was out of town, for instance, she suggested that he take his meals at "Mrs. Lee's table" instead of eating "cooked over . . . dishes" elsewhere. She also recommended Lee's establishment to friends as transitional housing when they relocated in Baltimore.[41]

The Calvert Street location did not remain Lee's only boardinghouse. Although it is not certain when she made the move, by 1876 "Mrs. Lee's" was on the corner of St. Paul and Read Streets. She had probably moved to 806 St. Paul Street by 1870, when the U.S. census lists twenty-three people living under her roof, including Laura Lee, brother-in-law Henry Lee and his wife, Anna, three families with young children, an attorney, and a "liquor dealer." In 1872 Lee sold the Winchester house for $3,625, but a lien of $2,643 on the building came out of the sale. The earlier loan may have been necessary to furnish the house on St. Paul Street. Clearly, a house large enough to accommodate twenty-three people required a great deal of furnishings.[42]

In 1886 the tax assessor recorded Lee as living at 119 Madison Street, and in 1889 Lee listed her boardinghouse, the "Shirley," at "Madison St. nr. Park Av." under "Principal Hotels" in Miss Remington's *Society Visiting List.* If Lee

40. Barringer et al., *University of Virginia*, 517–18; MGL, 886 (Oct. 29, 1865), 871 (Sept. 21, 1865); Stannard, *Richmond*, 192–93; Wolseley to McKim, Nov. 12, 1904, reprinted in McKim, *Soldiers Recollections*, 258–59 n.

41. Eliza Gildersleeve to Basil Gildersleeve, Europe, Oct. 21, Sept. 28, 1888, Gildersleeve Papers; MGL, 827 (May 22, 1865).

42. Handwritten notation on the back of an invoice from the Mount Vernon Hotel, Sept. 1, 1876, Rowland Papers; Ninth Census; Hopkins, "Extract from the Journal of Mrs. Hugh H. Lee," 381; Winchester Deed Book 13:273, 275–77, 283–85, 344–45, Frederick County Courthouse, Winchester, Va.

had the choice of naming her new boardinghouse, it is possible that her choice stemmed from her Virginia heritage, claiming association with the Tidewater economic giants of the Georgian era, such as the Hill and Carter families of Shirley Plantation. Nonetheless, by advertising her business, Lee's success no longer depended merely upon her *connexion*.[43]

The location of her boardinghouse was both a sign of, and possibly a contribution to, any success Lee may have had. The Madison Street house was located in a prominent section of the city, and men associated with the Peabody Conservatory of Music and several professors from Johns Hopkins University, including Herbert Baxter Adams, Joseph Ames, Daniel Colt Gilman, and Kirby Flower Smith, frequented the Shirley. Gildersleeve and Gen. Francis Pegram were also academic visitors to "Lee's table," but they had been known to her during the war.[44]

When Henry A. Rowland first came to Baltimore to teach at Johns Hopkins, he first stayed at the Mount Vernon Hotel but searched for a less expensive place to board. On the back of a September 1876 bill from the Mount Vernon, Rowland listed several options open to him, including "Mrs. Lee, St. Paul cor. Read," and "Mrs. Murdoch, 36 Hamilton." The next bill he paid was fifty dollars to Mrs. Murdoch for "two months rent of room." Whether because of the price, the location, or a lack of space, Rowland chose Murdoch's place over Lee's in 1876 but became a visitor to the Shirley later on.[45]

Although Lee could not have wanted for company in her busy boardinghouse, she probably did feel lonesome at times for family members. The summer after the war, while still in Staunton, as Lee took communion in church, kneeling "at the altar between Lute & Lal," she was saddened to think that they "might never meet there together again." Her thought at that time was that she could not "shake off the presentiment that" her "shattered family" would "never again be reunited." Lee was right.[46]

The Burwell children all married and made homes of their own. In 1866 Louisa Burwell married Benjamin M. Cromwell, the surgeon who had

43. Baltimore General Property Taxes, 1886, ledger 5, vol. 1, reel 424, p. 614, Baltimore City Archives; Miss Remington, *Society Visiting List of 1889 and 1890, Baltimore, Maryland* (Baltimore: Thomas E. Lycett, 1889), 214; Ruth S. Coski, "'Under Vines and Fig-Trees': Charles City County in the Georgian Age," in *Charles City County Virginia: An Official History*, ed. James P. Whittenburg and John M. Coski (Salem, W.Va.: Don Mills, 1989), 39.

44. Greenhow Family Papers, Genealogical Collection, CWM.

45. Ibid.; invoice from Mount Vernon Hotel, Sept. 1, 1876; receipt from M. L. Murdoch, Sept. 8, 1876, Rowland Papers.

46. MGL, 852 (Aug. 7, 1865).

boarded in the Lee household in 1864, a match that Lee herself had culti-vated. Louisa and Benjamin moved to western Maryland in 1882 when Cromwell took the position of resident physician at Consolidated Coal Com-pany at Eckhart Mines in Alleghany County. The Cromwells had six chil-dren. Lewis Burwell married Sarah "Sallie" Bastable of Clarksburg, West Virginia, also in 1866, and they made their home in Mount Savage, Mary-land, where they had five children: a son named after Lewis, a daughter named after Sarah, and Mary Burwell, Antoinette Lee Burwell, and Louisa Burwell, continuing the naming practices of the *connexion*. Laura Lee Burwell married Spencer Livingston Davidson of Washington, D.C., in 1868 and produced two children, Laura Lee Davidson and Spencer Livingston David-son Jr., who shared his home with Mary at the end of her life. Robert Burwell married Anne Elizabeth Clayton of Athens, Georgia, in 1870 and appears to have remained in Georgia, at least for a time, since his first child was born there in 1871. Robert and Anne had four children: Edward Clayton Burwell, Elizabeth Lee Burwell, Mary Burwell, and Lewis Carter Burwell.[47]

Antoinette and Laura Lee moved to Baltimore initially, but Antoinette did not stay. In September 1866, while visiting with George's family in Clarks-burg, Laura and Antoinette told their niece Hortensia Lee that they planned on "returning to Winchester in October." It is not certain when Antoinette left or where she went, but she is not listed on the 1870 Census with Mary. Antoinette died in Brooklyn, New York, in 1881; she might have been living with relatives at the time or just visiting. In any case, Mary Greenhow Lee's "presentiment that" her "shattered family" would "never again be reunited" was correct. Except for Laura Lee and Henry and Anna for a time, Lee's household consisted mostly of boarders for the last half of her life.[48]

Lee wrote on November 17, 1865, "no one knows how I dread the new life before me," and in a letter to Mary Williams on June 7, 1866, she admit-ted, "I never felt it so much as now, being amongst strangers & . . . having really no interest in the world around me." Somehow she overcame these dreary notions, however, because she became involved in numerous associa-tions. In 1895, at age seventy-six, "Mrs. Hugh H. Lee, of Winchester, Va." became a charter member and one of the managers of the newly organized Baltimore Chapter of the United Daughters of the Confederacy. By 1896, she was secretary of the UDC, which in April 1898 held a bazaar for the ben-

47. *Confederate Veteran*, Aug. 1917, 374; Carlton, *Known Descendants of Robert Carter*, 133, 134; Brown, *Burwell*, 31.

48. Hortensia Lee to John J. Williams, Sept. 6, 1866, Williams Papers; gravestone, Marie Antoinette Lee, Mount Hebron Cemetery, Winchester, Va.; MGL, 852 (Aug. 7, 1865).

efit of Confederate veterans, mothers, and widows. In 1904, at age eighty-five, Lee was still listed as recording secretary for the chapter, now grown to 736 members.[49]

In an undated letter to Lucy Parke Bagby, widow of George Bagby of Richmond, Lee wrote that she "must decline" taking on the position of vice president of a new association Bagby was forming. Since she understood how much depended "on the one at the helm" during the formative period of new organizations, she did not believe that she could offer enough attention to be an effective leader. Explaining that adding to the time she already gave to the Confederate Home, the Maryland Branch of Woman's Auxiliary to the Board of Missions, and other "charities" with which she had been involved for years, she would have very little to contribute to another cause. The only thing Lee could offer to the position, given her "home duties," would be "good will and a very limited portion of time," so she suggested that Bagby ask someone else. Besides these groups, Lee was active in her church and served as secretary for the Southern Education Association, organized to help build schools in the South.[50]

In 1889 Mary Greenhow Lee's name appeared in Miss Remington's *Society Visiting List*, a public signal to Baltimore society that she was *visitable*. Despite the turmoil that had propelled her there, she had successfully transferred her status from Virginia to Baltimore and continued on her independent path, even as she remained steadfast in her service to the South.[51]

Among the members of Mary Greenhow Lee's Winchester household, it appears that only Lewis Burwell outlived her, dying in 1909. There is some question as to the date of Robert's death. The year listed in the Greenhow genealogy is 1870, yet all of his children were born in years subsequent to that. Louisa Burwell Cromwell died in March 1883 and was buried in Winchester near her mother's grave. Laura Burwell Davidson died in 1887.[52]

49. MGL, 891 (Nov. 17, 1865); Mary Greenhow Lee to Mary Williams, June 7, 1866, Williams Papers; *Confederate Veteran* 3, no. 8, Aug. 1895, 226; *Confederate Veteran* 3, no. 11, Nov. 1895, 331; *Confederate Veteran* 4, no. 4, Apr. 1896, 133; *Confederate Veteran* 5, no. 12, Dec. 1897, 602; *Minutes of the Eleventh Annual Meeting of the United Daughters of the Confederacy Held in St. Louis, Missouri, Oct. 4–8, 1904* (Nashville, Tenn.: Press of Foster and Webb, 1905), 35, 312.

50. Mary Greenhow Lee to Lucy Parke (Chamberlayne) Bagby, n.d., Bagby Family Papers (Mss1B1463b), VHS; Mary Greenhow Lee obituary, *Evening Star and Morning News*, May 27, 1907; Hopkins, "Extract from the Journal of Mrs. Hugh H. Lee," 380.

51. Miss Remington, *Society Visiting List*, 82.

52. Brown, *Burwell*, 31; Carlton, *Known Descendants of Robert Carter*, 133–34; *Confederate Veteran*, Aug. 1917, 374; gravestone, Louisa Carter Burwell Cromwell, Mount Hebron Cemetery, Winchester, Va.

Laura Lee died on June 24, 1902, of a cerebral hemorrhage brought on by arteriosclerosis. A funeral service, conducted for "only the nearest relatives and most intimate friends," took place at her home in Baltimore, then her body was transported to Winchester, where she was buried at Mount Hebron Cemetery next to Antoinette. By the time of Laura's death, Mary was over eighty-two years old and too feeble to travel far, which was probably one reason for the Baltimore service. Mary is not mentioned among those who attended Laura's burial in Winchester. Many of those who did, however, also attended Mary's services five years later.[53]

At nine in the morning of May 25, 1907, Mary Greenhow Lee died at the home of Spencer L. Davidson Jr., her great-nephew, at 1119 Park Avenue after being "confined to her bed for four months." The primary reason given for her death appears to be kidney failure, a condition of her "advanced age." As with Laura Lee, funeral services were held for Mary in Baltimore, this time at Emmanuel Protestant Episcopal Church, accommodating the *connexion* nearby. Then she finally returned to Winchester, her casket met at the train depot by old friends who followed to Mount Hebron Cemetery for burial next to Hugh Holmes Lee. Fittingly, the funeral director in charge of the arrangements was George Kurtz, a former Confederate hero and surely someone she would have entrusted with her final ceremony. Instead of separate gravestones, Mary and Hugh share one, marred by a bullet hole left from the war. Earlier, during the war, Lee had written, "went to the cemetery this evening & amongst other signs of war observed a bullet, embedded in the centre of the shaft of the monument, which marks the spot where my last home will be—where my heart is now." A small stone labeled "M.G.L." marks her actual grave.[54]

One of Lee's most valuable possessions had been her family silver, which comprised two-thirds of her estate. Three-fourths of it came to her after the death of her sister-in-law, Rose O'Neal Greenhow, who had died during the Civil War as she returned from a trip to England, where she had been promoting both the Confederacy and her new book, the story of her imprisonment for spying for the Confederacy. The ship Greenhow traveled on ran aground off the coast of Wilmington, North Carolina. Before boarding a small rowboat to make it to shore, she had wrapped the proceeds from her book, mostly gold, around her waist to save it. Unfortunately, that boat also

53. Certificate of Death, Laura Lee, Baltimore City Archives; *The Evening Star*, June 26, 1902.

54. Certificate of Death, Mary Greenhow Lee, Baltimore City Archives; *Evening Star and Morning News Item*, May 27, 1907; MGL, 556 (Apr. 12–15, 1864).

capsized and she drowned, weighted down by the gold. At some point, Mary Greenhow Lee had received possession of this "old silver," originally owned by her grandfather, John Greenhow, and left to her brother Robert upon the death of their father. She willed this heirloom, in turn, to Robert's grandson Capt. Tredwell Moore.[55]

Very few items belonging to Mary Greenhow Lee now exist. Her diaries, the Civil War journal, and a few letters remain, preserved in various archives. One of Louisa and Benjamin's granddaughters, Mary Greenhow Lee Poe Skinner, donated Mary Greenhow Lee's Civil War journal to the Winchester–Frederick County Historical Society, indicating that Lee's namesake had been the beneficiary of this historical document. In addition to the written sources, a pair of stockings that Lee knitted from tenting material during the war is now owned by the Museum of the Confederacy in Richmond, Virginia.[56]

In 1915 Laura Lee Davidson, Mary's great-niece, wrote from Barridge, Ontario, to Mrs. Thomas Baxter Gresham of Park Avenue in Baltimore. In the course of catching up on news, Davidson remarked: "I am so very glad that the chair, that Aunt Lee cherished so, is in your care. It was . . . the chair in which General [Stonewall] Jackson sat, forever sacred on that account. I remember that dear Aunt Lee never liked to have any one use it."[57]

With so few sources available to reflect the last half of Mary Greenhow Lee's life, this one mention of the care she gave the chair Jackson sat in when he visited her on October 27, 1862, may give the clearest indication of her last years. That chair was a reminder to Lee of the dedication she gave to the cause, signified by the fact that Jackson had come in person to thank her for her "soldier work." It is also significant that Davidson understood clearly that "dear Aunt Lee" wanted no one to sit in the chair. Typically, Mary had made her likes and dislikes known right to the last.[58]

Clearly, Lee remained loyal to the South, valuing the heritage of the cause

55. Sigaud, "Mrs. Greenhow and the Rebel Spy Ring," 197; *Harper's Weekly,* Sept. 7, 1861, Jan. 18, 1862; Richmond Circuit Court Book 1:166, LOV; Richmond Hustings Court Book 8:263, LOV; "Last Will and Testament of Mary G. Lee," in "Register of Wills of Orphans Court, Baltimore City, State of Maryland," Baltimore Register of Wills, 387; Administration of Estate, Mary Lee, 1908, MSA.

56. Carlton, *Known Descendants of Robert Carter,* 133; *Winchester Evening Star,* Mar. 5, 1963.

57. Laura Lee Davidson to Mrs. Thomas Baxter Gresham, May 16, 1915, Stonewall Jackson Papers, Virginia Military Institute Archives, Lexington. Although not stated, Davidson implies in the letter that Gresham received the chair because of all her "kindnesses during the last years of Aunt Lee's life" and that "Aunt Lee" had become very attached to her through that time.

58. MGL, 246 (Oct. 22, 1862).

she continued to serve to the end of her life. She also remained a member of the *connexion*. Even though war knocked the economic pins out from under many members of the old southern aristocracy, they still maintained an advantaged attitude in their genteel poverty because they could rely upon the other characteristics that had made them *visitable* before the rebellion. Lee's life illuminates this stubborn retention of prestige and influence when the Old South faded and the New South appeared. Born into one of the wealthiest Richmond families, Mary Greenhow Lee was judged "worthless" by Baltimore's tax assessor in 1905, just two years before her death, when the assessment of her estate was valued at less than three hundred dollars.[59]

The criteria of tax assessors, fortunately, are not those of historians. Lee's obituary gave her credit for the various charities she contributed her energy to and especially for giving "her heart and soul to the Confederate cause," styling her home into a "barometer of the fortunes of the Confederacy." Yet even this praise does not reveal her full historical value, which comes from the record she left of her personal reactions to life in the nineteenth-century South. Rather than a life lived well within the generalized notions we have about women of her class, her region, and her era, hers shows the exposed places in that social construction where women claimed the advantage. Her example complicates the picture we think we have of the past. The story of Mary Greenhow Lee adds to our understanding about the southern world of the nineteenth century and women's part in creating that world, and it connects people of all eras with the timelessness of human effort to confront and resist change.[60]

59. Miss Remington, *Society Visiting List*, 82; Baltimore General Property Taxes, Baltimore City Archives, 1905, ledger 8, vol. 1, p. 448; Administration of Estate, Mary Lee, 1908; "Last Will and Testament of Mary G. Lee," 387; Richmond Circuit Court Book 1:166; Richmond Hustings Court Book 8:263.

60. *Evening Star and Morning News Item*, May 27, 1907; MGL, 461 (Aug. 1863), 477 (Sept. 1863), 518 (Nov. 1986).

Bibliography

MANUSCRIPT COLLECTIONS

The Albert and Shirley Small Special Collections Library, University of Virginia Library, Charlottesville

Brooke Family Correspondence
"Chapel Hill Farm for Sale" Handbill
Richard Bland Lee Papers
James and John Murray Mason Papers (No. 5036)
Gen. John Mason Papers
Stuart Family Papers

Archives, Library of Virginia, Richmond

W. Eugene Ferslew, "Map of the City of Richmond, Henrico County, Virginia," 1859
Thomas S. Latimer Papers
"Plan of the City of Richmond," 1838
Emma Wood Richardson, "Civil War Remembrances"
Henry S. Shanklin Letters
W. Barrett Sydnor Papers

Archives Room, Handley Library, Winchester, Virginia

Portia Baldwin Baker Diary
David Bard Papers (361 WFCHS)
James W. Beeler Diary, Rubye Hall Collection (73 THL), typescript
James M. Cadwallader Diary, J. Paul Cadwallader Collection (683 THL)
Julia Chase, "War Time Diary of Miss Julia Chase, Winchester, Virginia," Julia Chase
    Collection (544 THL), typescript
John Peyton Clark Journal, Louisa Crawford Collection (424 WFCHS), typescript
Owen J. Edwards Diary (253 THL)
Harriet Hollingsworth Griffith Diary, Louisa Crawford Collection (424 WFCHS)
Ann Cary Randolph Jones Papers
Mrs. Hugh Lee Collection (1182 WFCHS)
Ben Ritter Collection (12 WFCHS)
Kate Sperry, "Surrender, Never Surrender!" Kate Sperry Papers (80 WFCHS), type-
    script
Philip Williams Family Papers (172 WFCHS)

Eleanor S. Brockenbrough Library, Museum of the Confederacy, Richmond, Virginia

Scrapbook of Mrs. Holmes Conrad, Scrapbook Collections
Mary De Renne Letterbook
Richard Ewell to Lizinka Brown, March 5, 1862, Confederate Military Leaders Col-
    lection
Stonewall Jackson Collection
Robert E. Lee to Robert Y. Conrad, James Marshall, Edmund Pendleton, Hugh Nel-
    son, and Alfred M. Barbour, April 27, 1861, R. E. Lee Collection
Medical and Hospital Collection
Col. J. Q. A. Nadenbousch Letters, Soldier Letters Collections

Manuscripts and Archives, Virginia Historical Society, Richmond

Ambler Family Papers (Mss1Am167c)
Turner Ashby Papers (Mss1As346a)
Bagby Family Papers (Mss1B1463b)
Bassett Family Papers
St. George Tucker Brooke, "Autobiography of St. George Tucker Brooke Written for
    His Children," 1907, typescript
Ida Mason Dorsey Brown Papers (Mss1B8134a)
Byrd Family Papers
Claiborne Family Papers
Holmes Conrad Papers (Mss1C7637b)
Robert Y. Conrad Papers (Mss1C7638a)
Henry Curtis Papers

Armistead Churchill Gordon Papers
Grymes Family Papers (Special Collections)
Gwathmey Family Papers (Mss1G9957a)
Harrison Family Papers
Robert Mercer Taliaferro Hunter Papers (Mss2H9185a1)
Robert Edward Lee Papers
James Marshall Papers (Mss2 M35638b)
Mason Family Papers (Mss1M3816c/a)
McDonald Family Papers
McIntosh Family Papers (Mss1M1895a)
Sherwin McRae Papers
Preston Family Papers (Mss1P9267fFA2)
Conway Robinson Papers
Seddon Family Papers
Frederica Holmes Trapnel Papers

Manuscripts Department, Maryland Historical Society, Baltimore

Mary Greenhow Diary, 1837, Greenhow-Lee Papers (MS 534), typescript
Mary Lorraine Greenhow (Mrs. Robert Greenhow Sr.) Commonplace Book,
    1829–50 (MS 534)
Mary Greenhow Lee Papers

*Manuscripts Department, Southern Historical Collection, Wilson Library, University of
North Carolina at Chapel Hill*

John Y. Mason Correspondence (No. 496)
David Gregg McIntosh, "A Ride on Horseback in the Summer of 1910," 1910 (No.
    1889)
William Groves Morris Papers (No. 3626), photocopy
William Nelson Pendleton Papers (No. 1466)
Henry Alexander Wise Papers (No. 2380; owned by Eastern Shore of Virginia His-
    torical Society), photocopy

Manuscripts Division, Library of Congress, Washington, D.C.

Nathaniel P. Banks Papers
Cutts Family Papers
Jubal Anderson Early Papers
Mary Greenhow Lee Papers
Rodgers Family Papers

Maryland State Archives, Annapolis

Administration of Estate, Mary Lee, 1908

Special Collections, Swem Library, College of William and Mary,
Williamsburg, Virginia

Blair Family Papers
Dew Family Papers
Greenhow Family Papers (Genealogical Collection)
Robert Greenhow Jr. "Diary giving an account of his journey from Washington,
    D.C., to Mexico City in 1837"
Robert Greenhow Jr. Papers
Laura Lee Diary, "The History of Our Captivity," March 1862–April 1865
Cassie Moncure Lyne Scrapbook
"Minutes of the Cerulean Society"
Tucker-Brooke Family Papers
Tyler Family Papers (Women of Virginia Project Records)
Asa John Wyatt Civil War Diary, June 19, 1861–July 29, 1862

Special Collections, Leyburn Library, Washington and Lee University,
Lexington, Virginia

William P. Parker, "Diary of a Surgeon of the 7th Tennessee Regiment in Virginia,
    May 20, 1861–May 21, 1862"

Special Collections, Milton S. Eisenhower Library, Johns Hopkins University,
Baltimore, Maryland

Herbert Baxter Adams Papers
Joseph Sweetman Ames Papers
Basil Lanneau Gildersleeve Papers (Ms. 5)
Daniel Colt Gilman Papers
Henry Augustus Rowland Papers (Ms. 6)

Special Collections Division, The University of Georgia Libraries, Athens

Gordon Family Papers

Virginia Military Institute Archives, Lexington

Stonewall Jackson Papers

MICROFILM EDITIONS OF MANUSCRIPT COLLECTIONS

Mary Greenhow (Mrs. Hugh Holmes Lee) Diary, 1837. Manuscripts Division, Library of Congress, Washington, D.C.

Thomas Jefferson Papers. Presidential Series. Manuscripts Division, Library of Congress, Washington, D.C. (Manuscripts and Archives, Virginia Historical Society, Richmond.)

William Lee Letterbook, 1739–95. Manuscripts and Archives, Virginia Historical Society, Richmond.

Papers of Dolley Madison. Manuscripts Division, Library of Congress, Washington, D.C.

Betty Herndon Maury Diary, 1861–63. Manuscripts Division, Library of Congress, Washington, D.C.

Hunter Holmes McGuire Papers. The Albert and Shirley Small Special Collections Library, University of Virginia, Charlottesville.

Minor Family Papers. Manuscripts and Archives, Virginia Historical Society, Richmond.

Papers of Gen. Philip Sheridan. Manuscripts Division, Library of Congress, Washington, D.C.

MICROFILM AND MICROFICHE EDITIONS OF PUBLISHED PRIMARY SOURCES

Ellyson's Business Directory, and Almanac, for the Year 1845. Richmond: H. K. Ellyson, 1845. Library of Virginia, Richmond.

Ferslew, W. Eugene. *Second Annual Directory for the City of Richmond, to Which Is Added a Business Directory for 1860.* Richmond: W. Eugene Ferslew, 1860. Library of Virginia, Richmond.

A Full Directory, for Washington City, Georgetown, and Alexandria. Washington, [D.C.]: E. A. Cohen, 1834. Library of Virginia, Richmond.

Matchett's Baltimore Director [sic], Corrected up to September, 1835. For 1835–6. Containing . . . a Plan of the City. Library of Virginia, Richmond.

Matchett's Baltimore Director [sic], for 1840–1. Library of Virginia, Richmond.

"A Month's Visit to the Confederate Headquarters." *Blackwood's Edinburgh Magazine.* 92, no. 567 (January 1863): 1–29. The Albert and Shirley Small Special Collections Library, University of Virginia, Charlottesville.

The Richmond Directory, Register, and Almanac, for the Year 1819. Richmond: John Maddox, 1819. Library of Virginia, Richmond.

The Washington Directory, and Governmental Register, for 1843. Washington, D.C.: Anthony Reintze, 1843. Library of Virginia, Richmond.

Woods' Baltimore Directory, for 1858–'59. Baltimore: John W. Woods, 1858. Library of Virginia, Richmond.

GOVERNMENT DOCUMENTS AND PUBLICATIONS

Federal Records

U.S. Bureau of the Census. Fourth, Fifth, Sixth, Seventh, Eighth, and Ninth U.S. Census. Library of Virginia, Richmond, microfilm.

U.S. Senate. *Remarks of Senator Mason, of Virginia, and Senator Trumbull, of Illinois, on the Extension of Slavery into Free Territory.* December 2, 1856. Washington, D.C.: Buell and Blanchard, 1856.

———. *Speech of Hon. J. M. Mason, of Virginia, on the Admission of Kansas.* March 15, 1858. Washington, D.C.: Geo. S. Gideon, 1858.

U.S. War Department. *The War of the Rebellion: A Compilation of the Official Records of the Union and Confederate Armies.* 70 vols. in 128 parts. Washington, D.C.: Government Printing Office, 1880–1901.

County Records

Albemarle County, Virginia. Land Tax Registers, 1855, 1860. Library of Virginia, Richmond.

———. Personal Property Tax Lists, 1855, 1860. Library of Virginia, Richmond.

Augusta County, Virginia. Deed Books, 1816, 1822, 1823. Library of Virginia, Richmond. Microfilm.

———. Land Tax Registers, 1820, 1823, 1824, 1825. Library of Virginia, Richmond. Microfilm.

———. Personal Property Tax Lists, 1820. Library of Virginia, Richmond. Microfilm.

Clark County, Virginia. Land Tax Registers, 1845, 1850, 1851, 1854, 1860. Library of Virginia, Richmond.

———. Personal Property Tax Lists, 1855, 1860. Library of Virginia, Richmond.

Dinwiddie County, Virginia. Land Tax Registers, 1855, 1860. Library of Virginia, Richmond.

———. Personal Property Tax Lists, 1855, 1860. Library of Virginia, Richmond.

Fairfax County, Virginia. Land Tax Registers, 1855, 1860. Library of Virginia, Richmond.

———. Personal Property Tax Lists, 1855, 1860. Library of Virginia, Richmond.

Fauquier County, Virginia. Land Tax Registers, 1855, 1860. Library of Virginia, Richmond.

———. Personal Property Tax Lists, 1855, 1860. Library of Virginia, Richmond.

Frederick County, Virginia. County Superior Court Books. Library of Virginia, Richmond.

———. Land Tax Registers, 1830, 1845, 1846–65. Library of Virginia, Richmond.

———. Personal Property Tax Lists, 1845, 1846, 1848–50, 1854, 1855, 1859, 1860. Library of Virginia, Richmond.

———. Will Books. Frederick County Courthouse, Winchester, Virginia.

Harrison County, Virginia. Personal Property Tax List, 1860. Library of Virginia, Richmond.

Henrico County, Virginia. Deed Books. Library of Virginia, Richmond.

———. Land Tax Registers, 1810–12, 1815–21, 1823, 1825–30, 1834, 1835, 1839–44, 1850, 1855, 1860. Library of Virginia, Richmond.

———. Personal Property Tax Lists, 1810, 1815, 1819, 1825, 1830, 1835, 1840, 1845, 1850, 1855, 1860. Library of Virginia, Richmond.

James City County, Virginia. Land Tax Registers, 1787–1818. Library of Virginia, Richmond. Microfilm.

———. Personal Property Tax Lists, 1782–1824. Library of Virginia, Richmond. Microfilm.

Loudoun County, Virginia. Land Tax Registers, 1855, 1860. Library of Virginia, Richmond.

———. Personal Property Tax Lists, 1855, 1860. Library of Virginia, Richmond.

New Kent County, Virginia. Land Tax Registers, 1835, 1837, 1840, 1845, 1850. Library of Virginia, Richmond. Microfilm.

Rockingham County, Virginia. Land Tax Registers, 1855, 1860. Library of Virginia, Richmond.

———. Personal Property Tax Lists, 1855, 1860. Library of Virginia, Richmond.

Shenandoah County, Virginia. Deed Books, 1802, 1809, 1810, 1812, 1818. Library of Virginia, Richmond.

———. Land Tax Registers, 1855, 1860. Library of Virginia, Richmond.

———. Personal Property Tax Lists, 1855, 1861. Library of Virginia, Richmond.

Surry County, Virginia. Land Tax Registers, 1855, 1860. Library of Virginia, Richmond.

———. Personal Property Tax Lists, 1855, 1860. Library of Virginia, Richmond.

Warren County, Virginia. Land Tax Registers, 1850. Library of Virginia, Richmond.

City Records

Baltimore, Maryland. General Property Taxes, 1886, 1896, 1905, 1907. Baltimore City Archives, Baltimore, Maryland. Microfilm.

"Last Will and Testament of Mary G. Lee." Baltimore City Register of Wills. Baltimore, Maryland.

Petersburg, Virginia. Land Tax Registers, 1855, 1860. Library of Virginia, Richmond.

———. Personal Property Tax Lists, 1855, 1860. Library of Virginia, Richmond.

"Register of Wills of Orphans Court, Baltimore City, State of Maryland." Baltimore City Archives, Baltimore, Maryland.

Richmond, Virginia. Circuit Court Books. Library of Virginia, Richmond.

———. Common Hall Records, Library of Virginia, Richmond.

———. Deed Books. Library of Virginia, Richmond.

———. Hustings Court Books. Library of Virginia, Richmond.

———. Land Tax Registers, 1809–15, 1819, 1825, 1830, 1835, 1839, 1840, 1945, 1850, 1855, 1860. Library of Virginia, Richmond.

———. Legislative Petitions, Library of Virginia, Richmond.

———. Personal Property Tax Lists, 1805, 1810, 1815, 1819, 1825, 1830, 1835, 1839–43, 1845, 1850, 1855, 1860. Library of Virginia, Richmond.

Staunton, Virginia. Land Tax Registers, 1855, 1860. Library of Virginia, Richmond.
————. Personal Property Tax Lists, 1850, 1855, 1860, 1863. Library of Virginia, Richmond.
Winchester, Virginia. Deed Books. Frederick County Courthouse, Winchester, Virginia.
————. Land Tax Registers, 1830, 1845, 1846–65. Library of Virginia, Richmond.
————. Personal Property Tax Lists, 1843–62. Library of Virginia, Richmond.

CONTEMPORARY PERIODICALS AND OTHER PUBLICATIONS

"A Catalogue of the Offices and Students of the University of Virginia, Tenth Session, 1833–1834." Charlottesville, Va.: Chronicle Steam Book Printing House, 1880.
Confederate Veteran. 3, no. 8 (August 1895); 3, no. 11 (November 1895); 4, no. 4 (April 1896); 5, no. 12 (December 1897).
Danforth, John B., and Herbert A. Claiborne. Historical Sketch of the Mutual Assurance Society of Richmond, Va., from Its Organization in 1794 to 1879. Richmond: William Ellis Jones, 1879. Reproduced by duopage process, Wooster, Ohio: Micropublishers, Micro-Photo Division, 1971. Original at the Library of Virginia.
DeBow's Review. January 1861.
Etiquette at Washington: Together with the Customs Adopted by Polite Society in the Other Cities of the United States. 3d ed. Baltimore: Murphy, 1857.
Fisher, George D. History and Reminiscences of the Monumental Church, Richmond, Virginia, from 1814 to 1878. Richmond: Whittet and Shepperson, 1880.
The Fundamental Rules and Regulations of the Lancastrian Institution. Richmond: Ritchie, Trueheart, and Du-Val, 1817. Rare Books, Virginia Historical Society, Richmond.
Greenhow, Robert, Jr. The Tri-Color; Devoted to the Politics, Literature, &c of Continental Europe. New York: Ludwig and Tolefree, 1830. Photostatic copy.
Lee, Edmund Jennings. The Lees of Virginia: The Descendants of Colonel Richard Lee. Philadelphia, 1895.
Macon, Emma Cassandra Riely, and Reuben Conway Macon. Reminiscences of the Civil War. Privately printed, 1911.
Magill, Mary Tucker. Women; or, Chronicles of the Late War. Baltimore: Turnbull Brothers, 1871.
McKim, Rev. Randolph Harrison. "In Memoriam. Good Men a Nation's Strength, a Sermon Preached on the Occasion of the Death of Gen. Robert E. Lee, in Christ Church, Alexandria, Va., October 16th, 1870." Baltimore: John Murphy, 1870.
————. The Proposal to Change the Name of the Protestant Episcopal Church. New York: E. P. Dutton, n.d.
————. A Soldier's Recollections: Leaves from the Diary of a Young Confederate. New York: Longmans, Green, 1911.
Moore, J. Quitman. "Southern Civilization; or, the Norman in America." DeBow's Review 32 (January–February 1862).

Munford, George Wythe. *The Two Parsons; Cupid's Sports; the Dream; and the Jewels of Virginia.* Richmond: J. D. K. Sleight, 1884.

A Provisional List of Alumni, Grammar School Students, Members of the Faculty, and Members of the Board of Visitors of the College of William and Mary in Virginia from 1693 to 1888. Richmond: Division of Purchase and Printing, 1941.

Randolph, Rev. Alfred Magill. "Address on a Day of Fasting and Prayer." Fredericksburg, Va.: Records Job Office, 1861.

Remington, Miss. *Society Visiting List of 1889 and 1890, Baltimore, Maryland.* Baltimore: Thomas E. Lycett, 1889.

Ritchie, Thomas Jr. *A Full Report, Embracing All the Evidence and Arguments in the Case of the Commonwealth of Virginia vs. Thomas Ritchie, Jr., Tried at the Spring Term of the Chesterfield Superior Court, 1846.* New York: Burgess, Stringer, 1846.

Sanborne Fire Insurance Company. *Map of Baltimore City.* Baltimore: Sanborne Fire Insurance, 1901.

United Daughters of the Confederacy. *Minutes of Annual Meeting.* Nashville: Press of Foster and Webb, 1897, 1899, 1903, 1905.

———. *Minutes of the Eleventh Annual Meeting of the United Daughters of the Confederacy Held in St. Louis, Missouri, October 4–8, 1904.* Nashville, Tenn.: Press of Foster and Webb, 1905.

NEWSPAPERS

Charleston Mercury, 1862

The Enquirer, 1812

New York Times, 1861, 1862

Richmond Enquirer, 1814, 1819, 1834, 1835, 1840, 1861

Virginia Free Press, 1856

Virginia Gazette, 1771

Winchester Evening Star, 1902, 1963

Winchester Evening Star and Morning News, 1907

Winchester Virginian, 1840, 1846, 1849, 1850, 1853, 1854, 1856

PUBLISHED PRIMARY SOURCES

Barclay, Ted. *Liberty Hall Volunteers: Letters from the Stonewall Brigade (1861–1864),* edited by Charles W. Turner. Berryville, Va.: Rockbridge, 1992.

Chesnut, Mary Boykin. *A Diary from Dixie,* edited by Ben Ames Williams. Boston: Houghton Mifflin, 1949.

Davis, Jefferson. *The Messages and Papers of Jefferson Davis and the Confederacy, Including Diplomatic Correspondence, 1861–1865.* 2 vols., edited by James D. Richardson. New York: Chelsea House–R. Hector, 1966.

Edmonds, Amanda. *Journals of Amanda Virginia Edmonds: Lass of the Mosby Confederacy,*

1859–1867, edited by Nancy Chappelear Baird. Stephens City, Va.: Commercial, 1984.

Edmondson, James K. *My Dear Emma: War Letters of Col. James K. Edmondson, 1861–1865)*, edited by Charles W. Turner. Staunton, Va.: McClure, 1978.

Hotchkiss, Jedediah. *Make Me a Map of the Valley: The Civil War Journal of Stonewall Jackson's Topographer*, edited by Archie P. McDonald. Dallas: Southern Methodist University Press, 1989.

Jefferson, Thomas. *Notes on the State of Virginia*, edited by William Peden. New York: W. W. Norton, 1982.

Mason, James M. *The Public Life and Diplomatic Correspondence of James M. Mason, with Some Personal History*, edited by Virginia Mason. New York: Neale, 1906.

McCarthy, Carlton. *Detailed Minutiae of Soldier Life in the Army of Northern Virginia, 1861–1865*. Richmond, Va.: Carlton McCarthy, 1882.

McDonald, Cornelia A. *Diary with Reminiscences of the War*, edited by Hunter McDonald. Nashville: Cellom and Glertner, 1934.

Sheridan, Philip H. *Personal Memoirs of P. H. Sheridan, General, United States Army*. 2 vols. New York: Charles L. Webster, 1888.

Smith, John David, and William Cooper Jr., eds. *A Union Woman in Civil War Kentucky: The Diary of Frances Peter*. Lexington: University Press of Kentucky, 2000.

Washington, George. *The Papers of George Washington*, edited by W. W. Abbot. Colonial Series, vol. 3, April–November 1756. Charlottesville: University Press of Virginia, 1983.

Wolseley, Garnett. *The Letters of Lord and Lady Wolseley, 1870–1911*, edited by Sir George Arthur. New York: Doubleday, Page, 1922. Reprint, New York: Kraus, 1972.

Secondary Sources

Books

Alexander, Bevin. *Lost Victories: The Military Genius of Stonewall Jackson*. New York: Henry Holt, 1992.

Ambler, John Jaquelin. *The Amblers of Virginia*. Richmond, 1972.

Ames, William E. *A History of the National Intelligencer*. Chapel Hill: University of North Carolina Press, 1972.

Aries, Philippe. *Centuries of Childhood: A Social History of Family Life*, translated by Robert Baldick. New York: Alfred A. Knopf, 1962.

Atack, Jeremy, and Peter Passell. *A New Economic View of American History from Colonial Times to 1940*. 2d ed. New York: W. W. Norton, 1994.

Ball, Douglas B. *Financial Failure and Confederate Defeat*. Urbana: University of Illinois Press, 1991.

Barringer, Paul Brandon; James Mercer Garnett; and Rosewell Page, eds. *University of Virginia: Its History, Influence, Equipment, and Characteristics, with Biographical*

Sketches and Portraits of Founders, Benefactors, Officers, and Alumni. New York: Lewis, 1904.

Bateman, Fred, and Thomas Weiss. *A Deplorable Scarcity: The Failure of Industrialization in the Slave Economy.* Chapel Hill: University of North Carolina Press, 1981.

Bean, W. G. *Stonewall's Man: Sandie Pendleton.* Wilmington, N.C.: Broadfoot, 1987.

Bepko, Claudia, and Jo-Ann Krestan. *Too Good for Her Own Good.* New York: Harper Collins, 1991.

Bertsch, Gary K.; Robert P. Clark; and David M. Wood. *Comparing Political Systems: Power and Policy in Three Worlds.* New York: Macmillan, 1986.

Blanton, Wyndham B. *Medicine in Virginia in the Nineteenth Century.* Richmond, Va.: Garrett and Massie, 1933.

Brown, Stuart E., Jr. *Burwell: Kith and Kin of the Immigrant Lewis Burwell (1621–1653) and Burwell Virginia Tidewater Plantation Mansions.* [Berryville, Va.]: Virginia Book, [1994].

Bynum, Victoria E. *"Unruly Women": The Politics of Social and Sexual Control in the Old South.* Chapel Hill: University of North Carolina Press, 1992.

Carlton, Florence Tyler. *A Genealogy of the Known Descendants of Robert Carter of Corotoman.* Richmond, Va.: Whittet and Shepperson, 1982.

Cartmell, T. K. *Shenandoah Valley Pioneers and Their Descendants: A History of Frederick County, Virginia.* Berryville, Va.: Chesapeake, 1909.

Cash, W. J. *The Mind of the South.* New York: Alfred A. Knopf, 1941.

Cashin, Joan E. *A Family Venture: Men and Women on the Southern Frontier.* Baltimore: Johns Hopkins University Press, 1991.

Cecil-Fronsman, Bill. *The Common Whites: Class and Culture in Antebellum North Carolina.* Ann Arbor, Mich.: University Microfilms International, 1985.

Censer, Jane Turner. *North Carolina Planters and Their Children.* Baton Rouge: Louisiana State University Press, 1984.

Chambers-Schiller, Lee Virginia. *"Liberty, A Better Husband": Single Women in America, the Generations of 1789–1840.* New Haven: Yale University Press, 1984.

Chodorow, Nancy J. *Feminism and Psychoanalytic Theory.* New Haven: Yale University Press, 1989.

Christian, Andrew H., Jr. *A Brief History of the Christian, Dunscomb, and Duval Families.* Richmond, Va.: Dietz, 1909.

Christian, W. Asbury, D.D. *Richmond, Her Past and Present.* Spartanburg, S.C.: Reprint Company, 1973.

Christian Family of Virginia. Richmond, Va.: Whittet and Shepperson, 1901.

Clinton, Catherine. *The Other Civil War: American Woman in the Nineteenth Century.* New York: Hill and Wang, 1984.

Colt, Margaretta Barton. *Defend the Valley: A Shenandoah Family in the Civil War.* New York: Crown, 1994.

Cott, Nancy F. *The Bonds of Womanhood: "Woman's Sphere" in New England, 1780–1835.* New Haven: Yale University Press, 1977.

Dabney, Virginius. *Richmond: The Story of a City*. Rev. and exp. ed. Charlottesville: University Press of Virginia, 1990.

———. *Virginia: The New Dominion*. Charlottesville: University Press of Virginia, 1989.

Degler, Carl N. *At Odds: Women and the Family in America from the Revolution to the Present*. New York: Oxford University Press, 1980.

———. *Place over Time: The Continuity of Southern Distinctiveness*. Baton Rouge: Louisiana State University Press, 1977.

Delauter, Roger U., Jr. *Winchester in the Civil War*. Lynchburg, Va.: H. E. Howard, 1992.

Demos, John. *Past, Present, and Personal: The Family and the Life Course in American History*. New York: Oxford University Press, 1986.

D'Otrange Mastai, Boleslaw, and Marie-Louise D'Otrange. *The Stars and the Stripes: The American Flag as Art and as History from the Birth of the Republic to the Present*. New York: Alfred A. Knopf, 1973.

Eaton, Clement. *A History of the Southern Confederacy*. New York: Free Press, 1954.

Eggenberger, David. *Flags of the U.S.A.* New York: Thomas Y. Crowell, 1959.

Elkins, Stanley, and Eric McKitrick. *The Age of Federalism*. New York: Oxford University Press, 1993.

Farnham, Christie Anne. *The Education of the Southern Belle: Higher Education and Student Socialization in the Antebellum South*. New York: New York University Press, 1994.

Faust, Drew Gilpin. *The Creation of Confederate Nationalism: Ideology and Identity in the Civil War South*. Baton Rouge: Louisiana State University Press, 1988.

———. *Mothers of Invention: Women of the Slaveholding South in the American Civil War*. Chapel Hill: University of North Carolina Press, 1996.

Fischer, David Hackett. *Albion's Seed: Four British Folkways in America*. New York: Oxford University Press, 1989.

Fisher, Noel C. *War at Every Door: Partisan Politics and Guerrilla Violence in East Tennessee, 1860–1869*. Chapel Hill: University of North Carolina Press, 1997.

Foner, Eric. *Reconstruction: America's Unfinished Revolution, 1863–1877*. New York: Harper and Row, 1988.

———. *A Short History of Reconstruction, 1863–1877*. New York: Harper and Row, 1990.

Fox-Genovese, Elizabeth. *Within the Plantation Household: Black and White Women of the Old South*. Chapel Hill: University of North Carolina Press, 1988.

Frank, John P. *Justice Daniel Dissenting: A Biography of Peter V. Daniel, 1784–1860*. Cambridge: Harvard University Press, 1964.

Gallagher, Gary. *The Confederate War*. Cambridge: Harvard University Press, 1997.

Genealogies of Virginia Families: From the William and Mary College Quarterly Historical Magazine. Vols. 3-4. Baltimore: Genealogical Publishing, 1981.

Glave Newman Anderson and Associates, Inc., Architects. *An Adaptive Preservation Study for the Monumental Church*, 1974.

Goodwin, Maud Wilder. *Dolley Madison*. Women of Colonial and Revolutionary Times. New York: Charles Scribner's Sons, 1896. Reprint, Spartanburg, S.C.: Reprint Company, 1967.

Greene, Jack P. *Pursuits of Happiness: The Social Development of Early Modern British Colonies and the Formation of American Culture*. Chapel Hill: University of North Carolina Press, 1988.

Hall, Virginius Cornick, Jr. *Portraits in the Collection of the Virginia Historical Society: A Catalogue*. Charlottesville: University Press of Virginia, 1981.

Harrington, Fred Harvey. *Fighting Politician: Major General N. P. Banks*. Westport, Conn.: Greenwood, 1970.

Henderson, Col. G. F. R. *Stonewall Jackson and the American Civil War*. 1898. Reprint, 2 vols. in 1, New York: Longmans, Green, 1949.

Historical Atlas of the World. Newly rev. ed. Maplewood, N.J.: Hammond, 1995.

Hoole, W. Stanley. *Vizetelly Covers the Confederacy*. Tuscaloosa, Ala.: Confederate Publishing, 1957.

———. *Lawley Covers the Confederacy*. Tuscaloosa, Ala.: Confederate Publishing, 1964.

Isaac, Rhys. *The Transformation of Virginia, 1740–1790*. New York: W. W. Norton, 1982.

Jabour, Anya. *Marriage in the Early Republic: Elizabeth and William Wirt and the Companionate Ideal*. Baltimore: Johns Hopkins University Press, 1998.

Jones, Jacqueline. *Labor of Love, Labor of Sorrow: Black Women, Work, and the Family, from Slavery to the Present*. New York: Vintage, 1995.

Jordan, Daniel P. *Political Leadership in Jefferson's Virginia*. Charlottesville: University Press of Virginia, 1983.

Kasson, John F. *Rudeness and Civility: Manners in Nineteenth-Century Urban America*. New York: Hill and Wang, 1990.

Kerber, Linda K. *Women of the Republic: Intellect and Ideology in Revolutionary America*. Chapel Hill: University of North Carolina Press, 1980.

Kercheval, Samuel. *A History of the Valley of Virginia*. 4th ed. Strasburg, Va.: Shenandoah, 1925.

Lebsock, Suzanne. *The Free Women of Petersburg: Status and Culture in a Southern Town, 1784–1860*. New York: W. W. Norton, 1984.

———. *Virginia Women, 1600–1945: "A Share of Honour."* Richmond: Virginia State Library, 1987.

Lehmann, Joseph H. *The Model Major-General: A Biography of Field-Marshal Lord Wolseley*. Cambridge, U.K.: Riverside; Boston: Houghton Mifflin, 1964.

Leonard, Elizabeth D. *Yankee Women: Gender Battles in the Civil War*. New York: W. W. Norton, 1995.

Lippman, Walter. *A Preface to Politics*. Ann Arbor: University of Michigan Press, Ann Arbor Paperbacks, 1962.

Massey, Mary Elizabeth. *Refugee Life in the Confederacy*. Baton Rouge: Louisiana State University Press, 1964.

McCardell, John. *The Idea of a Southern Nation: Southern Nationalists and Southern Nationalism, 1830–1860.* New York: W. W. Norton, 1979.

McCoy, Drew R. *The Elusive Republic: Political Economy in Jeffersonian America.* New York: W. W. Norton, 1980.

McIlhany, Hugh Milton, Jr. *Some Virginia Families.* Baltimore: Genealogical Publishing, 1962.

Mitchell, Robert D. *Commercialism and Frontier: Perspectives on the Early Shenandoah Valley.* Charlottesville: University Press of Virginia, 1977.

Morton, Oren Frederic. *The Story of Winchester in Virginia: The Oldest Town in the Shenandoah Valley.* Strasburg, Va.: Shenandoah, 1925.

Morton, Richard L. *Colonial Virginia: Vol. II, Westward Expansion and Prelude to Revolution, 1710–1763.* Chapel Hill: University of North Carolina Press, 1960.

Munford, Beverley B. *Virginia's Attitude toward Slavery and Secession.* New York: Longmans, Green, 1910.

Munford, Robert Beverley, Jr., *Richmond Homes and Memories.* Richmond, Va.: Garrett and Massie, 1936.

Nagel, Paul C. *The Lees of Virginia: Seven Generations of an American Family.* New York: Oxford University Press, 1990.

Nash, Capt. Joseph Van Holt. *Students of the University of Virginia: A Semi-Centennial Catalogue, with Brief Biographical Sketches.* Baltimore: Charles Harvey, 1878.

Newton, Sarah E. *Learning to Behave: A Guide to American Conduct Books before 1900.* Bibliographies and Indexes in American History, no. 28. Westport, Conn.: Greenwood, 1994.

Niven, John. *Martin Van Buren: The Romantic Age of American Politics.* New York: Oxford University Press, 1983.

Norfleet, Fillmore. *Saint-Mémin in Virginia: Portraits and Biographies.* Richmond, Va.: Dietz, 1942.

Oakes, James. *The Ruling Race: A History of American Slaveholders.* New York: Knopf, 1982.

O'Brien, Michael. *An Evening When Alone: Four Journals of Single Women in the South, 1827–67.* Charlottesville, University Press of Virginia, 1993.

Paludan, Phillip Shaw. *"A People's Contest:" The Union and Civil War, 1861–1865.* New York: Harper and Row, 1988.

Philips, Edith. *Louis Hue Girardin and Nicholas Gouin Dufief and Their Relations with Thomas Jefferson, an Unknown Episode of the French Emigration in America.* Extra vol. no. 3. Baltimore: Johns Hopkins University Press, 1926.

Pollock, Michael E. *Marriage Bonds of Henrico County, Virginia, 1782–1853.* Baltimore: Genealogical Publishing, 1984.

Potter, David M. *The Impending Crisis: 1848–1861,* completed and edited by Don E. Fehrenbacher. New York: Harper and Row, 1976.

———. *The South and the Sectional Conflict.* Baton Rouge: Louisiana State University Press, 1968.

Preston, Adrian, ed. *The South African Diaries of Sir Garnet Wolseley, 1875.* Cape Town, S.A.: A. A. Balkema, 1971.

Quarles, Garland R. *The Churches of Winchester, Virginia: A Brief History of Those Established Prior to 1825.* Winchester, Va.: Farmers and Merchants National Bank, 1960.

————. *The Story of One Hundred Old Homes in Winchester, Virginia.* Winchester, Va.: Farmers and Merchants Bank, 1967.

————. *Occupied Winchester: 1861–1865.* Winchester, Va.: Farmers and Merchants Bank, 1976.

————. *Some Worthy Lives: Mini-Biographies, Winchester and Frederick County.* Winchester, Va.: Winchester–Frederick County Historical Society, 1988.

————. *Some Old Homes in Frederick County, Virginia.* Rev. ed. Winchester, Va.: Winchester–Frederick County Historical Society, 1990

————. *The Story of One Hundred Old Homes in Winchester, Virginia.* Rev. ed. Winchester, Va.: Winchester–Frederick County Historical Society, 1993.

Quarles, Garland R., and Lewis N. Barton, eds. *What I Know about Winchester: Recollections of William Greenway Russell, 1800–1891.* Vol. 2. Reprinted from *The Winchester News,* Winchester–Frederick County Historical Society. Staunton, Va.: McClure, 1953.

Quarles, Garland R.; Lewis N. Barton; C. Vernon Eddy; and Mildred Lee Grove, eds. *Diaries, Letters, and Recollections of the War between the States.* Winchester, Va.: Winchester–Frederick County Historical Society, 1955.

Rable, George C. *Civil Wars: Women and the Crisis of Southern Nationalism.* Urbana: University of Illinois Press, 1989.

Reynolds, Arlene. *The Civil War Memories of Elizabeth Bacon Custer.* Austin: University of Texas Press, 1994.

Richmond Portraits in an Exhibition of Makers of Richmond, 1737–1860. Richmond, Va.: Valentine Museum, 1949.

Risjord, Norman K. *Jefferson's America, 1760–1815.* Madison, Wis.: Madison House, 1991.

Robertson, Alexander F. *Alexander Hugh Holmes Stuart, 1807–1891: A Biography.* Richmond, Va.: William Byrd, 1925.

Robertson, James I. Jr. *Civil War Virginia: Battleground for a Nation.* Charlottesville: University Press of Virginia, 1991.

Rock, Paul. *The Making of Symbolic Interactionism.* Totowa, N.J.: Rowman and Littlefield, 1979.

Rothman, David J. *The Discovery of the Asylum: Social Order and Disorder in the New Republic.* Boston: Little, Brown, 1971.

Royster, Charles. *The Destructive War: William Tecumseh Sherman, Stonewall Jackson, and the Americans.* New York: Alfred A. Knopf, 1991.

Rudd, A. Bohmer, ed. *Shockoe Hill Cemetery, Richmond, Virginia:, Register of Interments, April 10, 1822–December 31, 1950.* Washington, D.C.: A. Bohmer Rudd, n.d.

Ryan, Mary P. *Cradle of the Middle Class: The Family in Oneida County, New York, 1790–1865.* Cambridge: Cambridge University Press, 1981.

————. *Women in Public: Between Banners and Ballots, 1825–1885.* Baltimore: John Hopkins University Press, 1990.

Salmon, John S., comp. *A Guidebook to Virginia's Historical Markers.* Rev. and exp. ed. Charlottesville: University Press of Virginia, 1994.

Schlotterbeck, John Thomas. *Plantation and Farm: Social and Economic Change in Orange and Greene Counties, Virginia, 1716 to 1850.* Ann Arbor, Mich.: University Microfilms International, 1980.

Scott, Anne Firor. *The Southern Lady: From Pedestal to Politics, 1830–1930.* Chicago: University of Chicago Press, 1970.

Scott, Joan W. *Gender and the Politics of History.* New York: Columbia University Press, 1988.

Scott, Mary Wingfield. *Houses of Old Richmond.* Richmond, Va.: Valentine Museum, 1941.

————. *Old Richmond Neighborhoods.* Richmond, Va.: Whittet and Shepperson, 1950.

Selby, John. *The Stonewall Brigade.* New York: Hippocrene, 1974.

Severa, Joan L. *Dressed for the Photographer: Ordinary Americans and Fashion, 1840–1900.* Kent, Ohio: Kent State University Press, 1995.

Shanks, Henry T. *The Secession Movement in Virginia, 1847–1861.* Richmond, Va.: Garrett and Massie, 1937.

Sheldon, Marianne Patricia Buroff. *Richmond, Virginia: The Town and Henrico County to 1820.* Ann Arbor, Mich.: Xerox University Microfilms, 1975.

Sherr, Lynn, and Jurate Kazickas. *Susan B. Anthony Slept Here: A Guide to American Women's Landmarks.* New York: Random House, Times Books, 1994.

Smith, Bonnie G. *Ladies of the Leisure Class: The Bourgeoises of Northern France in the Nineteenth Century.* Princeton, N.J.: Princeton University Press, 1981.

Stampp, Kenneth M. *The Imperiled Union: Essays on the Background of the Civil War.* New York: Oxford University Press, 1980.

Stannard, Mary Newton. *Richmond: Its People and Its Story.* Philadelphia: J. B. Lippincott, 1923.

Stephenson, Mary A. *Carter's Grove Plantation: A History.* [Williamsburg, Va.: Colonial Williamsburg Foundation, 1964].

Thompson, Edward P. *The Making of the English Working Class.* New York: Random House, 1963.

Tolbert, Lisa C. *Constructing Townscapes: Space and Society in Antebellum Tennessee.* Chapel Hill: University of North Carolina Press, 1999.

Tong, Rosemarie. *Feminist Thought: A Comprehensive Introduction.* Boulder, Col.: Westview, 1989.

Tripp, Steven Elliott. *Yankee Town, Southern City: Race and Class Relations in Civil War Lynchburg.* New York: New York University Press, 1997.

Tubbs, James Balfour. *Rennie Family Connections.* Vol. 1. Privately printed, 1993.

Tylor, Dola S. *Winchester, Virginia Abstracts of Wills, 1794–1894.* Bowie, Md.: Heritage, 1990.

Varg, Paul A. *United States Foreign Relations, 1820–1860.* East Lansing: Michigan State University Press, 1979.

Varon, Elizabeth R. *"We Mean to Be Counted": White Women and Politics in Antebellum Virginia.* Chapel Hill: University of North Carolina Press, 1998.

Watts, Steven. *The Republic Reborn: War and the Making of Liberal America, 1790–1820.* Baltimore: Johns Hopkins University Press, 1987.

Whites, LeeAnn. *The Civil War as a Crisis in Gender: Augusta, Georgia, 1860–1890.* Athens: University of Georgia Press, 1995.

Winchester Chamber of Commerce, *Winchester, Virginia: The Virginia Gateway to the Shenandoah Valley.* Strasburg, Va.: Shenandoah, 1929.

Wolfe, Margaret Ripley. *Daughters of Canaan: A Saga of Southern Women.* Lexington: University Press of Kentucky, 1995.

Woodward, C. Vann. *The Burden of Southern History.* Rev. ed. Baton Rouge: Louisiana State University Press, 1968.

Wyatt-Brown, Bertram. *Southern Honor: Ethics and Behavior in the Old South.* New York: Oxford University Press, 1982.

———. *Yankee Saints and Southern Sinners.* Baton Rouge: Louisiana State University Press, 1985.

Articles

Barbee, David Rankin. "Robert Greenhow." *William and Mary Quarterly*, 2d ser., 12, no. 1 (January 1933): 182–83.

Berry, Michael W., and Ann Arsell Wheat Hunter. "Collier and Christian of Charles City and New Kent Counties." *Virginia Genealogist* 34, no. 2 (April–June, 1990): 82–88.

Boyd, Julian P. "The Murder of George Wythe." *William and Mary Quarterly*, 3d ser., 12, no. 4 (October 1955): 512–42.

Breen, T. H. "Horses and Gentlemen: The Cultural Significance of Gambling among the Gentry of Virginia." *William and Mary Quarterly*, 3d ser., 34, no. 2 (April 1977): 239–57.

Campbell, Randolph B. "Planters and Plain Folks: The Social Structure of the Antebellum South." In *Interpreting Southern History: Historiographical Essays in Honor of Sanford W. Higginbotham*, edited by John B. Boles and Evelyn Thomas Nolen, 48–77. Baton Rouge: Louisiana State University Press, 1987.

Clinton, Catherine. "Sex and the Sectional Conflict." In *Taking Off the White Gloves: Southern Women and Women Historians*, edited by Michelle Gillespie and Catherine Clinton, 43–63. Columbia: University of Missouri Press, 1998.

Conrad, David Holmes. "Early History of Winchester." In *Annual Papers of Winchester Virginia Historical Society*. Vol. 1, 169–232. Winchester, Va.: Winchester–Frederick County Historical Society, 1931.

Coski, Ruth S. "'Under Vines and Fig-Trees': Charles City County in the Georgian

Age." In *Charles City County Virginia: An Official History*, edited by James P. Whittenburg and John M. Coski, 35–44. Salem, W.Va.: Don Mills, 1989.

Eaton, Clement. "Winifred and Joseph Gales, Liberals in the Old South." *Journal of Southern History* 10, no. 4 (November 1944): 461–74.

Erikson, Erik H. "Ego Development and Historical Change." *Psychoanalytic Study of the Child* 2 (1946): 373–95.

Faust, Drew Gilpin. "The Peculiar South Revisited: White Society, Culture, and Politics in the Antebellum Period, 1800–1860." In *Interpreting Southern History: Historiographical Essays in Honor of Sanford W. Higginbotham*, edited by John B. Boles and Evelyn Thomas Nolen, 454–509. Baton Rouge: Louisiana State University Press, 1987.

———. "Altars of Sacrifice: Confederate Women and the Narratives of War." *Journal of American History* 76, no. 4 (March 1990): 1200–1228.

———. Introduction to *Macaria; or, Altars of Sacrifice* by Augusta Jane Evans, xiii–xxvi. Baton Rouge: Louisiana State University Press, 1992.

Fields, Barbara Jeanne. "Slavery, Race, and Ideology in the United States of America." *New Left Review* 181 (May–June 1990): 95–118.

Foote, Nelson N. "Identification as the Basis for a Theory of Motivation." *American Sociological Review* 16 (February 1951): 14–21.

Genovese, Eugene. "Yeoman Farmers in a Slaveholder's Democracy." *Agricultural History* 49 (1975): 331–42.

———. "'Our Family, White and Black': Family and Household in the Southern Slaveholders' World View." In *In Joy and in Sorrow: Women, Family, and Marriage in the Victorian South, 1830–1900*, edited by Carol Blesser, 69–87. New York: Oxford University Press, 1991.

Gleason, Philip. "Identifying Identity: A Semantic History." *Journal of American History* 69, no. 4 (March 1983): 910–31.

Gordon, Linda. "What's New in Women's History." In *A Reader in Feminist Knowledge*, edited by Sneja Gunew, 73–82. London: Routledge, 1991.

Griffin, Barbara J. "Thomas Ritchie and the Founding of the Richmond Lancastrian School." *Virginia Magazine of History and Biography* 86, no. 4 (October 1978): 447–60.

Grubb, Alan. "House and Home in the Victorian South: The Cookbook as Guide." In *In Joy and in Sorrow: Women, Family, and Marriage in the Victorian South, 1830–1900*, edited by Carol Blesser, 154–75. New York: Oxford University Press, 1991.

Hall, Jacquelyn Dowd. "Partial Truths: Writing Southern Women's History." In *Southern Women: Histories and Identities*, edited by Virginia Berhard et al., 11–29. Columbia: University of Missouri Press, 1992.

Hall, Stuart. "Gramsci's Relevance for the Study of Race and Ethnicity." In *Stuart Hall: Critical Dialogues in Cultural Studies*, edited by David Morley and Kuan-Hsing Chen, 411–40. London: Routledge, 1996.

Hareven, Tamara K. "Family Time and Historical Time." In *The Family*, edited by

Alice S. Rossi, Jerome Kagan, and Tamara K. Hareven, 57–70. New York: W. W. Norton, 1978.

Hemphill, W. Edwin. "Examinations of George Wythe Swinney for Forgery and Murder: A Documentary Essay." *William and Mary Quarterly*, 3d ser., 12, no. 4 (October 1955): 543–74.

Hobsbawm, Eric. "Some Reflections on Nationalism." In *Imagination and Precision in the Social Sciences: Essays in Memory of Peter Nettl*, edited by T. J. Nossiter, A. H. Hanson, and Stein Rokkan, 384–97. London: Faber and Faber, 1972.

Hofstra, Warren R. "Land, Ethnicity, and Community at the Opequon Settlement, Virginia, 1730–1800." *Virginia Magazine of History and Biography* 98 (1990): 423–48.

Holstein, Suzy Clarkson. "'Offering Up Her Life': Confederate Women on the Altars of Sacrifice." *Southern Studies* 2, no. 2 (1991): 113–30.

Hopkins, C. A. Porter, ed. "An Extract from the Journal of Mrs. Hugh H. Lee of Winchester, Va., May 23–31, 1862." *Maryland Historical Magazine* 53 (1958): 380–93.

Johnson, Ludwell H. "How Not to Run a College, 1812–1825." In *The College of William and Mary: A History, Vol. I, 1693–1888*, edited by Susan H. Godson, Ludwell H. Johnson, Richard B. Sherman, Thad W. Tate, and Helen C. Walker, 199–226. Williamsburg, Va.: King and Queen, 1993.

Kenney, A. Bentley. "The Devil Diarists of Winchester." *Winchester–Frederick County Historical Society Journal* 5 (1990): 11–27.

Kerber, Linda K. "Separate Spheres, Female Worlds: The Rhetoric of Women's History." *Journal of American History* 75, no. 1 (June 1988): 9–39.

———. "The Revolutionary Generation: Ideology, Politics, and Culture in the Early Republic." In *The New American History*, edited for the American Historical Association by Eric Foner, 31–60. Rev. and exp. ed. Philadelphia: Temple University Press, 1997.

Kierner, Cynthia A. "Genteel Balls and Republican Parades: Gender and Early Southern Civic Rituals, 1677–1826." *Virginia Magazine of History and Biography* 104, no. 2 (spring 1996): 185–210.

———. "Hospitality, Sociability, and Gender in the Southern Colonies." *Journal of Southern History* 62, no. 3 (August 1996): 449–80.

Lewis, Jan. "Motherhood and the Construction of the Male Citizen in the United States, 1750–1850." In *Constructions of the Self*, edited by George Levine, 143–64. New Brunswick, N.J.: Rutgers University Press, 1992.

Logan, Richard D. "Reflections on Changes in Self-Apprehension and Construction of the 'Other' in Western History." *Psychohistory Review* 19, no. 3 (spring 1991): 296–323.

McCormick, Richard P. "New Perspectives on Jacksonian Politics." *American Historical Review* 65, no. 2 (1960): 288–301.

Mentzer, Melissa. "Rewriting Herself: Mary Chesnut's Narrative Strategies." *Connecticut Review* 14, no. 1 (1992): 49–56.

Pessen, Edward. "How Different from Each Other Were the Antebellum North and South?" *American Historical Review* 85 (December 1980): 1119–49.

Rable, George C. "'Missing in Action': Women of the Confederacy." In *Divided Houses: Gender and the Civil War*, edited by Catherine Clinton and Nina Silber, 134–46. New York: Oxford University Press, 1992.

Schultz, Jane E. "Mute Fury: Southern Women's Diaries of Sherman's March to the Sea, 1864–1865." In *Arms and the Woman: War, Gender, and Literary Representation*, edited by Helen M. Cooper, Adrienne Suslander Munich, and Susan Merrill Squier, 59–79. Chapel Hill: University of North Carolina Press, 1989.

Scott, Anne Firor. "Women's Perspective on the Patriarchy in the 1850s." In *Half Sisters of History: Southern Women and the American Past*, edited by Catherine Clinton, 76–92. Durham, N.C.: Duke University Press, 1994.

Sigaud, Louis A. "Mrs. Greenhow and the Rebel Spy Ring." *Maryland Historical Magazine* 41, no. 3 (September 1946): 173–98.

Smith-Rosenberg, Carroll. "The Female World of Love and Ritual: Relations between Women in Nineteenth-Century America." *Signs: Journal of Women in Culture and Society* 1 (1975): 1–30.

Stevenson, Brenda. "Distress and Discord in Virginia Slave Families, 1830–1860." In *In Joy and In Sorrow: Women, Family, and Marriage in the Victorian South, 1830–1900*, edited by Carol Blesser, 103–24. New York: Oxford University Press, 1991.

Thompson, Edward P. "Eighteenth-Century English Society: Class Struggle without Class?" *Social History* 3 (1978): 133–65.

Treadway, Sandra Gioia. "New Directions in Virginia Women's History." *Virginia Magazine of History and Biography* 100, no. 1 (January 1992): 5–28.

Wates, Wylma. "Precursor to the Victorian Age: The Concept of Marriage and Family as Revealed in the Correspondence of the Izard Family of South Carolina." In *In Joy and in Sorrow: Women, Family, and Marriage in the Victorian South, 1830–1900*, edited by Carol Blesser, 3–14. New York: Oxford University Press, 1991.

Weaver, George H., M.D. "Surgeons as Prisoners of War: Agreement Providing for Their Unconditional Release during the American Civil War." *Bulletin of the Society of Medical History of Chicago* 4, no. 3 (January 1933): 249–61.

Welter, Barbara. "The Cult of True Womanhood: 1820–1860." *American Quarterly* 18 (1966): 133–55.

Wilentz, Sean. "Society, Politics, and the Market Revolution, 1814–1848." In *The New American History*, edited by Eric Foner, 61–84. Rev. and exp. ed., American Historical Association. Philadelphia: Temple University Press, 1997.

Wood, Kirsten E. "'One Woman So Dangerous to Public Morals': Gender and Power in the Eaton Affair." *Journal of the Early Republic* 17, no. 2 (summer 1997): 237–75.

Woodward, C. Vann. "The Search for Southern Identity." *Virginia Quarterly Review* 3 (summer 1958): 321–38.

Wright, Gavin. "The Efficiency of Slavery: Another Interpretation." *American Economic Review* 69 (March 1979): 219–26.

Wyatt-Brown, Bertram. "W. J. Cash and Southern Culture." In *From the Old South to the New: Essays on the Transitional South*, edited by Walter J. Fraser Jr. and Winfred B. Moore Jr., 195–214. Westport, Conn.: Greenwood, 1981.

Dissertations, Theses, and Unpublished Papers

Burwell, George Harrison, III. "Sketch of Carter Burwell (1716–1756)," 1961. Research Library, Colonial Williamsburg Foundation, Williamsburg, Virginia.

DeLaney, Theodore C. "Julia Gardiner Tyler: A Nineteenth-Century Southern Woman." Ph.D. diss., College of William and Mary, 1995.

Shaffer, Wade Lee. "The Richmond Junto and Politics in Jacksonian Virginia." Ph.D. diss., College of William and Mary, 1993.

Slaughter, Jane C. "Louis Hue Girardin: Educator, Historian, and Man-of-Letters." Ph.D. diss., University of Virginia, 1935.

Smart, Ann Morgan. "The Urban/Rural Dichotomy of Status Consumption: Tidewater Virginia, 1815." Master's thesis, College of William and Mary, 1986.

Stephenson, Mary A. "The John Greenhow House Historical Report, Block 13-2, Building 23E, Lot 159." Report 1265. Research Department, Colonial Williamsburg Foundation, Williamsburg, Virginia, 1947.

———. "The General Store (18th Century)." Report 90. Research Department, Colonial Williamsburg Foundation, Williamsburg, Virginia, 1954.

Tyler, Lyon G. Williamsburg Plat, in "Williamsburg, the Old Colonial Capitol." Research Department, Colonial Williamsburg Foundation, Williamsburg, Virginia. Photostatic copy.

Index